Calgary's Best Walks

Lori Beattie

My Kind of Night, Sheila Kernan

Maps, book design, layout and illustration by Sergio Gaytan
Front cover artwork and interior artwork, as marked, copyright Sheila Kernan
Interior artwork, as marked, copyright Mandy Budan
Front and back cover design by Sergio Gaytan
Photographs by Lori Beattie except in Walk 2, Walk 24 and Walk 34
Photograph in Walk 2 (leaves with raindrops) and Walk 24 by Keith Dewing
Photograph in Walk 34 by Oscar Dewing
Editing by Meaghan Craven
Author photo by Trudie Lee

1 2 3 4 5

Library and Archives Canada Cataloguing in Publication

Beattie, Lori, author
Calgary's best walks / Lori Beattie.

ISBN 978-0-9939535-0-7 (pbk.)

1. Walking--Alberta--Calgary--Guidebooks.
2. Calgary (Alta.)--Guidebooks. I. Title.

GV199.44.C22C33 2015 917.123›38044 C2014-908206-1

Published by: Fit Frog Books
www.fitfrog.ca
lorib@fitfrog.ca
403.229.4299

Connect with the author at www.calgarysbestwalks.ca

Printed in Canada

Contents

Acknowledgements

Thanks to Sergio Gaytan, graphic designer extraordinaire, for his enthusiasm for this project and for his attention to detail in creating exceptional maps. The original artwork in the book and on the cover makes me very happy, ecstatic in fact, and I want to thank artists Sheila Kernan and Mandy Budan.

Thanks to John Gilchrist for sharing his self-publishing expertise. Fraser Seely offered some helpful publishing advice and I want to thank him. Tracey Etwell, north area parks at the City of Calgary, went out of her way to find me a map of Nose Hill with all the future signage marked. That was a big help. Thanks to Roland Kirzinger, parks planner for Fish Creek Provincial Park, who answered my multiple phone calls concerning flood restoration. Thanks to Peter Abramowicz for help with website set-up. Meaghan Craven, thanks for your attention to detail in editing my book.

And thanks to my family – Keith, Oscar and Eve Dewing. They have walked with me all over the city and beyond. When Oscar was two years old, he was asked what his mum did for work and he said "she walks". He is now thirteen and that still holds true.

A million thanks to my parents, Margaret and Donald Beattie of Woodstock, New Brunswick, who encouraged me to try new things, to be creative and to make things up. Don't follow the rules. Those lessons have come in very handy in creating this book.

Introduction

I love to walk, everywhere and anywhere. Walking makes me happy. I enjoy the fresh air, the time to think, and the freedom to explore. I also love the simplicity. You don't need special gear or skills to go for a walk, just practical footwear, a few layers of clothes, and the ability to put one foot in front of the other: left, right, left, right.

Exploring Calgary on foot is ideal for anyone, no matter their interests. Taking a walk in the city can help you satisfy your desire to explore and experience wilderness, art, and gardens; rivers, reservoirs, hills and flatlands; as well as the urban core and quiet communities, on trails that end at a local café, restaurant or ice cream shop. It is this vast range of treasures in such a small space that makes walking in Calgary so enjoyable, so stimulating. Walk through neighbourhoods and observe or interact with gardeners, front-porch sitters, or other walkers. See and be seen on a walk along a bustling commercial street. Or log off and reconnect with nature by getting off the beaten track and onto a more remote one.

Walking outside is the perfect way to clear your head, to shake up your routine and put things into perspective. It's also a great activity to engage in with your kids, your family, and your friends. Conversations flow when you walk. What else is there to do but chat and observe? And all that fresh air and Alberta sunshine does wonders for your mood.

The routes included in this book introduce you to parts of the city that may be new to you. Use the routes as guidelines and then expand on them. Change your route midstride and explore. The fun part about urban walking is the unknown, the surprises around unexplored corners. Create your own urban walkabouts, and let me know if you uncover hidden stairways, pathways, or secret neighbourhood cafés.

See you out there!

Lori

How to Use this Book

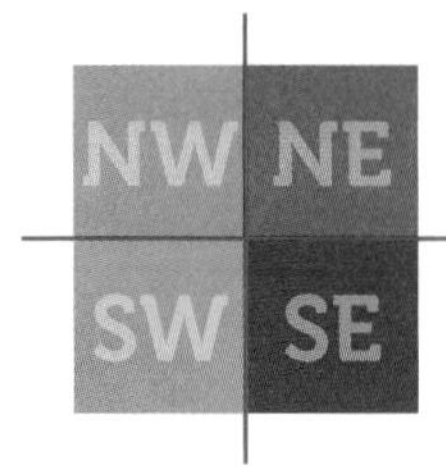

Walks are colour-coded by quadrant.

Walk Details

All the walk's details are included in this section. You'll find information on route categories, public transit options, parking, and the locations of public bathrooms. For current trail updates, including closures, check the City of Calgary website. (www.calgary.ca)

I provide route distances measured in kilometres. A person who walks regularly has an average pace of 5 km per hour. If the route is hilly, generally speaking, for every 100 m gained in elevation, you should add 10 minutes to your walk-time estimate. You gain between 35 and 60 metres in elevation when you climb from the river valley to the top of Calgary's escarpments. For those of you who enjoy counting steps as part of the 10,000/day step challenge, take note that with an average step length of 80 cm, you will walk 1,312 steps/km. If you complete a route that is 7.5 km or more, you will walk at least 10,000 steps.

See Category Descriptions (page 11) for information on the walk categories.

Seasonal Highlights/Cautions

The Highlights/Cautions section of each walk summarizes seasonal or general highlights or warnings.

Walk at a Glance

The Walk at a Glance is a route description that provides you with an overview of the walk, as well as information on items of note relative to the area the walk covers.

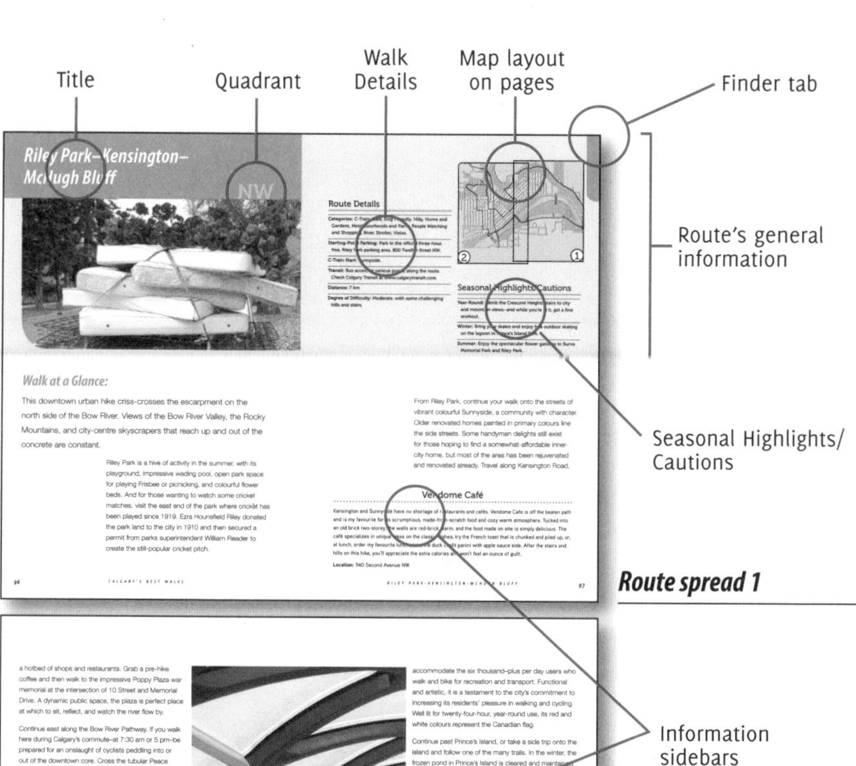

Walk at a Glance:

This downtown urban hike criss-crosses the escarpment on the north side of the Bow River. Views of the Bow River Valley, the Rocky Mountains, and city-centre skyscrapers that reach up and out of the concrete are constant.

Riley Park is a hive of activity in the summer, with its playground, impressive wading pool, open park space for playing Frisbee or picnicking, and colourful flower beds. And for those wanting to watch some cricket matches, visit the east end of the park where cricket has been played since 1919. Ezra Hounsfield Riley donated the park land to the city in 1910 and then secured a permit from parks superintendent William Reader to create the still-popular cricket pitch.

From Riley Park, continue your walk onto the streets of vibrant colourful Sunnyside, a community with character. Older renovated homes painted in primary colours line the side streets. Some handyman delights still exist for those hoping to find a somewhat-affordable inner-city home, but most of the area has been rejuvenated and renovated already. Travel along Kensington Road,

Vendome Café

Kensington and Sunnyside have no shortage of restaurants and cafés. Vendome Cafe is off the beaten path and is my favourite for its scrumptious, made-from-scratch food and cozy warm atmosphere. Tucked into an old brick two-storey, the walls are red-brick warm, and the food made on site is simply delicious. The café specializes in unique takes on the classic dishes; try the French toast that is chunked and piled up, or, at lunch, order my favourite lunch plate the duck confit panini with apple sauce side. After the stairs and hills on this hike, you'll appreciate the extra calories and won't feel an ounce of guilt.

Location: 940 Second Avenue NW

96 CALGARY'S BEST WALKS

RILEY PARK–KENSINGTON–MCHUGH BLUFF 97

Route spread 1

a hotbed of shops and restaurants. Grab a pre-hike coffee and then walk to the impressive Poppy Plaza war memorial at the intersection of 10 Street and Memorial Drive. A dynamic public space, the plaza is perfect place at which to sit, reflect, and watch the river flow by.

Continue east along the Bow River Pathway. If you walk here during Calgary's commute–at 7:30 am or 5 pm–be prepared for an onslaught of cyclists peddling into or out of the downtown core. Cross the tubular Peace Bridge, a pedestrian bridge that accommodates both walkers and cyclists in harmony. Designed by Spanish architect Santiago Calatrava, the bridge was built to

Training on the Crescent Heights Stairs

The Crescent Heights stairs on McHugh Bluff have become a year-round freeway full of Calgarians in training. Climbing stairs can make your muscles burn. When the intensity of an activity increases and you stop breathing comfortably, your cells start to rely on anaerobic (oxygen-free) respiration to function. A by-product of anaerobic exercise is an accumulation of lactic acid in your muscles. The burn you feel is caused by this accumulation; slow down or stop when you feel the burn. Fitness levels determine lactate thresholds so the fitter you are the more you can climb before your legs burn. If you want an alternative to the Crescent Heights stairs, try the paved path that gradually climbs the escarpment. Gradual hills are perfect for quadriceps training. Those big muscles in at the front of your legs are used constantly when alpine skiing or climbing a hill on a bike. Build quad strength by walking uphill backward for twenty steps and then forward for twenty steps. Keep alternating until you reach the top. The bigger the step you take, the tougher the workout.

accommodate the six thousand–plus per day users who walk and bike for recreation and transport. Functional and artistic, it is a testament to the city's commitment to increasing its residents' pleasure in walking and cycling. Well lit for twenty-four-hour, year-round use, its red and white colours represent the Canadian flag.

Continue past Prince's Island, or take a side trip onto the island and follow one of the many trails. In the winter, the frozen pond in Prince's Island is cleared and maintained for skating.

Onward past China Town, cross the Bow River and climb up the McHugh Bluff escarpment. Named after Felix McHugh, who homesteaded this property and was a prominent early entrepreneur, the bluff host views extending downtown west to the mountains. On a winter evening, the sights are dramatic and impressive. With every step up the hillside, the downtown skyscrapers rise into view, bright, compact, and towering. In December the colourful light displays on the houses makes this area the perfect spot for a Christmas lights hike. Follow the pathway to the popular Crescent Heights stairs, where a hotbed of sweaty Calgarians regularly keep fit. Across from Prince's Island Park, these stairs are easy access for downtown office workers–or visitors staying at downtown hotels–needing a quick, outdoor, training session.

Continue to the hillside trails and walk into the trees: willows, ashes, balsam poplar, and white spruce. This is a popular dog-walking area, so you'll likely meet a furry friend or two while following these treed escarpment trails. Or, if you choose to stay on top of the slope, you'll continue to enjoy the Rocky Mountain and Bow River vistas before descending to Sunnyside and deciding where to go for a nice meal or a social drink.

98 CALGARY'S BEST WALKS

RILEY PARK–KENSINGTON–MCHUGH BLUFF 99

Information sidebars

Route spread 2

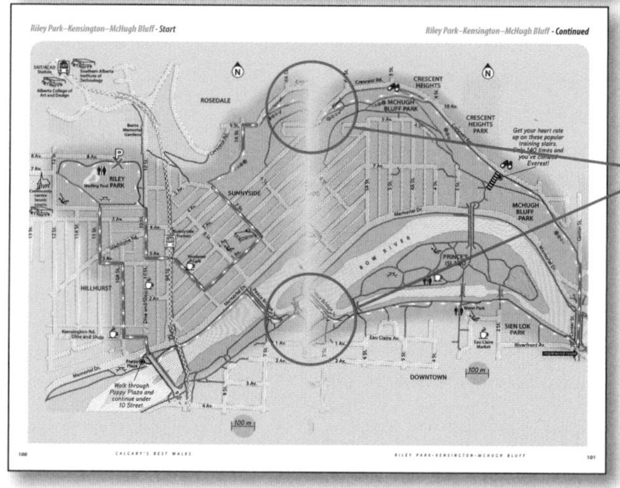

100 CALGARY'S BEST WALKS

RILEY PARK–KENSINGTON–MCHUGH BLUFF 101

Route spread 3

Map

Continuity-marks show map's overlapping points from one page to the next

Map Legend

Route pathway

Paved road

Paved path

Unpaved path

Alternate route

Nearby pathway

Paved road

Paved path

Unpaved path

Symbols

Uphill/Downhill

LRT station

LRT start

Commercial Area

Foot bridge

Traffic bridge

LRT

Railroad

Walk start

Parking

Restrooms

Stairs

Interpretative sign

Other sign

Viewpoint

Picnic area

Playground

On-leash area

Off-leash area

Coffee shop

Ice cream parlor

Powerline

Connection to another route, should you want a longer walk

Park Office

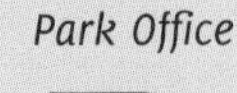

Landmark building

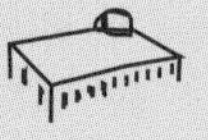

School

Church

House

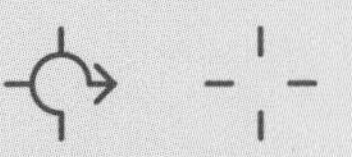

Continuity-marks show map's overlapping points from one page to the next

Category Descriptions

Families and Children

All of the routes in the book are great for kids, which is why I have not added a "kids" category. The varied terrain and the sights make all of the walks interesting. Make the walk more fun for kids by stopping for a picnic lunch, taking the single-track trail with the chickadees, or enjoying a playground. Of course, a post-walk ice cream guarantees success!

Café

If I include "café" in my description, you can be sure that a recommended, independent, coffee shop is along the route or close by.

Dog Friendly

The routes are mostly on-leash with the occasional off-leash park. Dogs are welcome on all routes except those in the Sandy Cross Conservation Area, Weaselhead Flats, the Jackrabbit Trail, and Inglewood Bird Sanctuary.

Hilly

If I use the word "hilly" in the category description, know that there is more than one significant hill climb.

Historic

Inner-city community walks are always historic.

Home and Gardens

The route travels through residential communities with canopies of trees, as well as varied landscaping, architecture, and colourful gardens from spring through fall.

C-Train

If "C-Train" is included in the category description, a LRT stop is along the route or close to it.

Nature

The word "Nature" indicates that most of or the entire walk is in the wilderness.

Neighbourhoods and Parks

This description tells you that the route will take you through natural area parks and green spaces, as well as along sidewalks through neighbourhoods.

People Watching and Shopping

The route passes by or travels along a pedestrian-friendly shopping street with independent shops, restaurants, and cafés.

River

You'll enjoy flowing water when walking "River" routes.

Trail Running

Much of the route is along earthy trails.

Stroller

This category description is one to watch out for if you are walking with a toddler or baby. Big-wheeled strollers can easily manage "Stroller" routes. Small-wheeled strollers should stick to the neighbourhood walks, not the natural areas with gravel pathways.

Vistas

If you want to see the Rocky Mountains and some river valley views, choose a route with "Vista" in the category description.

Category Descriptions Chart

	Route #	
NW	1	Glenbow Ranch Provincial Park
	2	Twelve-Mile Coulee Natural Environment Park
	3	Baker Park–Bowness Park–Valley Ridge Douglas Fir Trail
	4	Bowmont Natural Environment Park West
	5	Bowmont Natural Environment Park East
	6	Edgemont Hills and Ravines
	7	Nose Hill Park: Porcupine Valley and Aspen Grove
	8	Nose Hill Park: Meadowlark Prairie and Many Owls Valley
NE	9	West Nose Creek Park
	10	Vista Heights–Nose Creek–Renfrew–Winston Heights
	11	Bridgeland–Bow River–Nose Creek
NW	12	Confederation Park–Capitol Hill–Mount Pleasant
	13	Riley Park–Kensington–McHugh Bluff
	14	Briar Hill–Houghton Heights–West Hillhurst–Westmount
	15	Bow River–Parkdale–St. Andrews Heights
	16	Douglas Fir Trail and Wildwood
SW	17	Strathcona and Aspen Ravines
	18	Bankview–Scarboro–Connaught–Lower Mount Royal
	19	Downtown Art Walk
	20	Roxboro–Erlton–Ramsay
	21	Stanley Park–Roxboro–Mount Royal–East Elbow
	22	Sandy Beach–Elbow Park–Britannia
	23	Garrison Woods–Glenmore Dam–Altadore
	24	Weaselhead Flats Park–North Glenmore Park
	25	Jackrabbit Trail–South Glenmore Park
	26	Glenmore Reservoir Circumnavigation
	27	Griffith Woods
	28	Ann and Sandy Cross Conservation Area
	29	Fish Creek Park West
SE	30	Fish Creek Park–Bow Valley Ranche
	31	Fish Creek Park and Douglasdale Escarpment
	32	Carburn Park and Beaverdam Flats
	33	Elliston Park
	34	Inglewood–Pearce Estate Wetland–Inglewood Bird Sanctuary
	35	Inglewood–East Village RiverWalk–Bridgeland

C-train	Hilly	Nature	Home & Gardens	Neighbourhoods & Parks	Stroller	Café	Dog friendly	People watch & shop	Historic	Vistas	River	Trail running	**Route #**
	✔	✔			✔	✔	✔		✔	✔	✔	✔	1
✔	✔	✔					✔			✔		✔	2
		✔			✔	✔	✔				✔		3
	✔	✔				✔	✔			✔	✔	✔	4
	✔	✔				✔	✔			✔	✔	✔	5
	✔	✔		✔		✔	✔			✔		✔	6
	✔	✔				✔	✔			✔		✔	7
	✔	✔				✔	✔			✔		✔	8
		✔			✔		✔					✔	9
	✔		✔	✔	✔	✔	✔			✔	✔		10
✔	✔	✔	✔	✔	✔	✔	✔	✔	✔	✔	✔		11
		✔	✔	✔	✔	✔	✔						12
✔	✔		✔	✔	✔	✔	✔	✔	✔	✔	✔		13
✔	✔		✔	✔	✔	✔	✔	✔		✔	✔		14
	✔		✔	✔	✔	✔	✔			✔	✔		15
	✔	✔	✔	✔		✔	✔			✔	✔	✔	16
✔		✔		✔		✔	✔					✔	17
✔	✔		✔	✔	✔	✔	✔	✔		✔			18
✔				✔	✔	✔	✔	✔	✔		✔		19
✔	✔		✔	✔	✔	✔	✔	✔	✔	✔	✔		20
✔	✔	✔	✔	✔	✔	✔	✔			✔	✔		21
	✔	✔	✔	✔	✔	✔	✔			✔	✔		22
		✔	✔	✔	✔	✔	✔				✔		23
		✔			✔					✔	✔	✔	24
	✔	✔				✔					✔	✔	25
	✔	✔		✔	✔	✔	✔			✔	✔	✔	26
		✔			✔		✔				✔	✔	27
	✔	✔								✔		✔	28
✔	✔	✔			✔		✔			✔	✔	✔	29
✔	✔	✔			✔	✔	✔			✔	✔	✔	30
	✔	✔			✔	✔	✔			✔	✔	✔	31
		✔			✔		✔			✔	✔	✔	32
		✔			✔	✔		✔					33
		✔		✔	✔	✔		✔	✔		✔		34
✔	✔		✔	✔	✔	✔	✔	✔	✔	✔	✔		35

N
1
2
3
4
5
6
7
8
9
10
11
12
13
14
15
16
17
18
33
34
35

Overview Maps by Quadrant – NW and NE routes

NW

Walk		Page
1	Glenbow Ranch Provincial Park	20
2	Twelve-Mile Coulee Natural Environment Park	26
3	Baker Park–Bowness Park–Valley Ridge Douglas Fir Trail	32
4	Bowmont Natural Environment Park West	38
5	Bowmont Natural Environment Park East	44
6	Edgemont Hills and Ravines	50
7-8	Nose Hill Park - Overview of two routes	56
7	Nose Hill Park: Porcupine Valley and Aspen Grove	60
8	Nose Hill Park: Meadowlark Prairie and Many Owls Valley	66
12	Confederation Park–Capitol Hill–Mount Pleasant	90
13	Riley Park–Kensington–McHugh Bluff	96
14	Briar Hill–Houghton Heights–West Hillhurst–Westmount	102
15	Bow River–Parkdale–St. Andrews Heights	108
16	Douglas Fir Trail and Wildwood	114

NE

Walk		Page
9	West Nose Creek Park	72
10	Vista Heights–Nose Creek–Renfrew–Winston Heights	78
11	Bridgeland–Bow River–Nose Creek	84

Overview Maps by Quadrant – SW and SE routes

SW

SE

N
33
34
35
16
11
20
19
13
21
22
18
14
23
26
25
24
15
17
27
32
31
30
29
28

FARM
CALGARY'S BE
SHOP
DINE

The Routes

Glenbow Ranch Provincial Park

NW

Walk at a Glance:

Alberta's trademark, big, blue skies are a constant companion when you walk around Glenbow Ranch. And when the clouds roll in, the textures and patterns of the land juxtaposed to the blue backdrop draw your eyes high. The Chinook arch is especially impressive; its distinctive straight-line cloud formation and warm westerly winds provide welcome respite in mid-January.

Be prepared: the winds can be fierce here, especially pre-Chinook, when gusts foreshadow the rise in temperatures.

Vast and open, the park is situated along the north bank of the Bow River between Calgary and Cochrane in Rocky View County. Glenbow Ranch hosts 25 km of interconnecting paved and gravel pathways. Rolling

Route Details

Categories: Café, Dog Friendly, Hilly, Historic, Nature, River, Stroller, Trail Running, Vistas.

Starting-Point Parking: Glenbow Road, off of Highway 1A, about 4 km east of the town of Cochrane.

Transit: None.

Facilities: Bathrooms at trailhead. Visitor Centre on site. See www.albertaparks.ca/glenbow-ranch/ and Glenbow Ranch Parks Foundation, www.grpf.ca; or call 403-851-9053.

Distance: Route on north side of tracks: 9.18 km. Entire route (including south side of tracks): 14.34 km

Degree of Difficulty: Moderate, with lots of ups and downs.

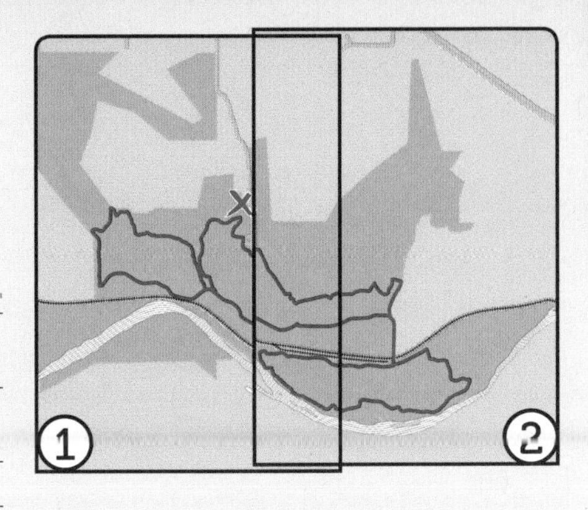

Seasonal Highlights/Cautions

Year-Round: Glenbow Ranch is open to the elements, without much shelter. Winds can be fierce here, especially before a Chinook. Trails are closed intermittently to allow cattle to graze the park's fescue grasslands. Animals in the park include everything from deer, elk, and moose, to badgers, coyotes, and ground squirrels, not to mention numerous species of birds and insects.

Spring, Summer, and Fall: Wildflowers begin in April and last through September. Fall foliage hits its peak in mid-to-late September.

grasslands lead to boundless views of the Bow River Valley and the Rockies beyond, and dips lead into aspen-filled coulees. And you will see trains. Since 1883 trains have travelled through this piece of prairie as part of their cross-Canada trek.

Cochrane Eats and Drinks

If you didn't bring your lunch to the ranch, head to Cochrane Coffee Traders post-walk for a cuppa fresh-roasted coffee and house-made lunches and baked goods. Popular with cyclists out for a day ride from Calgary, this is a nice spot to warm up by the fireplace on a cold day.

If it is a hot day and you feel the need for some ice cream, join the crowds at MacKay's ice cream shop. Serving house-made ice cream since 1948, MacKay's is a destination drive for Calgarians.

Location:

Cochrane Coffee Traders: 114 Second Avenue West

MacKay's: 220 First Street West

When you walk here, you follow in the footsteps of the First Nations peoples who lived and hunted in the area up to four thousand years ago. Evidence of tipi rings, cairns, and bison kills have been found at the ranch. The area was later established as western Canada's first big ranch, named the Cochrane Ranche in 1881. Here, ranchers discovered their cattle could not withstand the

harsh winters as the bison had; a lesson that was critical to the success of future southern Alberta ranches.

Cattle still roam the fields, as the park remains a working ranch. Grazing helps maintain the health and vigour of the fescue grassland landscape. In the fall and winter, the cattle eat the tall, protein-rich grasses. Their cropping of the grasses allows sunlight to reach the roots, leading to healthy grass growth in the spring. Interpretive signs along the route provide interesting background on Alberta's ranching heritage and geological history. A walk here calms the mind and refreshes the spirit.

Alberta Maverick: Eric Harvie

Eric Harvie's life changed in 1947 when the president of Imperial Oil called to tell him that the Leduc No. 1 exploration well had hit a gusher. Eric Harvie owned the mineral rights to that land.

A lawyer in his own private practice, Harvie had moved to the West a few years prior. He was a keen businessman and was always on the lookout for opportunities. In 1934 he purchased the Glenbow Sheep and Horse Ranch, and he spent weekends there with his wife Dorothy and their three children. He named his ranch Glenbow.

Eric Harvie was a collector of artifacts that told the story of the North American West. In 1954 he created the Glenbow Foundation, and in 1966 he donated his collection to the people of Alberta. The Glenbow Museum, the Calgary Zoo, Heritage Park, and other projects benefitted from his passion and generosity.

Hats off to Eric Harvie's son, Neil, and his family for donating this pristine piece of prairie heaven to the Government of Alberta in 2006. Albertans can now share in the beauty of this western landscape.

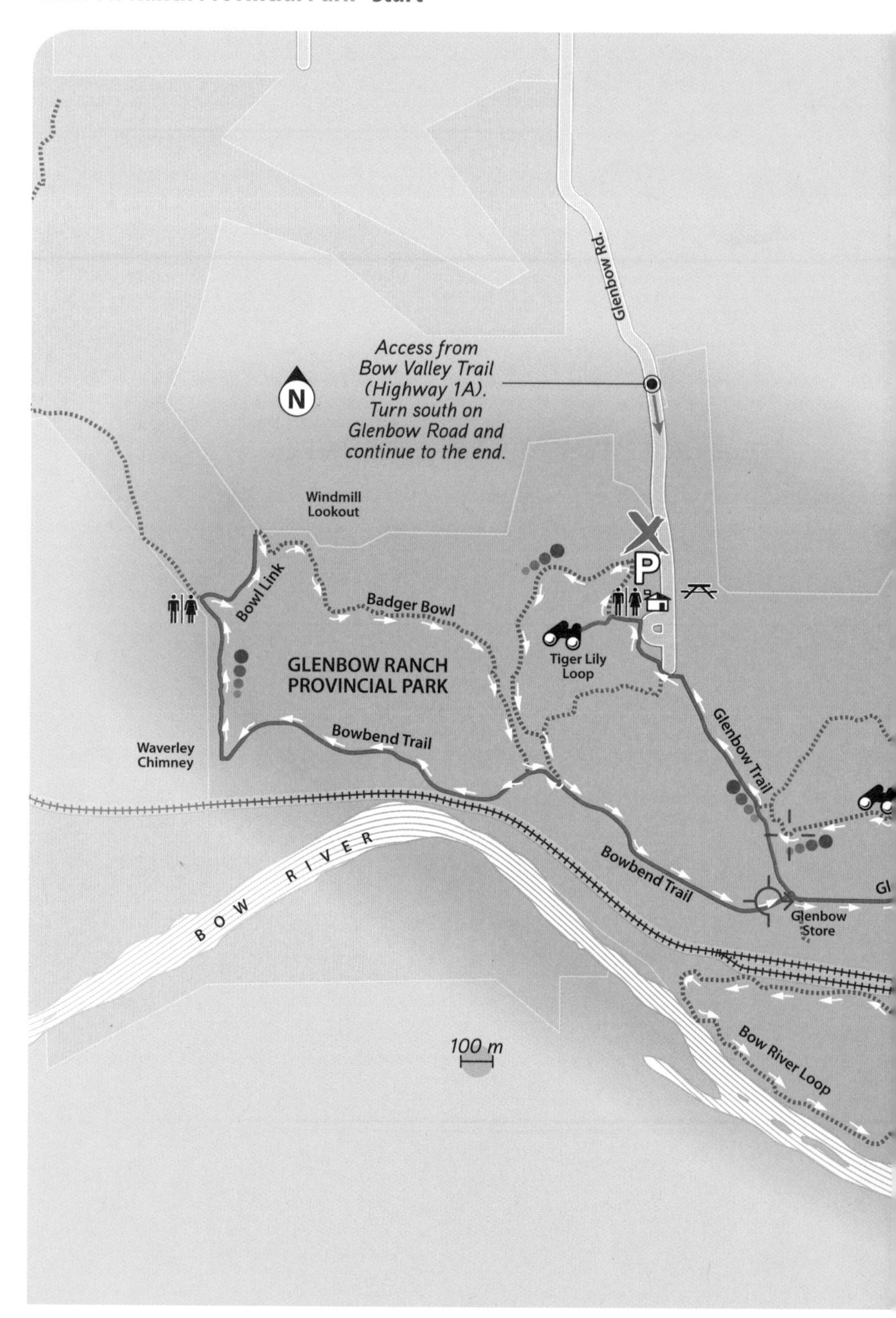
Glenbow Rd.
Access from
Bow Valley Trail
(Highway 1A).
Turn south on
Glenbow Road and
continue to the end.
N
Windmill
Lookout
Bowl Link
Badger Bowl
GLENBOW RANCH
PROVINCIAL PARK
Tiger Lily
Loop
P
Glenbow Trail
Waverley
Chimney
Bowbend Trail
Bowbend Trail
BOW RIVER
Glenbow
Store
Bow River Loop
100 m

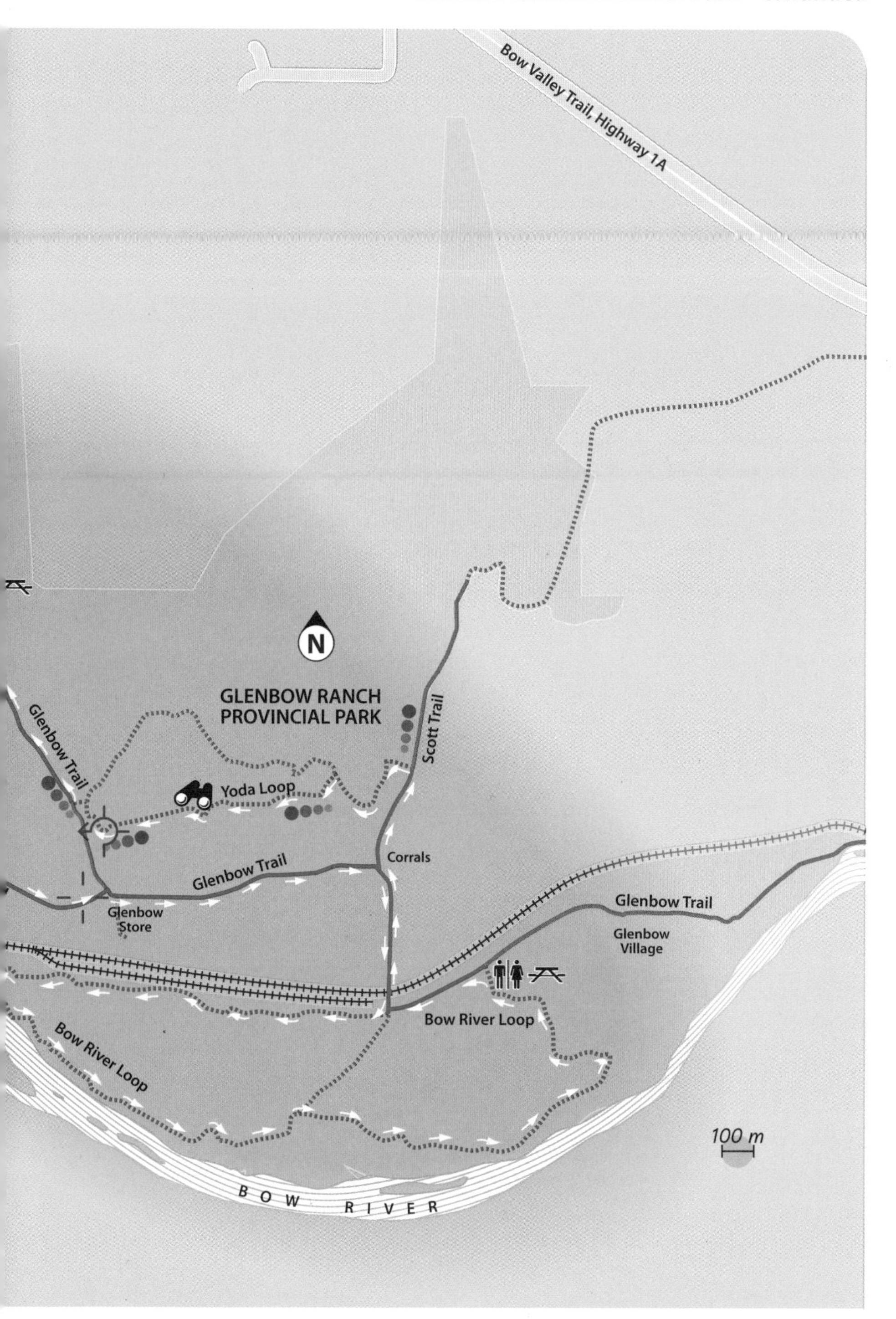
Bow Valley Trail, Highway 1A
GLENBOW RANCH PROVINCIAL PARK
Glenbow Trail
Yoda Loop
Scott Trail
Corrals
Glenbow Trail
Glenbow Store
Glenbow Trail
Glenbow Village
Bow River Loop
Bow River Loop
100 m
BOW RIVER

Twelve-Mile Coulee Natural Environment Park

NW

Walk at a Glance:

Wild walkabouts tucked into suburban neighbourhoods are always a pleasant surprise. Tuscany's Twelve-Mile Coulee Park got its name in the early days because it is approximately 12 miles (19 km) from Fort Calgary and was a convenient mileage marker on the stagecoach run from the Fort Calgary main post office to the mission church at Morleyville, a missionary outpost. The Metis used the term coulée, which means "small valley" or "gully," to describe the type of landscape in the park. It comes from the French verb couler, meaning "to flow," which is appropriate since the spring snow-melt leads to a rise in creek water level.

Route Details

Categories: Dog Friendly, Hilly, C-Train, Nature, Trail Running, Vistas.

Starting-Point Parking: Park in the official parking lot off Tuscany Boulevard, just north of Scenic Acres Link.

C-Train Start: Transit Bus access to Tuscany. Check Calgary Transit at www.calgarytransit.com.

Facilities: None. Nearby cafés: Cadence Coffe (description in Walk 5, page 47), Angel's Drive In (description in Walk 3, page 34).

Distance: 5.5 km
From C-Train: 8.5 km return

Degree of Difficulty: Moderate, with one challenging hill climb. Lots of optional hill climbs.

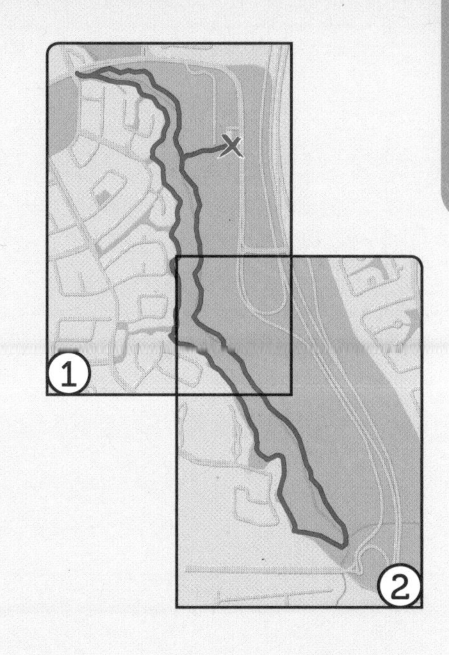

Seasonal Highlights/Cautions

Spring, Summer, and Fall: Bring your waterproof footwear if you want to creek hop. The creek is narrow and small however the current can be strong and the water levels can be high enough to soak your feet, well into the fall.

The route begins on high ground and descends into the treed coulee where a few trail options make for a varied walk. You can walk above the creek, on the newly

Urban Walking: A Legal High

This I know is true: going for a walk makes me feel good, great in fact. In his book *Happy City: Transforming Our Lives Through Urban Design*, Charles Montgomery points out that the effects of walking on mental health are clear: "Walking works like a drug, and it starts working even after a few steps."

Unfortunately, in Canada, we are engineering walking out of our lives. The majority of our children are driven everywhere. Currently, only about 12 per cent of North American kids walk or cycle for transportation. Just one generation ago, those figures were completely the opposite. Most kids walked, strolled, and chatted with friends on their way to school or the bus stop. They did this without parents, and if they were late, it was their own fault. The independence, the sense of freedom, that walking provides to kids trumps all the other benefits of self-propelled travel. It gives children some time away from the controlling world of hovering adults.

The sense of freedom and happiness walking provides to everyone is legal, simple, and cheap. It works like a charm to bring happiness to all who choose to take that first step.

constructed, slope-side trail, or along the coulee bottom. Adventurous creek-hoppers will enjoy using their creative navigating skills since the trail diverges in many areas and, depending on how much water is in the creek, you may have to backtrack and choose a higher route. This is the kind of exploring that kids love!

Those who choose to stay high and dry will walk through shrubs of willows, red-osier dogwoods, and American silverberry, as well as stands of trembling aspen, balsam poplar, and white spruce while on the north-facing slopes. The south-facing slopes are drier and host native prairie plants: rough fescue, Perry oat grass, and spear grasses thrive here. If you're a rock hound, check out the large, bedrock, sandstone outcroppings at the south end of the park. This is Calgary's best and most accessible example of the Porcupine Hills Formation that underlies the entire city.

You can easily adjust your walk length by taking any one of the many trails that climb out of the coulee, all of them unmarked but well used. Just be aware that some of these trails may be closed for rehabilitation as the park is being redeveloped. Too many informal trails may lead to erosion and the loss of a valuable park space.

Walk to the end of the coulee, near Nose Hill Drive, and begin the long gradual climb to the community of Tuscany and to views of the Rocky Mountains, Canada Olympic Park, and the downtown core. Continue along the paved path at the top of the coulee, or pick a trail and descend back into the wilderness. Creek-hop back to your starting point.

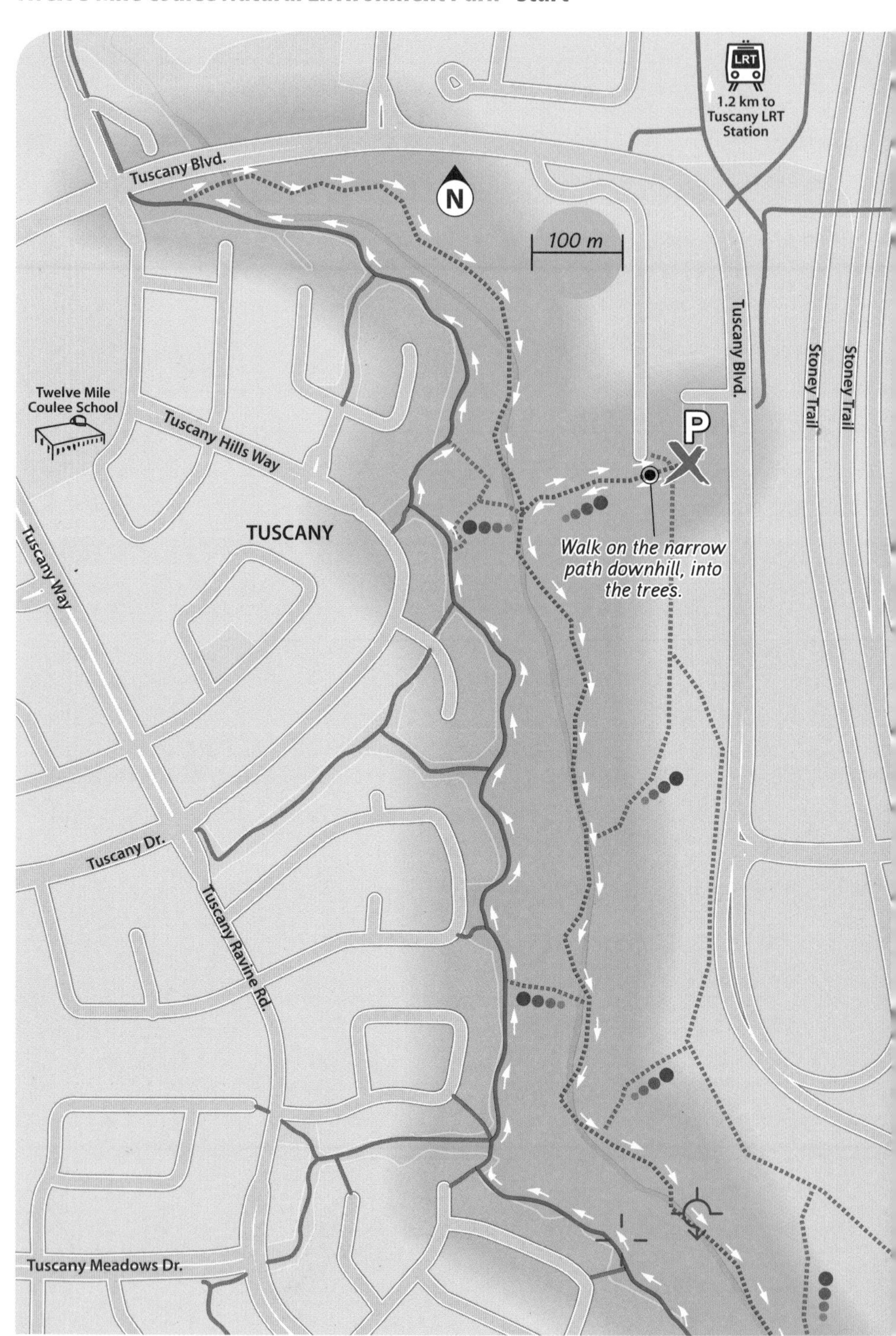
LRT
1.2 km to Tuscany LRT Station
Tuscany Blvd.
N
100 m
Tuscany Blvd.
Stoney Trail
Stoney Trail
P
Twelve Mile Coulee School
Tuscany Hills Way
TUSCANY
Walk on the narrow path downhill, into the trees.
Tuscany Way
Tuscany Dr.
Tuscany Ravine Rd.
Tuscany Meadows Dr.

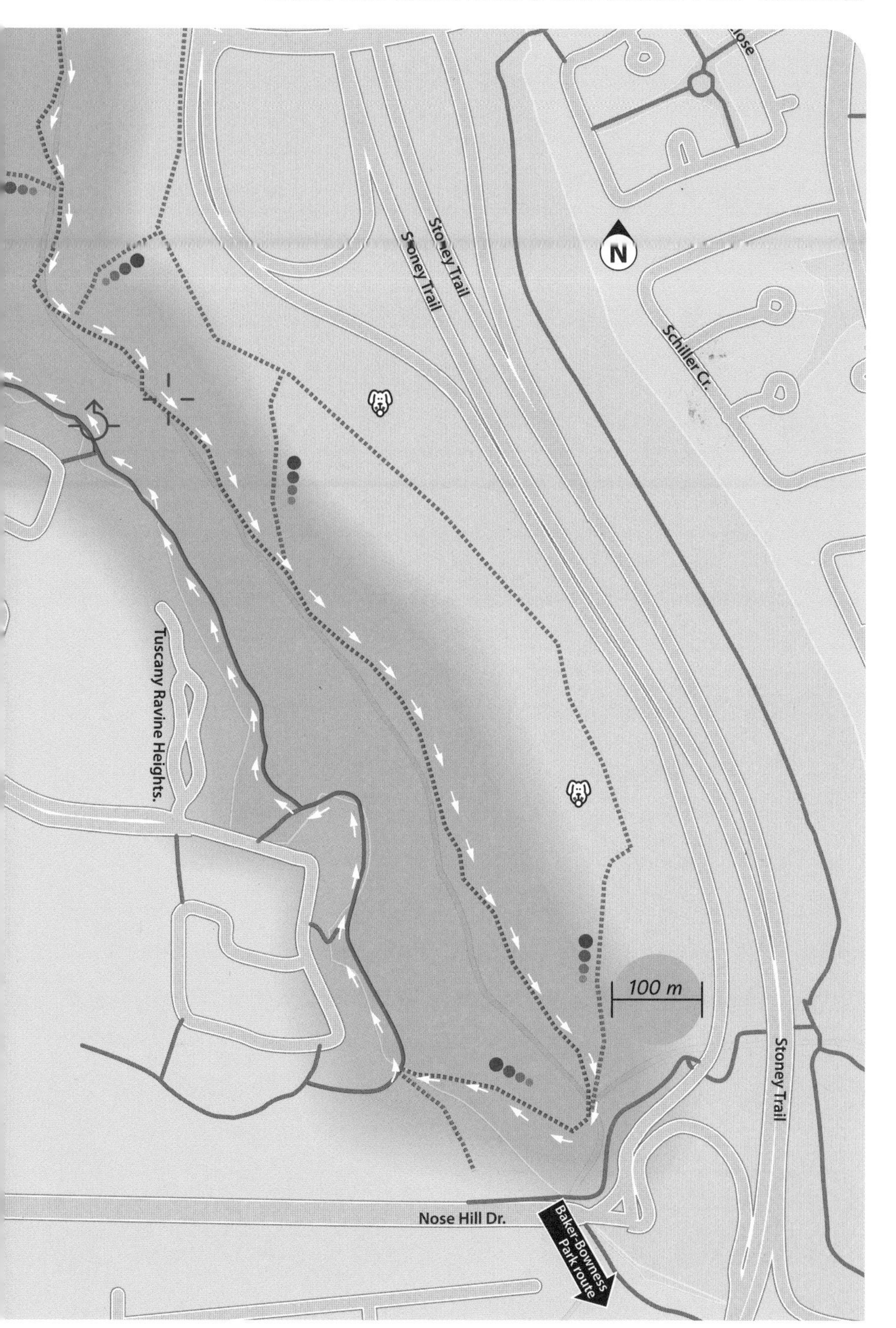
Stoney Trail
Stoney Trail
Schiller Cr.
N
Tuscany Ravine Heights.
100 m
Stoney Trail
Nose Hill Dr.
Baker-Bowness Park route

Baker Park–Bowness Park–Valley Ridge Douglas Fir Trail

NW

Walk at a Glance:

Baker Park, the little park across the river from Bowness Park, is a great place for listening to gaggling gossiping geese in the fall. Listen for the sounds of cocktail-party chatter and then look up to see Canada geese practicing their V formation. Walk east along the paved Bow River Pathway, and soon you'll enter Bowmont Natural Environment Park. Your visit to Bowmont Park is brief, but if you like the looks of it you can switch to the Bowmont Natural Environment Park West route (see page 38) and walk to Waterfall Valley.

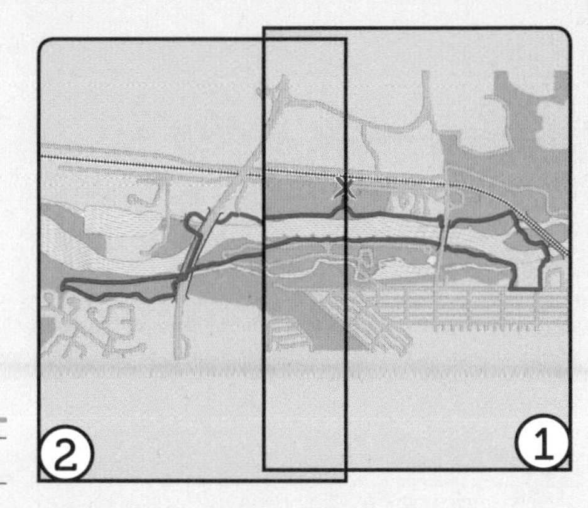

Route Details

Categories: Café, Dog Friendly, Nature, River, Stroller.

Starting-Point Parking: Baker Park, 9333 Scenic Bow Road NW; Bowness Park, 8900 Forty-Eighth Avenue NW.

Transit: Bus access at various points along the route. Check Calgary Transit at www.calgarytransit.com.

Facilities: Bowness Park: bathrooms, café, ice skating on lagoon, ice-skate rentals, fire pits, picnic areas, playgrounds, spray park, wading pool.

Distance: 7.5 km

Degree of Difficulty: Easy and mostly flat, with one optional hill climb.

Seasonal Highlights/Cautions

Winter: Ice skating on the lagoon is fantastic!

Spring, Summer, and Fall: Plan a post-walk picnic at Bowness Park.

To continue on to the route, cross the Bow River and make your way along side streets before entering Bowness Park, one of Calgary's most popular outdoor areas for family and friends to congregate. The place is a hive of activity in the summer picnic season so be prepared for a sensory explosion; bonfires, the smell of burgers, and the sound of friends and families having

Historic Streetcars to Bowness Park

In a time when automobiles were rare, Bowness Park had a streetcar that took Calgarians from the city to the town of Bowness (Bowness did not become a community in the city of Calgary until 1963). The park became a destination in the early 1920s and 1930s, even before it had many services. Thousands would visit the park on a warm summer weekend. The streetcar that extended to Bowness was the brainchild of landowner John Hextall, an Englishman turned owner of the Bowness Ranche. He donated the two islands that are Bowness Park to the City of Calgary in 1911 in a deal that ensured streetcar service to his new subdivision for the high-end Bowness Estates. The streetcar service was maintained from 1913 to 1950.

fun. In the winter, bring your skates and glide along the Bowness Lagoon, a frozen outdoor maze equipped with fire pits so you can warm up your hands. Don't forget to bring a Thermos of hot chocolate!

Before crossing back to the north side of the Bow River, you have the option of climbing to the community of Valley Ridge on a side trail through a Douglas fir forest. This wilderness add-on immerses you in nature and it provides the only hill climb on the route. Loop back from Valley Ridge along the paved pathway and continue under Stoney Trail back to Baker Park.

Angel's Drive In

Detour to Angel's Drive In for breakfast, lunch, or dinner. Offering a multitude of burgers, milkshakes, fruit shakes, and the classic Breyer's ice-cream cones, this is a perfect stop if you did not have time to make a picnic before leaving home.

Location: 8603 Forty-Seventh Avenue NW, www.angelsdrivein.com
Phone: 403-288-1009
Hours: 7 am–9 pm (weekdays), 7:30 am–9 pm (weekends)

Among Friends by Mandy Budan

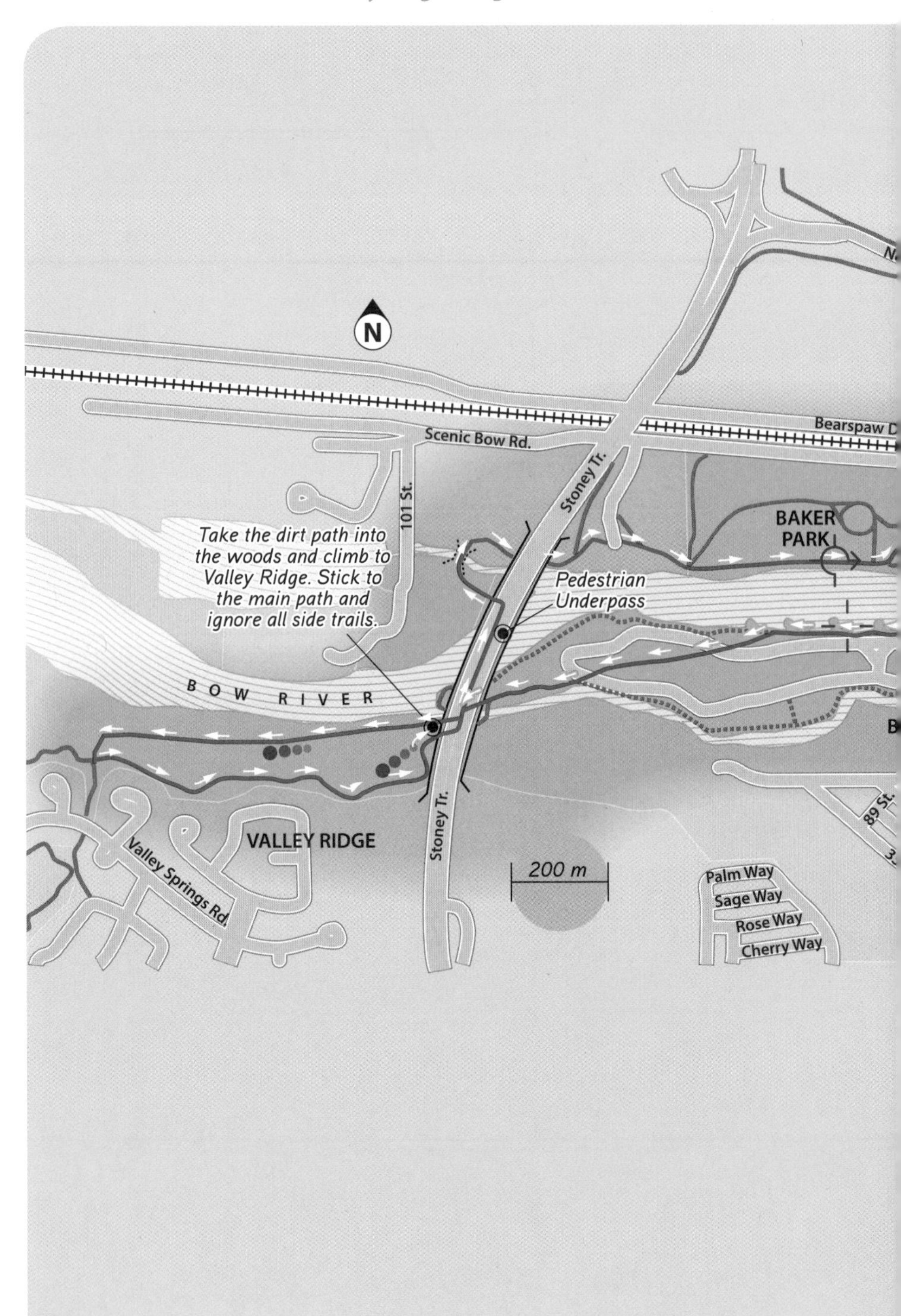
N
Bearspaw D
Scenic Bow Rd.
101 St.
Stoney Tr.
BAKER PARK
Take the dirt path into the woods and climb to Valley Ridge. Stick to the main path and ignore all side trails.
Pedestrian Underpass
BOW RIVER
VALLEY RIDGE
Valley Springs Rd.
Stoney Tr.
200 m
89 St.
Palm Way
Sage Way
Rose Way
Cherry Way

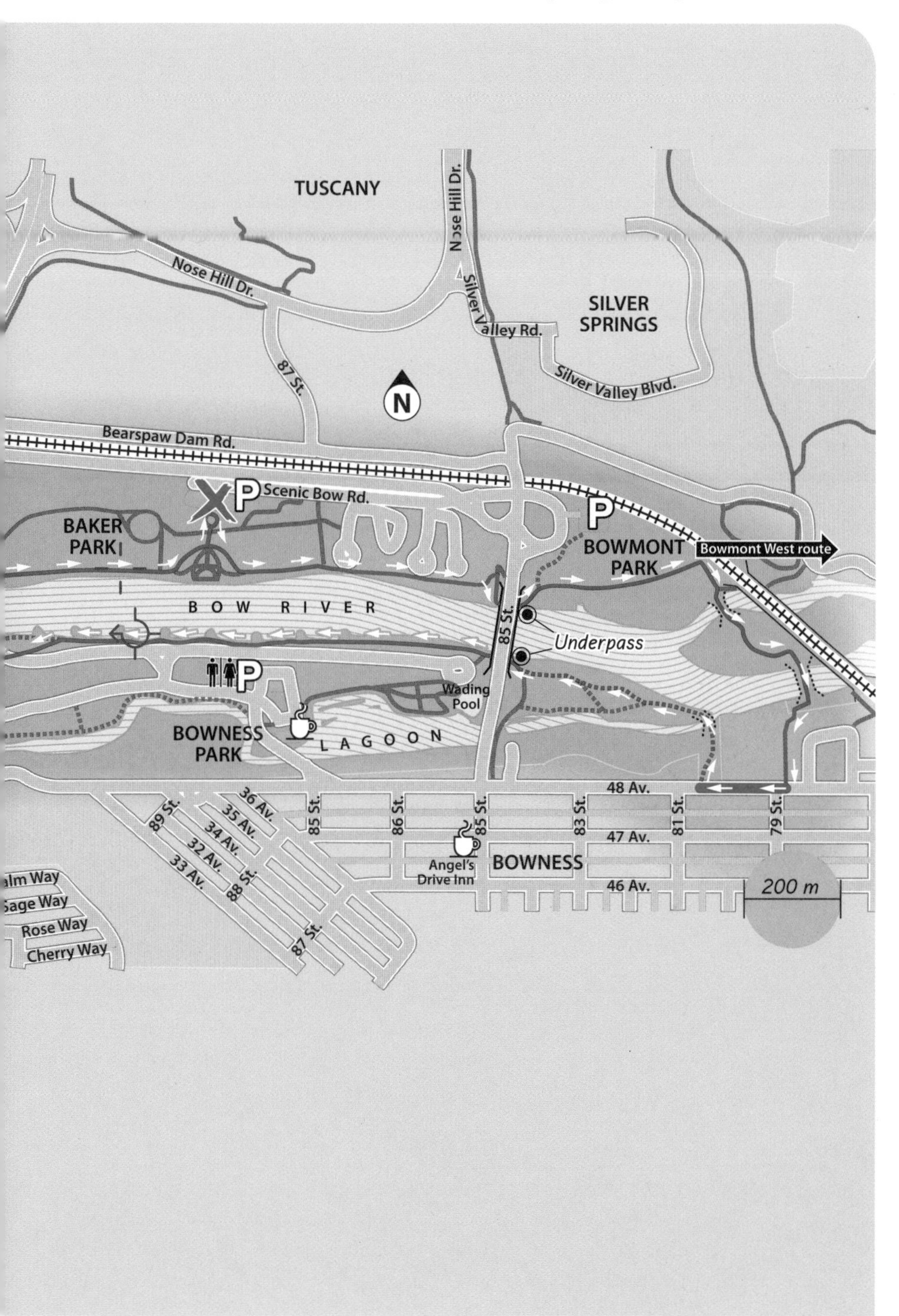

TUSCANY
Nose Hill Dr.
Nose Hill Dr.
Silver Valley Rd.
SILVER SPRINGS
Silver Valley Blvd.
87 St.
N
Bearspaw Dam Rd.
Scenic Bow Rd.
BAKER PARK
BOWMONT PARK
Bowmont West route
BOW RIVER
85 St.
Underpass
Wading Pool
BOWNESS PARK
LAGOON
48 Av.
36 Av.
35 Av.
34 Av.
32 Av.
33 Av.
89 St.
88 St.
87 St.
85 St.
86 St.
85 St.
83 St.
81 St.
79 St.
47 Av.
46 Av.
Angel's Drive Inn
BOWNESS
200 m
alm Way
Sage Way
Rose Way
Cherry Way

Bowmont Natural Environment Park West

NW

Walk at a Glance:

Waterfall Valley is your halfway point on this single-track walkabout that skirts the edges of escarpments and descends into ravines. Take the rolling hilly start or warm up slowly on the paved path before climbing to Bow River views.

Bowmont Natural Environment Park is a mix of grasslands, valleys fed with permanent sources of spring water, and shrub-filled offshore islands. Balsam poplar riparian forests still exist here. Once common along riverbanks in the North American prairies, this type of forest is now rare since it depends on flooding for regeneration, and rivers in Alberta flood far less commonly now that they are dammed.

Route Details

Categories: Café, Dog Friendly, Hilly, Nature, River, Trail Running, Vistas.

Starting-Point Parking: Park at the official parking area on Scenic Bow Road, just off Eighty-Fifth Street. The parking area is a pull-off on a sharp corner. A Bowmont Park sign hangs on the fence at the park entrance.

Transit: Bus access along to Silver Springs. Check Calgary Transit at www.calgarytransit.com.

Facilities: Café en route.

Distance: 5.3 km

Degree of Difficulty: Moderate, with lots of rolling hills and some challenging steep hills.

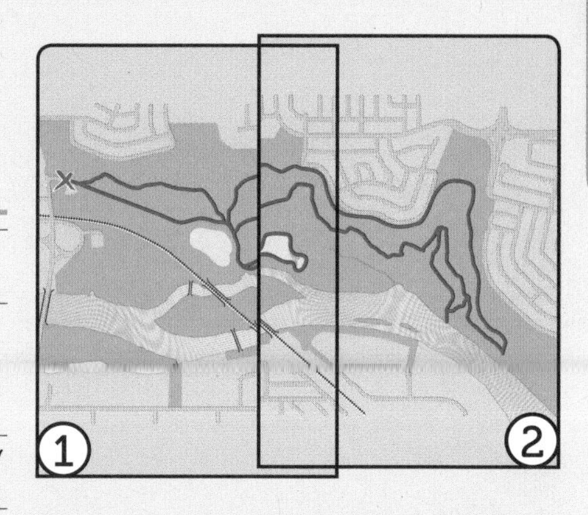

Seasonal Highlights/Cautions

Winter: Frozen waterfall in Waterfall Valley. Bring your hiking poles and/or traction devices for your shoes since single-track trails can be slippery.

Spring and Summer: Alberta wildflowers blanket the hillside from April through August.

Fall: Hillside shrubbery and prairie grasses turn golden yellow, burnt orange, and rich red.

Wildflowers are abundant in the grasslands and appear in April, starting with the purple-headed prairie crocus, followed by the yellow buffalo bean. These blooms are such a welcome sight after many months of the white-and-brown landscape. Follow the boardwalk trail and descend into Waterfall Valley where a 3-m cascading falls flows over a spongy-looking deposit of tufa. The

Pole It for Stability!

Avoid knee injuries and get an upper body workout by hiking with two poles on this hilly Bowmont trek. Two poles are better than one because four points of contact make you more stable than three. It is important to adjust pole length to suit the terrain. When hanging onto the handle, your forearm should be parallel to the ground. That means you must shorten the pole on the climb and lengthen it on descent. As you press the poles down and away behind you, you'll feel your abdominal, back, and arm muscles getting a workout. Poles not only increase your calorie burn and offer downhill stability but they also significantly reduce the lower-body impact of hiking. Your knees will thank you.

Geological Calgary

The grasslands in Bowmont Natural Environment Park lie atop 18 m of sediment that was once at the bottom of Glacial Lake Calgary. This lake was formed when the glaciers melted about 12,000 years ago and an ice dam blocked the flow of the runoff. The bedrock below the sediment is called the Porcupine Hills Formation, formed about 65 million years ago. When water seeps through the sediment, it strikes bedrock and then flows sideways, creating the waterfall in Waterfall Valley. The water absorbs calcium carbonate as it travels through the sediment. The mineral is deposited on the algae-covered rocks when the water surfaces, producing tufa. You will see examples of this in Waterfall Valley.

Café Le Matin

If you are in need of some breakfast midway through your walk, hike straight north out of Waterfall Valley all the way to Silver Springs Road and cross the intersection to get to Silver Spring Boulevard and the strip mall that is home to the tiny Café Le Matin. Locals flock to this friendly little restaurant with top-notch food. The Silver Springs community website lauds the restaurant and says that visitors are always greeted with a smile and a gentle "hello" or "good morning." Owners Mikyung and Jae Lee treat everyone as their friend. Mikyung expresses her restaurant's philosophy thus: "Please come to my house, and I will cook for you." And cook she does; breakfast, lunch, and pastries are tasty and fresh. The eggs Benedict is the café specialty. So climb an extra hill if your plan on treating yourself. Bon appetite!

Location: 1, 5720 Silver Spring Boulevard NW
Phone: 403-247-6647
Hours: 8:30 am –5 pm Monday-Saturday, Closed Sundays

tufa is composed of mineral deposits that result when spring water precipitates calcium carbonate over algae-covered rocks. On a very cold winter day when the falls are frozen and the spring water is warmer than the air, you are immersed in a glacial steam bath.

Climb back to the escarpment trail and continue east into the poplar stands, dropping closer to the river and then climbing back to the paved Bow River Pathway. This could be the turnaround point, or, you could make this a half-day hike by extending your walk along th57e Bowmont Natural Environment Park East route (see page 44).

Continue west along the paved path, enjoying Rocky Mountain views, before descending to the inland ponds. A nice spot for a picnic, the ponds are home to the familiar croak of amphibians. Listen for the boreal chorus frogs and tiger salamanders as you enjoy a snack.

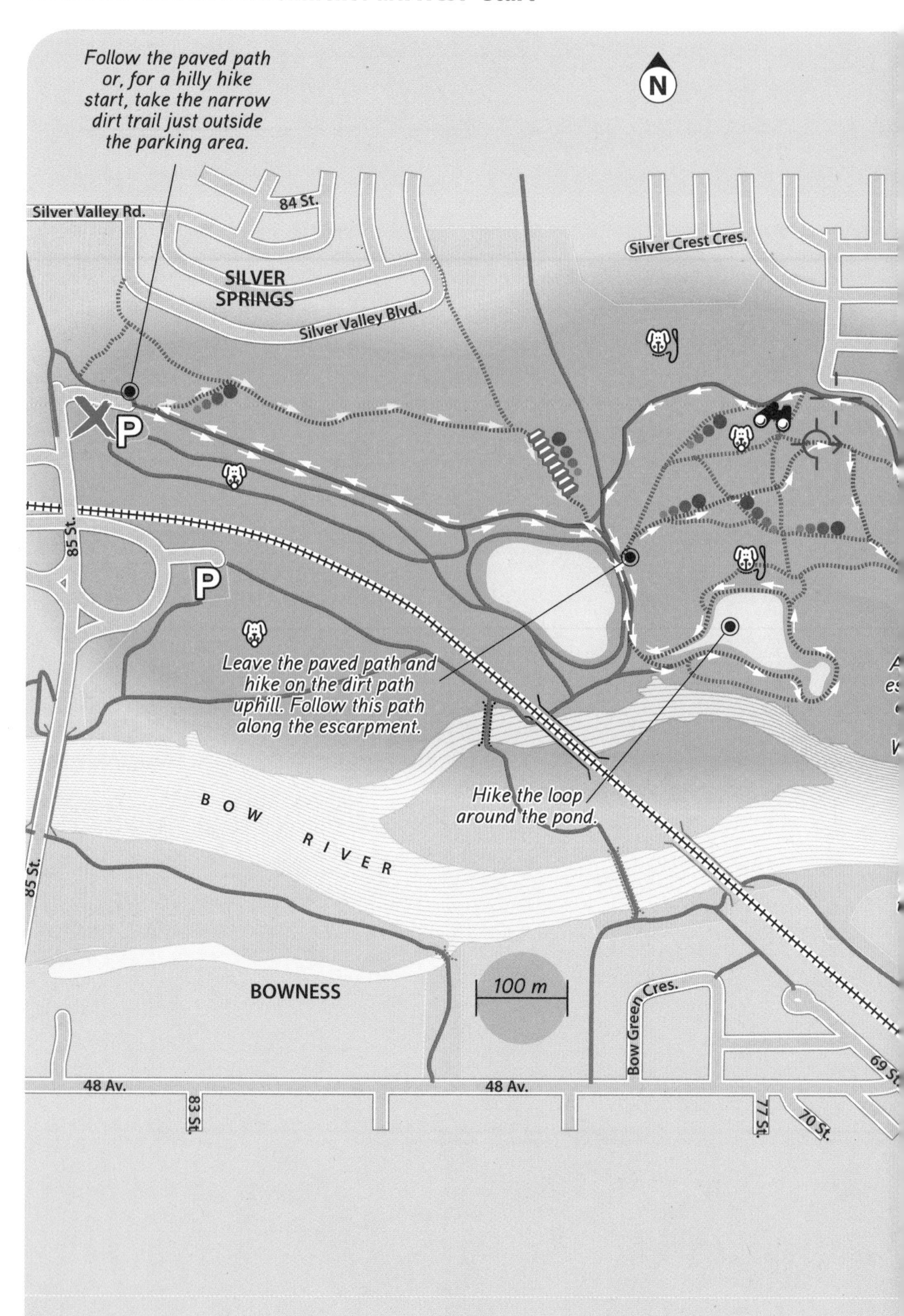
Follow the paved path or, for a hilly hike start, take the narrow dirt trail just outside the parking area.
N
Silver Valley Rd.
84 St.
Silver Crest Cres.
SILVER SPRINGS
Silver Valley Blvd.
P
85 St.
P
Leave the paved path and hike on the dirt path uphill. Follow this path along the escarpment.
Hike the loop around the pond.
BOW RIVER
85 St.
BOWNESS
100 m
Bow Green Cres.
48 Av.
48 Av.
83 St.
77 St.
70 St.
69 St.

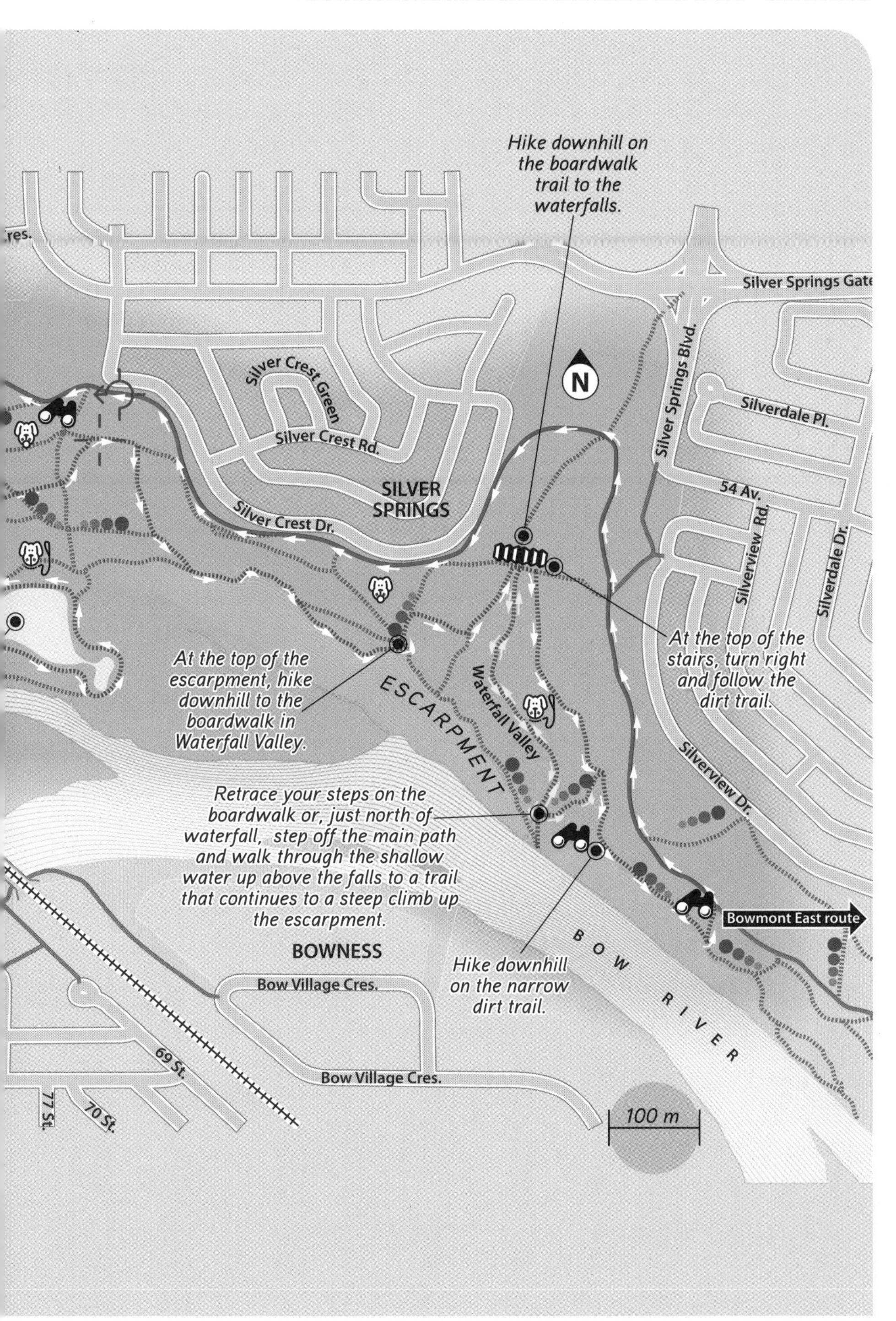
Hike downhill on the boardwalk trail to the waterfalls.
Cres.
Silver Springs Gate
Silver Springs Blvd.
Silver Crest Green
Silver Crest Rd.
Silverdale Pl.
N
SILVER SPRINGS
Silver Crest Dr.
54 Av.
Silverview Rd.
Silverdale Dr.
At the top of the stairs, turn right and follow the dirt trail.
At the top of the escarpment, hike downhill to the boardwalk in Waterfall Valley.
ESCARPMENT
Waterfall Valley
Silverview Dr.
Retrace your steps on the boardwalk or, just north of waterfall, step off the main path and walk through the shallow water up above the falls to a trail that continues to a steep climb up the escarpment.
Bowmont East route
BOWNESS
BOW RIVER
Hike downhill on the narrow dirt trail.
Bow Village Cres.
Bow Village Cres.
69 St.
77 St.
70 St.
100 m

Bowmont Natural Environment Park East

NW

Walk at a Glance:

Tucked in between the community of Silver Springs and the Bow River, Bowmont Natural Environment Park offers a nature break, with grassland trails and paved pathways. Start the hike on the paved Bow River Pathway and continue past the soon-to-be-reclaimed gravel pit along the Bow River before navigating inland onto the rollercoaster grassland pathways.

Route Details

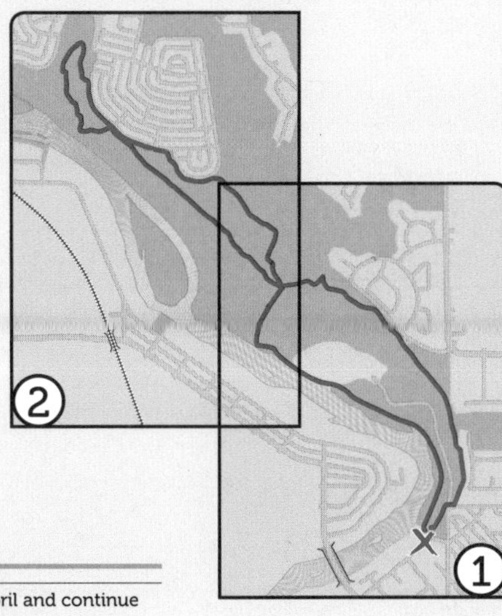

Categories: Café, Dog Friendly, Hilly, Nature, River, Stroller, Trail Running, Vistas.

Starting-Point Parking: Park at the official parking area on Fifty-Second Street (one-way) just off Home Road. There is no sign at the parking entrance.

Transit: Bus access. Check Calgary Transit at www.calgarytransit.com.

Facilities: None.

Distance: 7.3 km

Degree of Difficulty: Moderate, with many hills but with an option to stay on the paved regional pathway for a more gradual walk.

Seasonal Highlights/Cautions

Spring and Summer: Wildflowers start blooming in early April and continue throughout the summer.

Fall and Winter: In late September and early October, the grasses turn autumnal reds and oranges while the aspen groves host yellow leaves–always spectacular against a blue sky. Enjoy the solitude on the trails in the cooler months.

The rolling grassland trail is perfect for hikers in training, with its multiple climbs and descents. The high points on the trail offer a bird's eye view of some of the vast and impressive properties along the river in Bowness. Post-climb rest breaks allow you to soak up the Rocky Mountain views, which are hard to beat.

Hilly Hiking Techniques

Practice the "mountaineer" or "rest" step when climbing stairs or hills. Take a step uphill, straighten the stepping leg by letting your heel come back to the ground and then take your next uphill step. If the hill is really steep you may want to count one second in between steps. This endurance technique lets you relax your calf muscles and breathe easy so you have lots of energy for the long haul. The endurance step is a technique used by long-haul hikers.

While a slow and consistent pace is the key to endurance, a faster pace will help you build muscle strength and improve your anaerobic threshold. There is a benefit to the muscle burn you feel while hiking uphill. The strong muscles that result from the "burn" help support you on steep slope descents, or when you need a quick burst of energy.

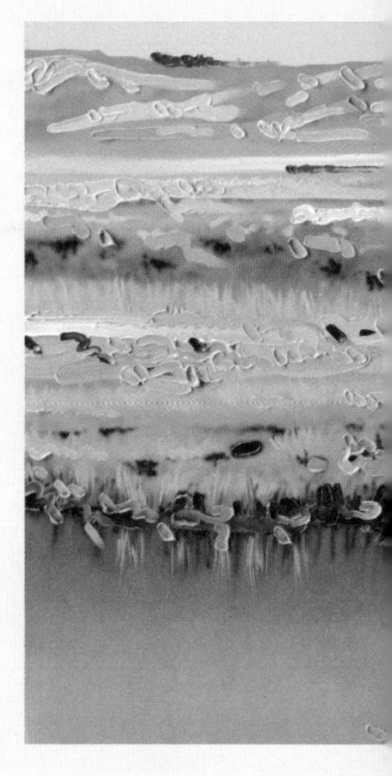

Along The Way I Stopped To See You
by Sheila Kernan

Loop back along the top of the escarpment, past the homes with million-dollar views. Cut inland along narrow pathways, descend the slope, and climb back up again along the switchback trail. Continue through the park to conclude your walk. Now you are all set to visit Bowness for a post-walk drink or meal, or just to check out the shops along Bowness Road.

Cadence Coffee

Self-described as "a 21st century diner located in the heart of Bowness, where friends meet to enjoy great food, superfine coffee, and fresh baking," Cadence is a local hot spot. Popular for breakfasts or a cup of coffee and freshly baked muffin, it is a wonderful post-walk destination. It is my favourite post Bowmont Park stop with groups of walkers that join me on guided walks. Cadence is also a great place to grab a picnic lunch before your walk. Made-to-order sandwiches, fresh soups, and lots of salads are available; grab some tasty food and enjoy it during a break at one of the sight-seeing lookouts perched on the Bowmont Park escarpments.

Location: 6407 Bowness Road NW, www. cadencecoffee.com
Hours: 7 am–5 pm (weekdays), 8 am–4 pm (weekends)

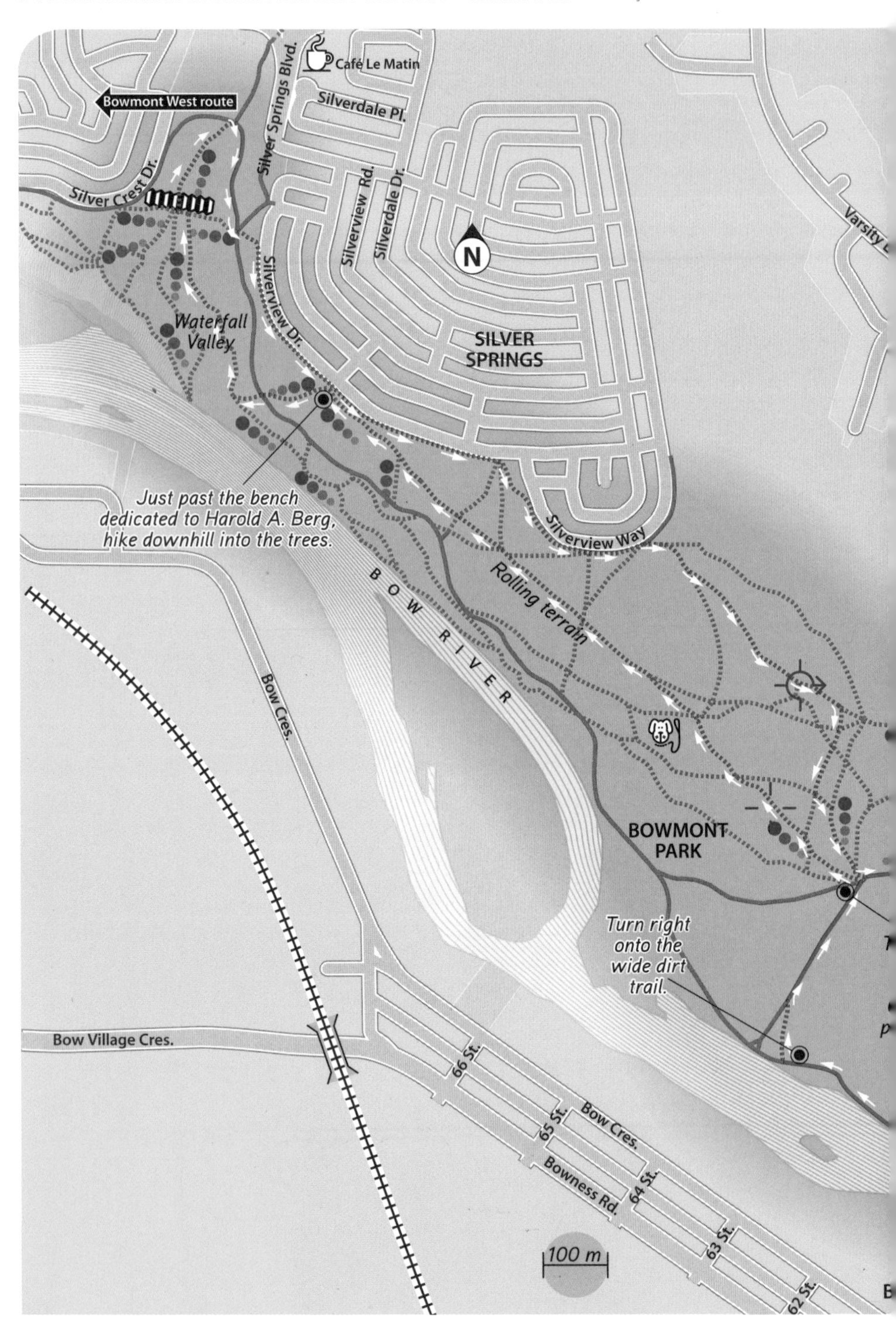
Café Le Matin
Bowmont West route
Silverdale Pl.
Silver Springs Blvd.
Silver Crest Dr.
Silverview Rd.
Silverdale Dr.
N
Varsity
Silverview Dr.
Waterfall Valley
SILVER SPRINGS
Just past the bench dedicated to Harold A. Berg, hike downhill into the trees.
Silverview Way
Rolling terrain
BOW RIVER
Bow Cres.
BOWMONT PARK
Turn right onto the wide dirt trail.
Bow Village Cres.
66 St.
65 St.
Bow Cres.
Bowness Rd.
64 St.
63 St.
62 St.
100 m

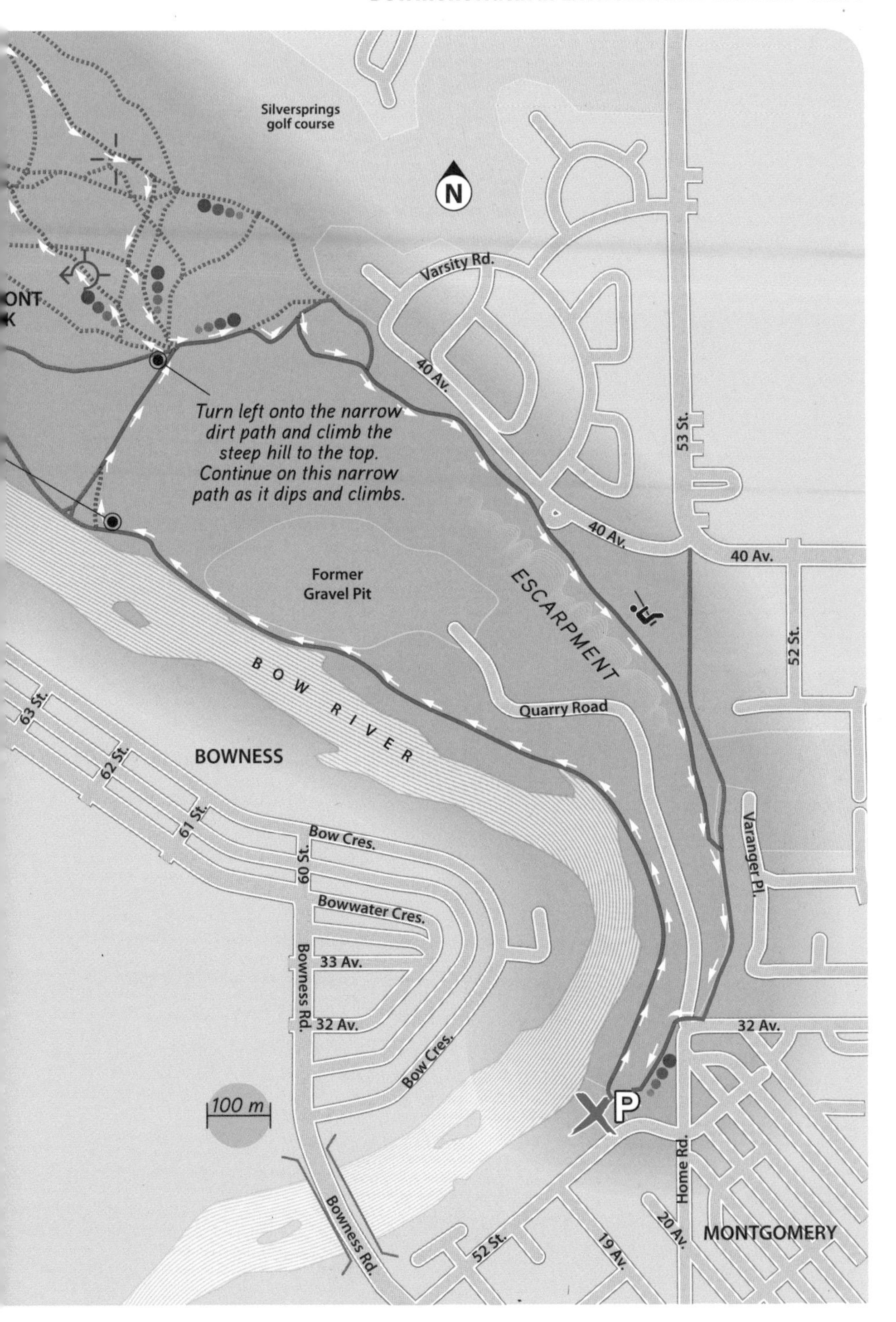

Silversprings golf course
N
Varsity Rd.
40 Av.
53 St.
Turn left onto the narrow dirt path and climb the steep hill to the top. Continue on this narrow path as it dips and climbs.
40 Av.
40 Av.
Former Gravel Pit
ESCARPMENT
52 St.
BOW RIVER
Quarry Road
63 St.
62 St.
BOWNESS
61 St.
Varanger Pl.
Bow Cres.
60 St.
Bowwater Cres.
33 Av.
Bowness Rd.
32 Av.
32 Av.
Bow Cres.
100 m
P
Home Rd.
Bowness Rd.
52 St.
19 Av.
20 Av.
MONTGOMERY

Edgemont Hills and Ravines

NW

Walk at a Glance

At its highest point of 1245 m, Edgemont offers expansive views of Calgary. Exposed slopes fill with wildflowers from April through August and host impressive windswept snowdrifts throughout the winter.

This route begins with a short walk through the neighbourhood, followed by a wide-open green-space climb. Post climb, the route continues west on one of the many dirt paths that crisscross the hill. Stay high and enjoy views throughout or drop low and climb up again for a physical challenge.

Route Details

Categories: Café, Dog Friendly, Hilly, Nature, Neighbourhoods and Parks, Trail Running, Vistas.

Starting point parking: Official parking lot on Edgemont Drive, just north of John Laurie Boulevard.

Transit: Bus access at various points along the route. Check Calgary Transit at www.calgarytransit.com.

Facilities: Seasonal bathrooms at trailhead.

Distance: 10.6 km

Degree of Difficulty: Moderate, with many optional hills.

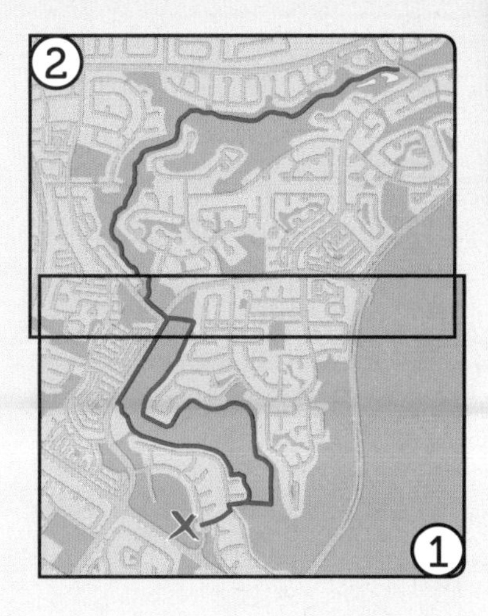

Seasonal Highlights/Cautions

Winter: After a big snowfall, snowdrifts can be waist high on the initial hill.

Spring: Enjoy wildflowers on the slopes, starting with the purple-headed prairie crocus in early April. Listen for red-winged blackbirds in the ravine wetlands.

Cross Edgemont Boulevard and follow the pathway into Edgemont Park Ravines, a manicured multi-use park with paved paths, art installations, and playgrounds. The ravine trail offers a relatively flat trek through a pleasant green space. Hikers in training will find many hill options where they can challenge their legs with some ravine-slope climbs.

Turn the corner at the T-junction and the park becomes less manicured, more natural. Thick willow shrubs consume the north-facing hillside, creating a sheltered home for mule deer. Listen for the Edgemont Park Ravine. Before reaching the ponds, the bird chatter is loud and clear. Cattails line the sides of the water and attract red-winged blackbirds, which have a distinctive sing-song call.

This is a linear route, an out-and-back walk. After you get your nature fix, turn on your heels and follow your breadcrumbs back to your car.

Friends Cappuccino Bar and Bakeshop

Warm up at this comfy local café tucked into the Edgemont. A popular spot for fresh, house-made muffins and good cup of coffee in the mornings, it also serves sandwiches and paninis to walkers in need of calories. And for dessert, grab one of the shop's "colossal" chocolate chip cookies, or a square with enough sugar to keep you going all week, or treat yourself to a slice of cake.

Location: 104, 45 Edenwold Drive NW, www.friendscafe.ca
Hours: 7 am- 5pm (weekdays), 8 am- 5 pm Saturday, 9 am-4 pm Sunday

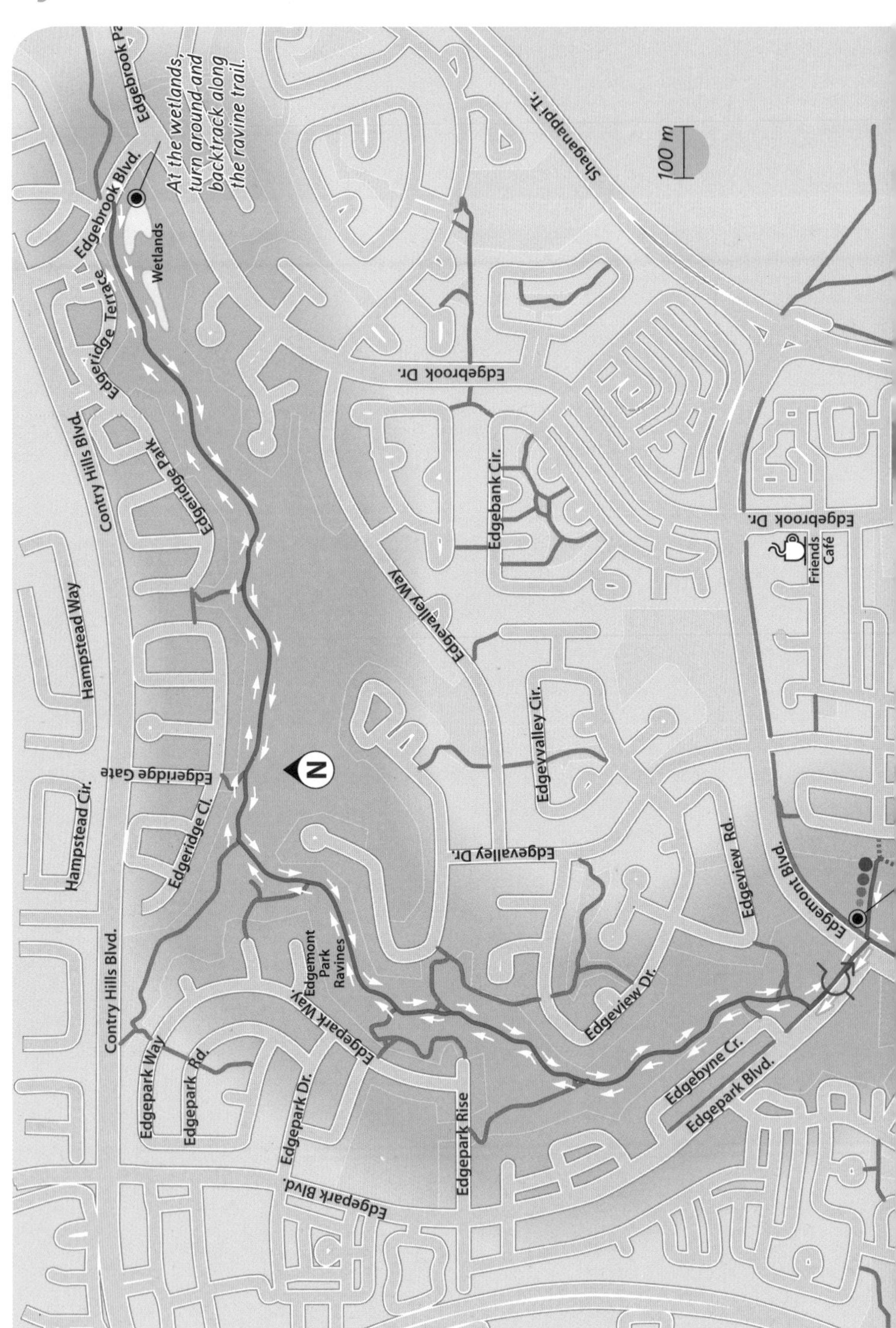
At the wetlands, turn around and backtrack along the ravine trail.
Edgebrook Blvd.
Edgebrook Pa
Wetlands
Shaganappi Tr.
100 m
Edgeridge Terrace
Edgebrook Dr.
Edgebank Cir.
Contry Hills Blvd.
Edgeridge Park
Edgebrook Dr.
Friends Café
Edgevalley Way
Hampstead Way
Edgevalley Cir.
Edgeridge Gate
N
Edgeridge Cl.
Hampstead Cir.
Edgevalley Dr.
Edgeview Rd.
Edgemont Blvd.
Edgemont Park Ravines
Edgeview Dr.
Edgepark Way
Edgepark Way
Edgepark Rd.
Edgepark Dr.
Edgebyne Cr.
Edgepark Blvd.
Edgepark Rise
Edgepark Blvd.

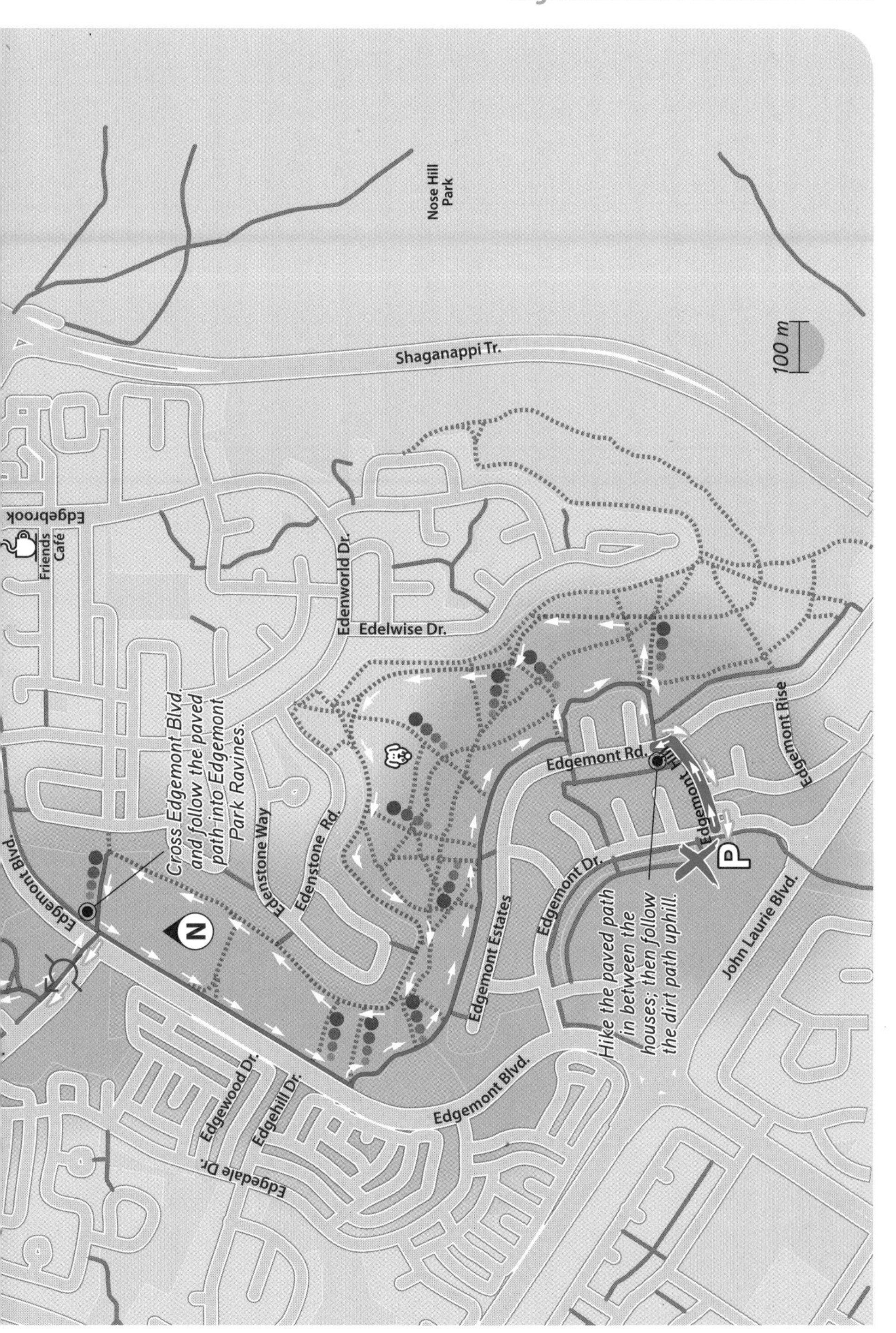
Nose Hill Park
Shaganappi Tr.
100 m
Edgebrook
Friends Café
Edenworld Dr.
Edelwise Dr.
Cross Edgemont Blvd. and follow the paved path into Edgemont Park Ravines.
Edenstone Way
Edenstone Rd.
Edgemont Rd.
Edgemont Hill
Edgemont Rise
Edgemont Estates
Edgemont Dr.
Edgemont Blvd.
Hike the paved path in between the houses; then follow the dirt path uphill.
John Laurie Blvd.
Edgewood Dr.
Edgehill Dr.
Edgedale Dr.
N
P

Nose Hill Park

NW

Overview:

The Nose Hill plateau is the highest point in Calgary, and it is wide open to the elements. This exposure makes for a refreshing and breezy walk on a hot summer day and a bone-chilling Arctic–like adventure during a –20°C January chill. The post-winter colour begins in April when the purple-headed prairie crocus peeks out, even through the fresh spring snow, and brings a smile to the faces of warmth-anticipating, winter-weary Calgarians.

Seasonal Highlights/Cautions

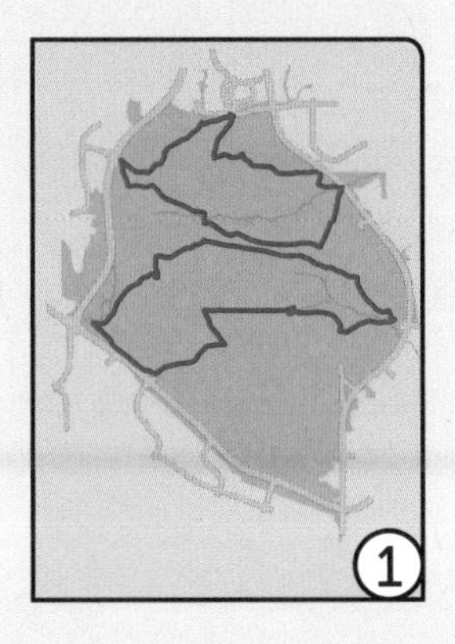

Year-Round: Navigating Nose Hill is challenging. If you are new to the hill, pay attention to the landmarks and do not attempt to walk the hill in poor visibility (snowstorms, fog, or darkness). The trail maps on the hill are difficult to use for orientation, so I suggest you use my map along with the on-trail maps, as well as landmarks, to help you navigate. The power lines at the far north end of the hill extend from the Berkley Gate parking lot to the Edgemont parking lot. If you can see the airport, you are on the Fourteenth Street side of the hill. There is an antenna visible on the hill, which is close to the Calgary Winter Club parking lot, off Fourteenth Street.

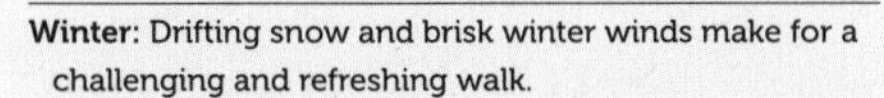

Winter: Drifting snow and brisk winter winds make for a challenging and refreshing walk.

Spring: Purple-headed prairie crocuses emerge on the Fourteenth Street side of the hill in early April. The yellow buffalo bean follows soon after.

Summer: Alberta wildflowers are abundant.

Fall: Shrubs and grasses turn rich shades of yellows, oranges, and reds.

This section of the book includes two routes that cover about three quarters of the hill. The Porcupine Valley and Aspen Grove route (see page 60) starts with a gradual climb to the wide-open plateau trail. Enjoy the mountain views before descending the open slopes into a shady aspen-filled coulee. The coulee trail offers a break from the wind on a winter day and relief from the hot sun in the summer. Back on the plateau, soak up panoramic views for the rest of this trek. The Meadowlark Prairie and Many Owls Valley route (see page 66) starts at the top of the plateau and offers a mix of gradual climbs, flat stretches, and dips into aspen-filled coulees.

From afar, Nose Hill seems plain, a bump on the horizon. It is only when you take the first step that the abundance and variety of vegetation in visible. Over two hundred flowering plants colour the hill's landscape throughout the summer and into the fall. Amongst the prairie grasses that dominate Nose Hill you'll also find mushrooms, mosses, and many animals. In the fall, shrubs and grasses become a kaleidoscope of rich red, burnt orange, and golden yellow. Wildlife is abundant on the hill, and I often see groups of white-tailed deer and the occasional waddling porcupine at dusk. Birders should be excited to hear that ninety-one bird species have been seen on Nose Hill–bring your binoculars. There are many geologically interesting features on Nose Hill, as well. Glacial erratics (rocks that were transported to a place by glaciers and then left behind after the glaciers melted) that have been rubbed smooth by buffaloes can be found throughout the park. And hikers in training will enjoy the drops into coulees followed by some stiff climbs that challenge the heart and legs.

At 11 square km, Nose Hill Park is one of the largest municipal parks in Canada. Due to the growth of the city, Nose Hill needed a trail-management plan that supported recreational use. Three trail types now cover the hill and trail maps have been placed at many intersections. Despite these maps (and my handy-dandy guidebook), the size of the area and the abundance of unofficial dirt paths make getting disoriented a possibility. In order to find your car at the end of your walk, route-finding 101 suggests that you always pay attention to the landmarks on the hill such as the mountain ranges in the west, the airport in the east, the power line that cross the hill in the north, the antenna that stands near the quarry, and the downtown office towers. Using landmarks also helps you make sense of the trailside maps, since long summer grasses can cover trails and deer and coyotes can create new ones. Pay attention to where you are and you can confidently slog through snowdrifts or follow new pathways without fear of an overnight urban adventure.

Bring your camera! Both routes offer superb views. And depending on where you are on the hill, you'll see the Front Range of the Rocky Mountains and the foothills, the prairies stretching out to the east, the compact downtown core rising prominently in the south, Canada Olympic Park ski and mountain-bike hill, and flights arriving and departing from the airport. Enjoy the solitude of this natural wilderness wonder in the heart of the city.

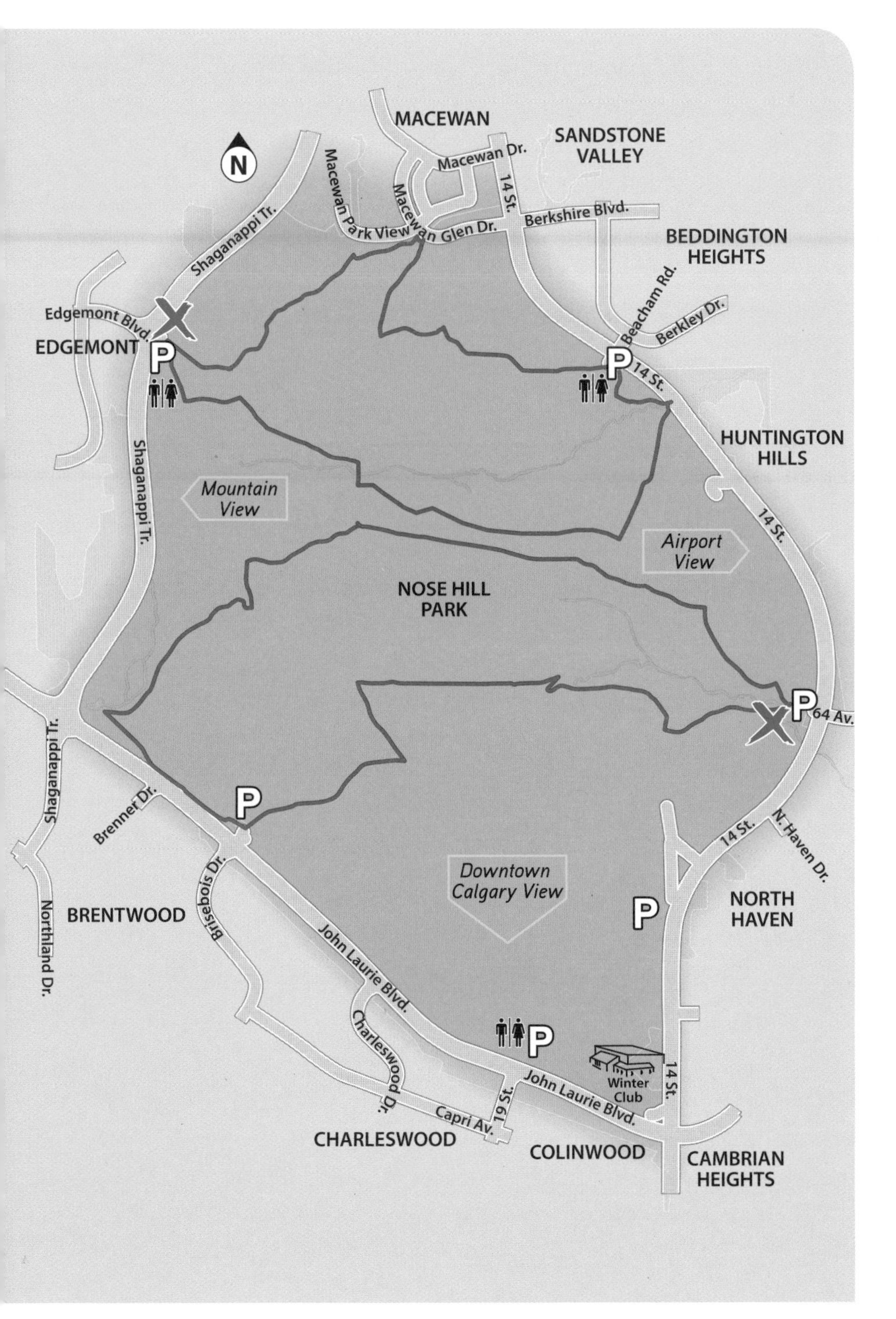
N
MACEWAN
SANDSTONE VALLEY
Macewan Dr.
Macewan Park View
Macewan Glen Dr.
14 St.
Berkshire Blvd.
BEDDINGTON HEIGHTS
Shaganappi Tr.
Beacham Rd.
Berkley Dr.
Edgemont Blvd.
EDGEMONT
P
14 St.
HUNTINGTON HILLS
Mountain View
Airport View
NOSE HILL PARK
64 Av.
Shaganappi Tr.
Brenner Dr.
14 St.
N. Haven Dr.
Brisebois Dr.
Downtown Calgary View
NORTH HAVEN
Northland Dr.
BRENTWOOD
John Laurie Blvd.
Charleswood Dr.
Winter Club
14 St.
John Laurie Blvd.
Capri Av.
19 St.
CHARLESWOOD
COLINWOOD
CAMBRIAN HEIGHTS

Nose Hill Park: Porcupine Valley and Aspen Grove

NW

Walk at a Glance:

Starting with a hill climb, pace for pleasure, enjoy the views, and soon you will be on the top of the plateau. Once on top, take a look around and you will see that Broadcast Hill (the hill where Canada Olympic Park is built) is also flat and at the same elevation as Nose Hill.

Hills south of the city near Priddis are the same. These plateaus are the remnants of a 60-million-year-old, swampy, forested landscape into which the Bow and Elbow rivers, and the glaciers that followed their valleys, have incised by 175 m. That is something to think about while you catch your breath.

Route Details

Categories: Café, Dog Friendly, Hilly, Nature, Trail Running, Vistas.

Starting-Point Parking: Official parking lot at Fourteenth Street and Sixty-Fourth Avenue NW.

Transit: Bus access into surrounding communities. Check Calgary Transit at www.calgarytransit.com.

Facilities: None at this trailhead. Café (Edelweiss, see Walk 12 on page 92; or Lina's, See Walk 10 on page 80)

Distance: 9.8 km

Degree of Difficulty: Moderate, with hills.

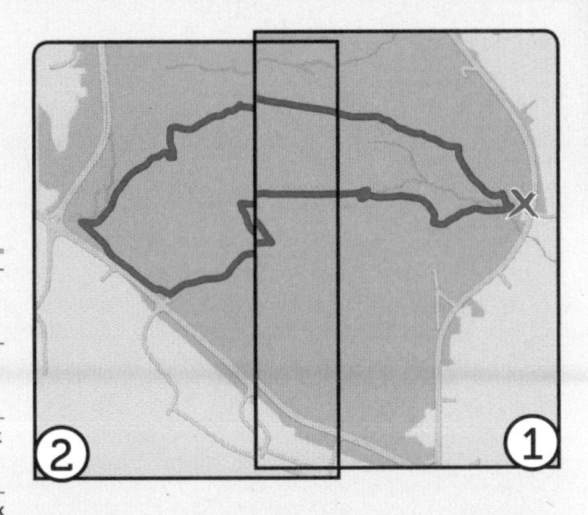

Seasonal Highlights/Cautions

Year-Round: Pay attention to your landmarks! The power lines at the far north end extend from the Berkley Gate parking lot to the Edgemont parking lot. If you can see the airport, you are on the Fourteenth Street side of the hill. There is an antenna visible on the hill and that is close to the Calgary Winter Club parking lot off Fourteenth Street.

Enjoy a flat walk on the plateau before descending into an aspen-filled coulee. Hone your senses while you walk. Listen for coyotes howling at passing sirens, and in the spring and summer, enjoy the colourful explosion of wildflowers. The little treasures are not visible from the road, only those on foot experience the purple-headed prairie crocuses and yellow buffalo beans, pink wild roses, orange lilies, and purple lupines all mixed up in the grassy landscape of the hill.

Itchy Buffalo and Erratics

When the glaciers carved their way across Nose Hill, they left behind many large boulders known as glacial erratics, which bear no compositional resemblance to local rocks. One hundred years ago, buffalo roamed Nose Hill. In the spring, the buffalo would rub against these stones as they began to molt, trying to remove irritating hairs. You can see the evidence in the form of deep, smooth depressions and shiny spots that remain on the stones today.

Trembling Aspen Clones

Parts of Nose Hill are covered with groves of trembling aspen, native trees with round leaves that are easily coerced into movement by the wind. Trembling aspen leaves are a fresh green in the spring and turn a vibrant yellow in the fall. All aspens within a grove are genetically identical. The original tree clones itself by sending out suckers from underground roots, each of which becomes a new aspen. Some trembling aspen colonies in Alberta are over six thousand years old. All clones within a colony change colour at the same time in the fall.

Trembling aspen groves make great hiding spots for animals and add sparkling colour to this grassland hike.

Blue Glass by Sheila Kernan

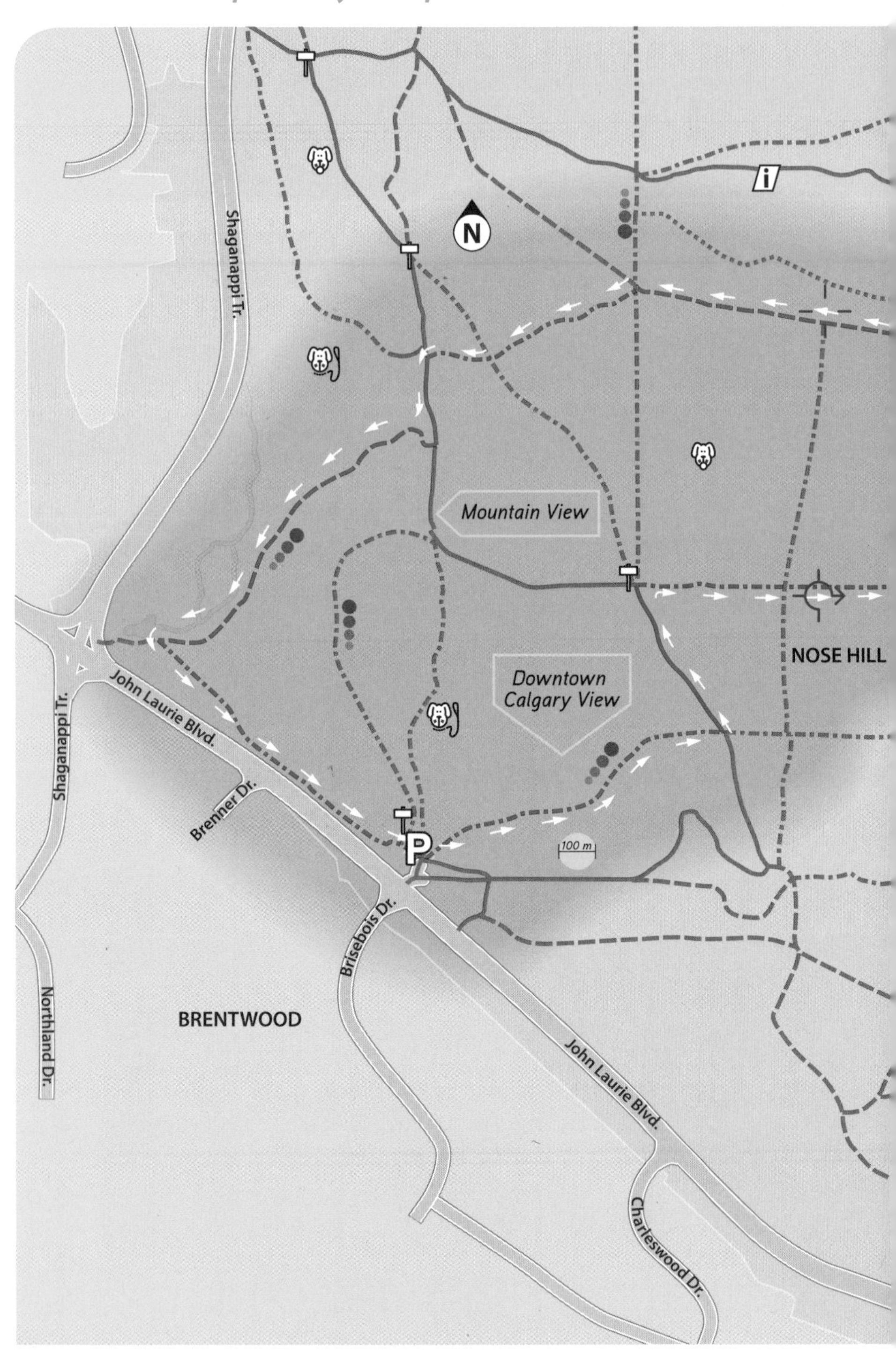

Shaganappi Tr.
N
Mountain View
NOSE HILL
Downtown Calgary View
John Laurie Blvd.
Shaganappi Tr.
Brenner Dr.
P
100 m
Brisebois Dr.
BRENTWOOD
Northland Dr.
John Laurie Blvd.
Charleswood Dr.

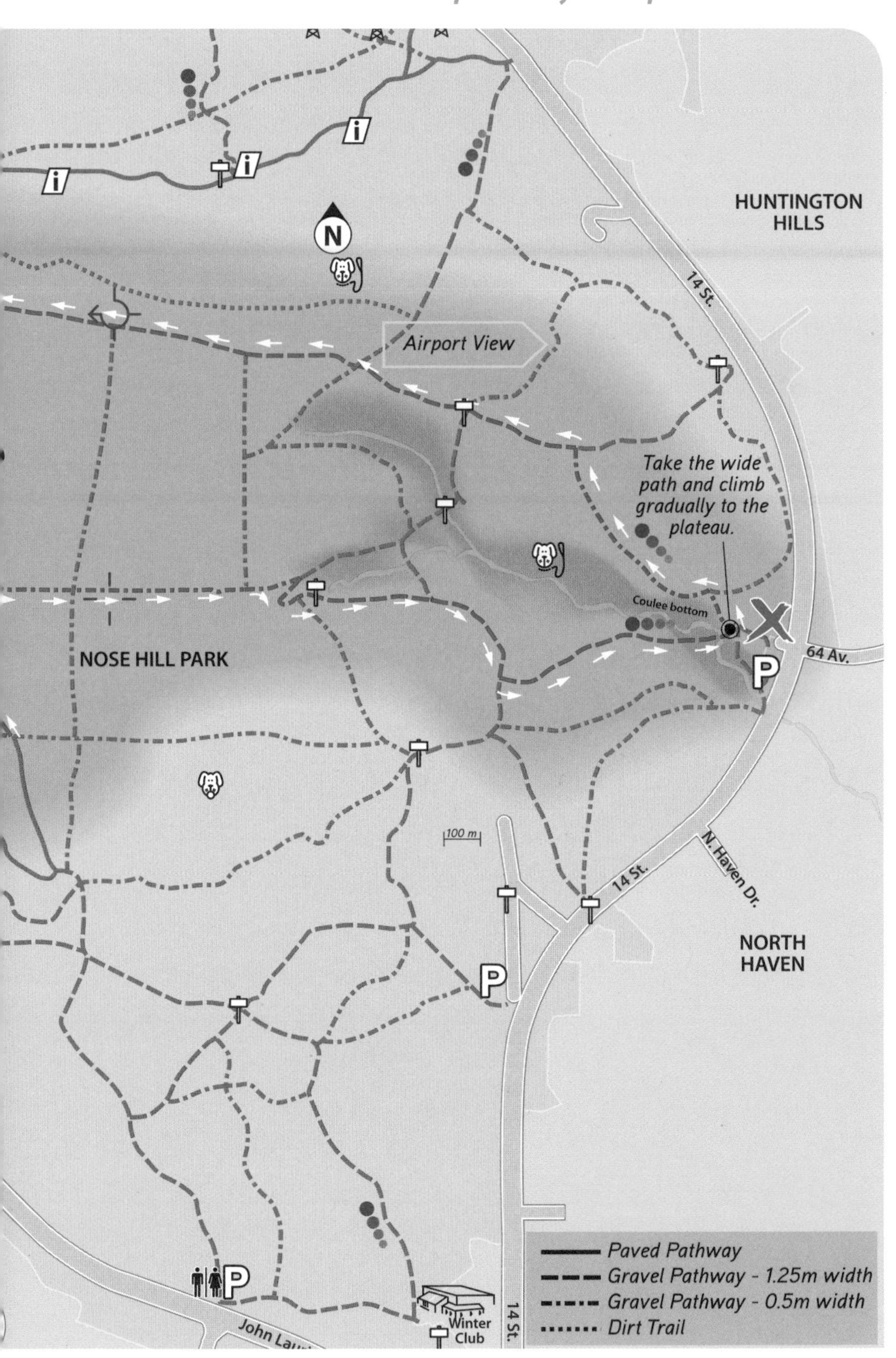
HUNTINGTON HILLS
14 St.
Airport View
Take the wide path and climb gradually to the plateau.
Coulee bottom
64 Av.
NOSE HILL PARK
100 m
N. Haven Dr.
14 St.
NORTH HAVEN
John Lau
Winter Club
14 St.
Paved Pathway
Gravel Pathway - 1.25m width
Gravel Pathway - 0.5m width
Dirt Trail

Nose Hill Park: Meadowlark Prairie and Many Owls Valley

NW

Walk at a Glance:

This route starts on the top of the plateau, the only route on Nose Hill that does not begin with a hill climb. Soak up panoramic plateau views and enjoy the flat-walk warm-up before dipping into aspen-filled coulees. Aspen groves give shelter to a wide variety of plants and animals from the winds that frequently buffet Nose Hill.

Route Details

Categories: Café, Dog Friendly, Hilly, Nature, Trail Running, Vistas.

Starting-Point Parking: Official parking lot at Shaganappi Trail and Edgemont Boulevard NW.

Transit: Bus access into surrounding communities. Check Calgary Transit at www.calgarytransit.com.

Facilities: Year-round bathroom, Café (Friends Café, see Walk 6 on page 52)

Distance: 7.3 km

Degree of Difficulty: Moderate, with hills.

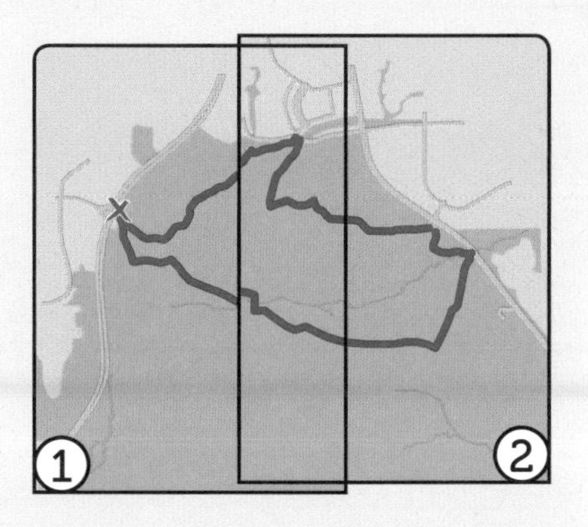

Seasonal Highlights/Cautions

Year-Round: Pay attention to your landmarks! The power lines at the far north end of the hill extend from the Berkley Gate parking lot to the Edgemont parking lot. If you can see the airport, you are on the Fourteenth Street side of the hill. There is an antenna visible on the hill, which is located close to the Calgary Winter Club parking lot off Fourteenth Street.

While in the coulees, keep a lookout for sheltering great horned owls, American robins, song sparrows, deer, white-tailed hare, and prairie long-tailed weasels.

Climb back to the plateau and enjoy the wide-open grassy landscape. Take to the trails after supper in September when the autumnal hues warm the hill. Burnt-yellow aspen groves, prairie grasses that turn rich red at the tips, and Calgary's trademark big blue sky makes this route the perfect fall frolic!

Grass Facts

Hardy grasses dominate the prairies and make up a large part of Nose Hill. These flowering plants are pollinated by the wind. They have no colourful flowers because they do not need to attract insects for pollination. Grasses benefit from grazing by large mammals like cattle and deer. Grazing removes the dead plants (the dry grass we see above ground) and allows the sun to reach new growth in the spring. Seeds eaten by grazing animals are dispersed, ready to go, with their own supply of fertilizer.

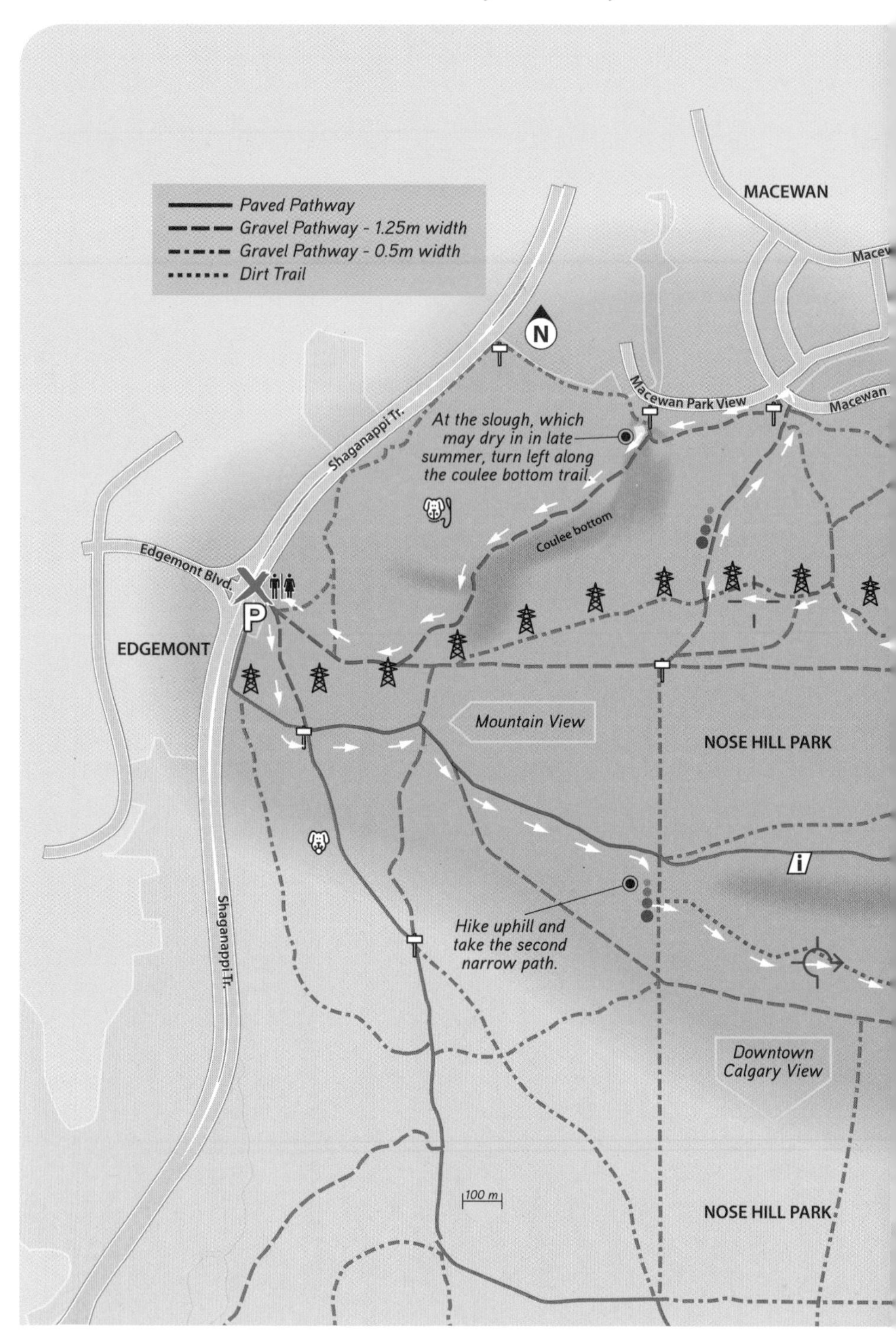
Paved Pathway
Gravel Pathway - 1.25m width
Gravel Pathway - 0.5m width
Dirt Trail
MACEWAN
Macewan Park View
Macewan
N
Shaganappi Tr.
At the slough, which may dry in in late summer, turn left along the coulee bottom trail.
Coulee bottom
Edgemont Blvd.
P
EDGEMONT
Mountain View
NOSE HILL PARK
Hike uphill and take the second narrow path.
Shaganappi Tr.
Downtown Calgary View
100 m
NOSE HILL PARK

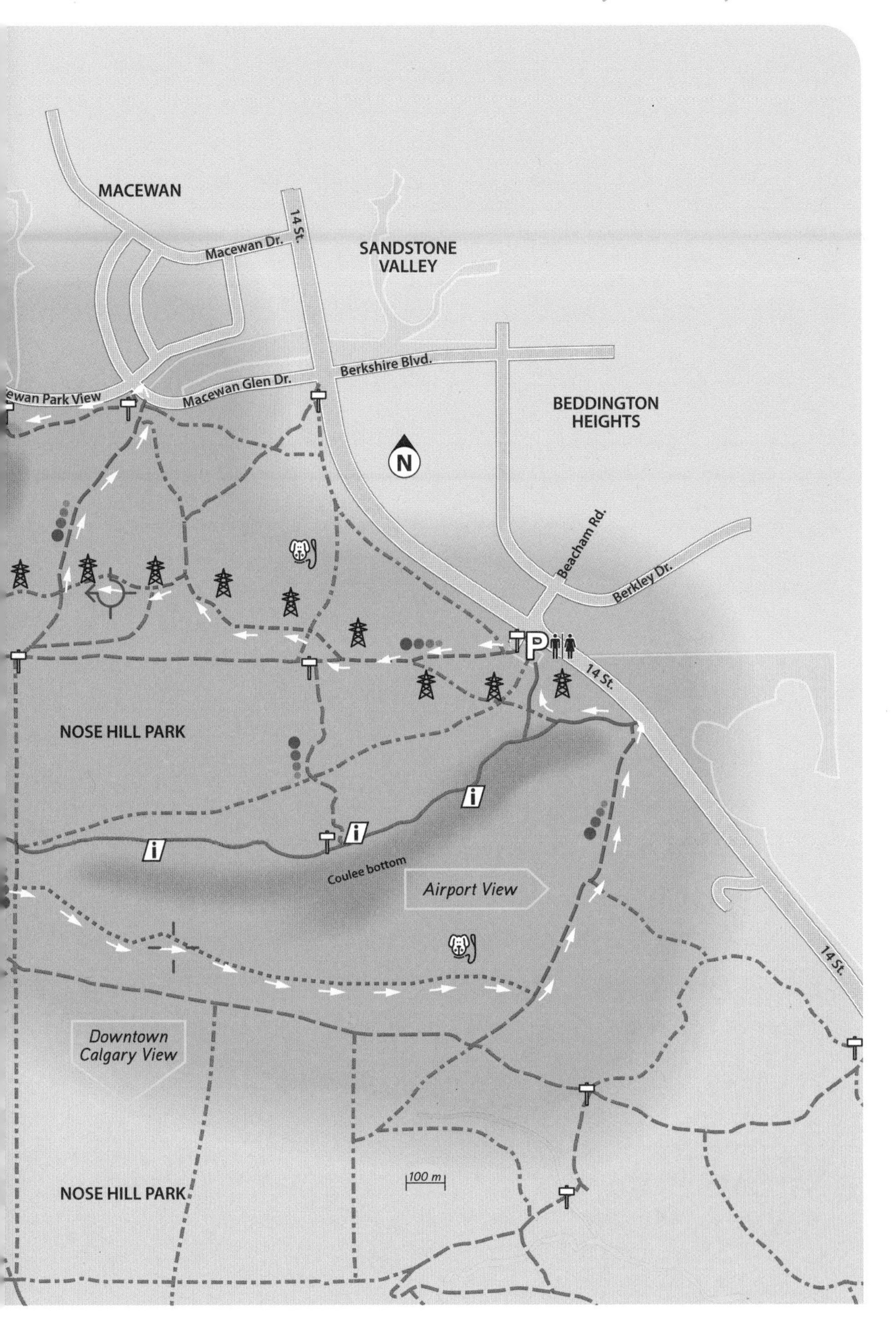
MACEWAN
14 St.
Macewan Dr.
SANDSTONE
VALLEY
Berkshire Blvd.
Macewan Glen Dr.
ewan Park View
BEDDINGTON
HEIGHTS
N
Beacham Rd.
Berkley Dr.
P
14 St.
NOSE HILL PARK
i
Coulee bottom
Airport View
14 St.
Downtown
Calgary View
100 m
NOSE HILL PARK

West Nose Creek Park

NE

Walk at a Glance:

A burbling creek has cut a valley worthy of the river that it once was, offering you views of sandstone escarpments. The route follows paved and gravel paths just below busy city streets, but make no mistake, this is a wilderness walk. Meander along the valley floor, through rough fescue grassland, alongside and across Nose Creek. The valley was forged by runoff from the last glaciation and, therefore, is considerably younger than the Bow and Elbow river valleys. Split Rock, a 2-m-high glacial erratic, is a significant feature along the route. Once part of Mount Edith Cavell in Jasper National Park, the boulder had a long ride on glaciers to arrive in Calgary.

Route Details

Categories: Dog Friendly, Nature, Stroller, Trail Running.

Starting-Point Parking: Official parking lot at the corner of Beddington Trail and Beddington Boulevard NE.

Transit: Bus access to the surrounding communities. Check Calgary Transit at www.calgarytransit.com.

Facilities: None.

Distance: 5 km

Degree of Difficulty: Easy, with gradual hills.

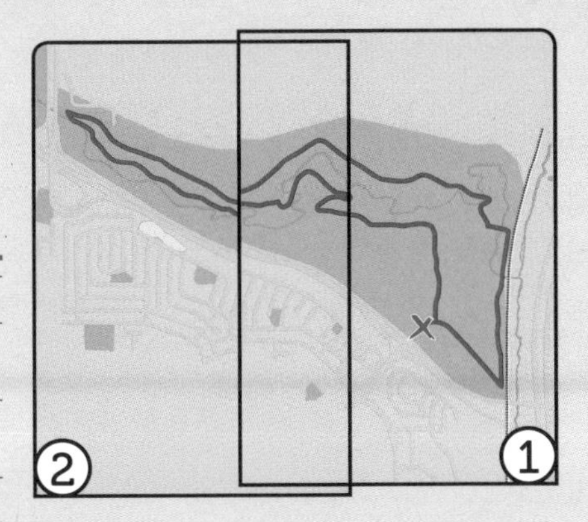

Seasonal Highlights/Cautions

Year-Round: Aviation addicts will enjoy the low-flying planes. With its proximity to the airport, I have nicknamed this route the "flight-path walk."

Winter: The landscape is open to the elements, so bundle up.

Add a Bounce to Your Step to Feel Happy

Feeling glum? Add a bounce to your step on your next walk. If you walk like a happy person, light on your feet, shoulders back, head up, and arms relaxed and swinging by your side, then you will feel happier.

We know that going for a walk, even a short walk, can make us feel better. Research shows that the mood benefits of regular, modest exercise, including walking, are a result of improved brain function, perhaps due to increased blood flow to the brain.

A new study published in the *Journal of Behaviour Therapy and Experimental Psychiatry* suggests your gait may also affect your frame of mind. The study adds to the growing body of research regarding the power of body language on the mind. Previous studies have shown that you can reduce stress and feel happier simply by smiling. Want to feel more confident and assertive? Practice some "power poses" like leaning over a desk with hands planted in front you.

If you walk like a depressed person, slumped shoulders, head positioned forward, and only swinging your arms slightly, you are more inclined to focus on the negative. Depression can be a self-perpetuating cycle: because you feel bad, you remember bad things, and because you remember bad things, you feel bad.

So, think like an actor and get into character. Project to the world how you want feel, even if you do not feel that way inside. Walk like a happy person, and you will feel happier.

West Nose Creek Park is home to a riparian zone, a narrow green space along the edge of a body of water. The diverse group of plants and animals found in this habitat are different from those a few metres away on either side. You'll walk past willows along the riverbanks and shrubs along the north-facing slope.

Keep an eye out for beavers. The park is one of the best locations in Calgary to view beaver dams and lodges. Birders will be pleased to learn that a variety of waterfowl, and several species of swallows and raptors call West Nose Creek Park home.

Loving The Long Summer Days
by Sheila Kernan

Interpretive signs along the route offer historical tidbits. One to note is that a stone quarry operated near the west end of the park for many years, and stone from the quarry was used to build many of the historic buildings in Calgary: the first and second courthouses, the McDougall Block in the downtown core, and Victoria and King Edward schools, to name a few.

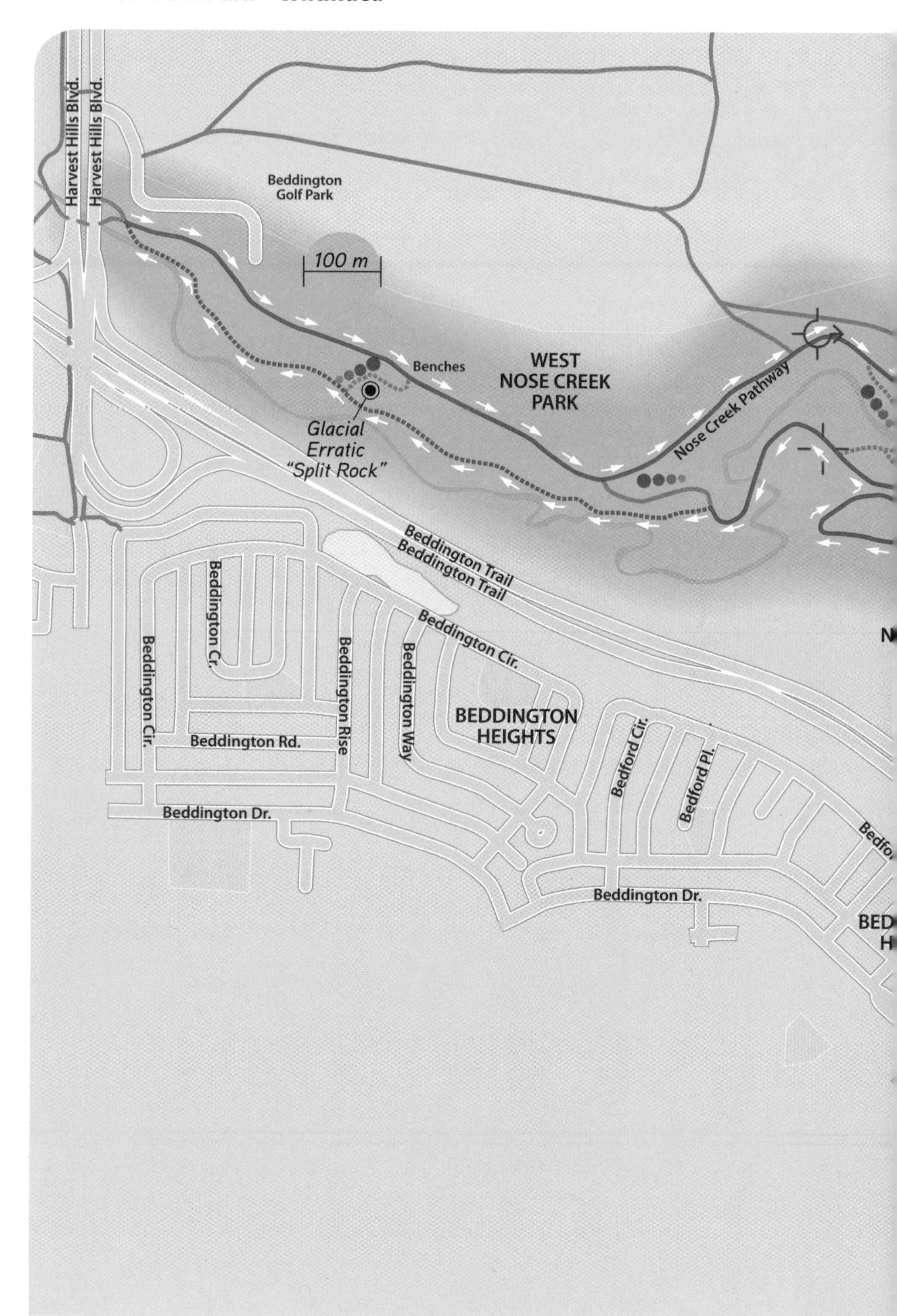
Harvest Hills Blvd.
Harvest Hills Blvd.
Beddington
Golf Park
100 m
Benches
WEST
NOSE CREEK
PARK
Glacial
Erratic
"Split Rock"
Nose Creek Pathway
Beddington Trail
Beddington Trail
Beddington Cr.
Beddington Cir.
Beddington Rise
Beddington Way
Beddington Cir.
BEDDINGTON
HEIGHTS
Beddington Rd.
Bedford Cir.
Bedford Pl.
Beddington Dr.
Beddington Dr.

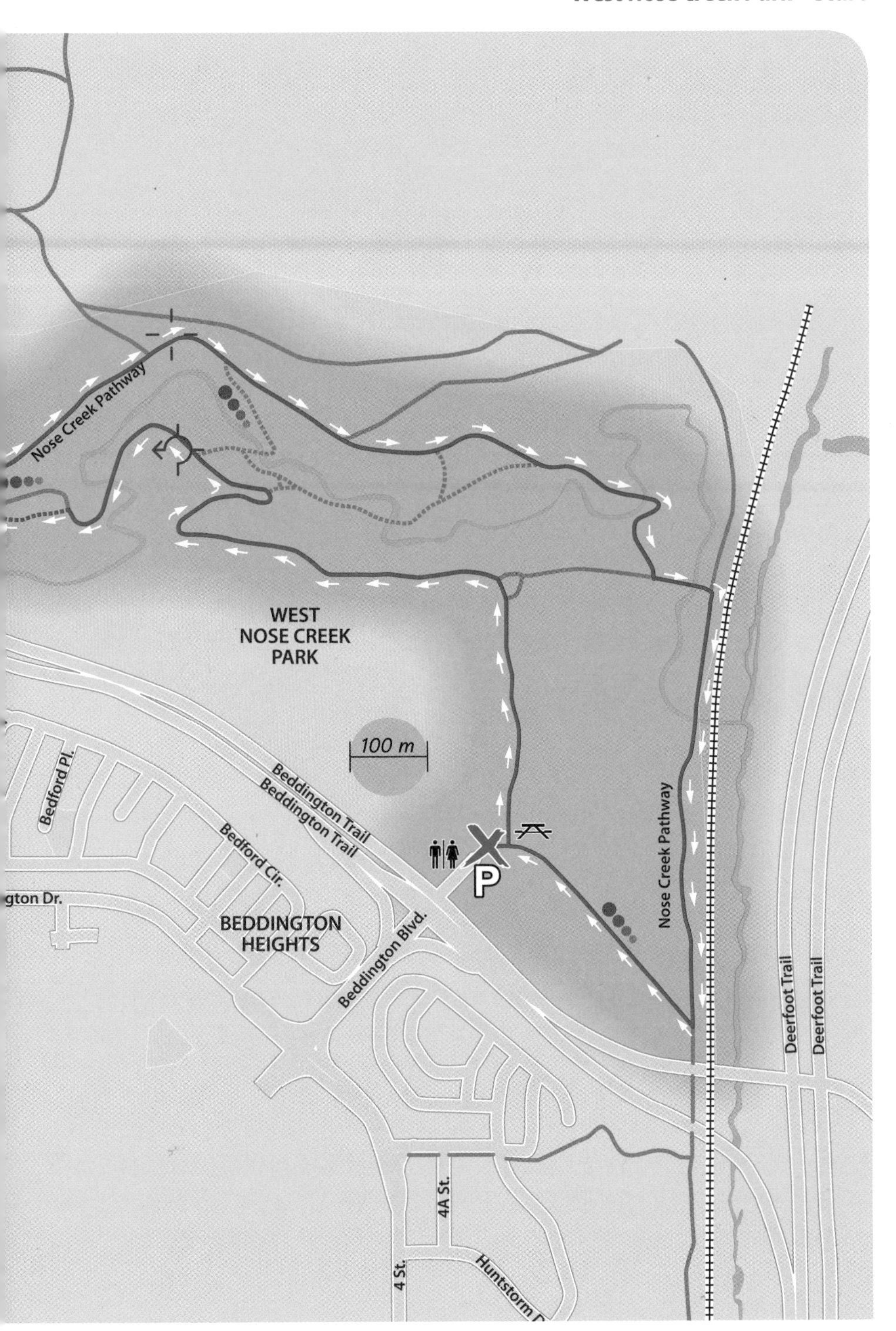
Nose Creek Pathway
WEST
NOSE CREEK
PARK
100 m
Beddington Trail
Beddington Trail
Bedford Pl.
Bedford Cir.
gton Dr.
BEDDINGTON
HEIGHTS
Beddington Blvd.
P
Nose Creek Pathway
Deerfoot Trail
Deerfoot Trail
4A St.
4 St.
Huntstorm

Vista Heights–Nose Creek–Renfrew–Winston Heights

NE

Walk at a Glance:

Larger than life: that is my first impression when I look west from Airways Park in Vista Heights. From this northeast viewpoint, the Rocky Mountains tower above Calgary's compact core. Walking the paved path along the escarpment, you hear the roar of a jet engine flying just above your head. Is the plane landing on the pathway? It's an exciting walk already!

The Calgary International Airport is just north, and the flights arriving and departing are steady. This is not surprising since Calgary is a hotbed of economic activity, a destination for work and recreation. Continue down the winding trail, cross over Calgary's busiest highway and continue south along the Nose Creek Pathway, a pleasant strip of nature that runs parallel to Deerfoot Trail.

Route Details

Categories: Café, Dog Friendly, Hilly, Home and Gardens, Neighbourhoods and Parks, River, Stroller, Vistas.

Starting-Point Parking: Street parking on Vista Street near Valleyview Road NE.

Optional Starting Point, Shorter Route: Street parking at Victory Park, Twentieth Avenue and Eighth Street SE.

Transit: Bus access at various points along the route. Check Calgary Transit at www.calgarytransit.com.

Facilities: None.

Distance: Main route: 9.3 km
Shorter route: 7.4 km

Degree of Difficulty: Moderate, with hills.

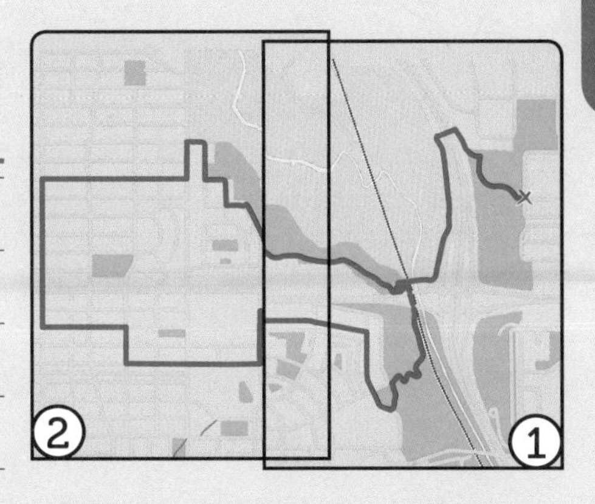

Seasonal Highlights/Cautions

Winter: The pedestrian bridge over Deerfoot Trail can be slippery.

Climb the switchback path to the community of Renfrew. Watch out for groups of long boarders on Wednesday nights, when Royal Board Shop, on Edmonton Trail, offers free skills classes to all newbie long boarders. My son took to the Renfrew side streets with them many a night, and this hill was ideal for practicing his slide turns.

Renfrew was developed in the 1940s and is now an inner-city neighbourhood, attractive for its convenient location. During the Second World War, Renfrew was home to the Royal Canadian Air Force training base and the Calgary Airport. You'll notice that the community's original homes stand out for their conservative size as new builds rise up and out, expanding to fill lots. The tree canopy spreads across many streets, creating an urban forest. Cross Edmonton Trail, a street with all services and some interesting shops. If you are hungry, stroll south along this street to Diner Deluxe at Eighth Avenue, or try other restaurants nearby that offer Mexican tacos, burgers, and sushi. Meander farther along Renfrew's side streets before crossing the Trans Canada into Tuxedo Park. Continue north and be sure to take a side-trip to my favourite Italian eatery and supermarket, Lina's on Centre Street.

After visiting Lina's, walk east through neighbourhoods in transition. Close proximity to Calgary's core means that real estate in Winston Heights / Mountview is increasing in value, and new homes reach high and wide alongside the 1950s bungalows and small wartime houses. You are now back at the Nose Creek Valley escarpment, where you can choose the off-leash single-track path or the paved path along the top of the slope. Walk past one of Calgary's few trailer parks before you descend into the Nose Creek valley. Enjoy the slow pace of the creek before the sensory explosion of Deerfoot hits and you climb back into the roar of Calgary's success.

Lina's Italian Market and Café

Lina will most likely be there when you visit her supermarket café. She runs a superb business, feeding customers tasty Italian pastas, pizzas, pastries, specialty coffees, and gelato. Lina's friendly upbeat energy is fun for kids and adults. The cafeteria-style restaurant is excellent. All you have to do is try and decide what to eat; that's a tough one since it is all so good. The individual-sized pizzas are exceptional–my favourite is the roasted veggie. After your meal, you can go shopping. Prepared lasagne, pasta sauces, and tiramisu are all made on site. Or grab some bread, meat, and cheese and have a picnic. Rows of quality Italian ingredients provide all you need for dinner planning. Continue your walk, well fed and happy.

Location: 2202 Centre Street NE, www.linasmarket.com
Hours: 9 am –7 pm (weekdays), 9 am–5 pm (weekends)

Twilight City Lights by Sheila Kernan

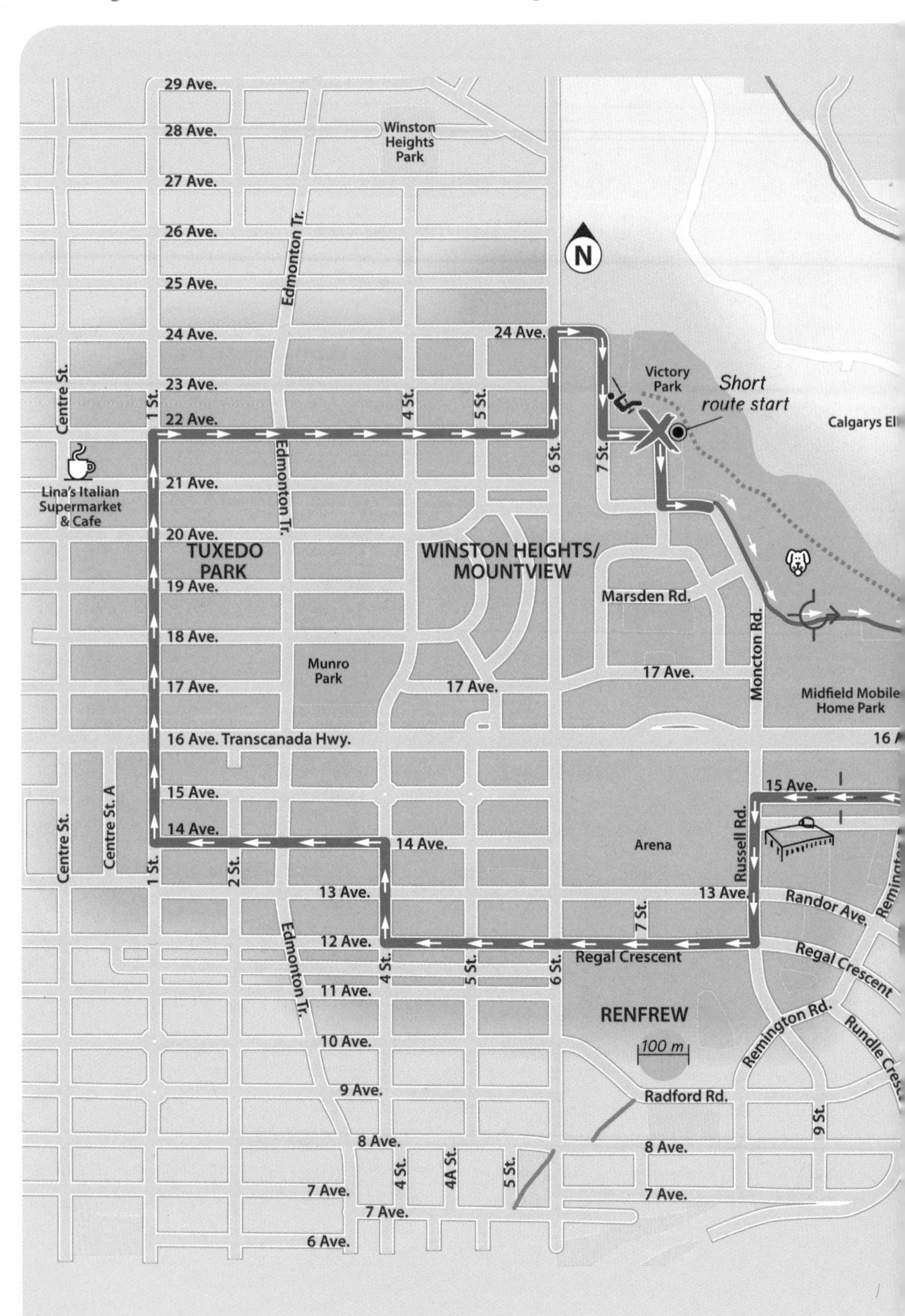
29 Ave.
28 Ave.
Winston Heights Park
27 Ave.
26 Ave.
Edmonton Tr.
25 Ave.
N
24 Ave.
24 Ave.
Centre St.
Victory Park
Short route start
23 Ave.
1 St.
4 St.
5 St.
22 Ave.
Calgarys El
6 St.
7 St.
Edmonton Tr.
21 Ave.
Lina's Italian Supermarket & Cafe
20 Ave.
TUXEDO PARK
WINSTON HEIGHTS/ MOUNTVIEW
19 Ave.
Marsden Rd.
18 Ave.
Munro Park
17 Ave.
17 Ave.
17 Ave.
Moncton Rd.
Midfield Mobile Home Park
16 Ave. Transcanada Hwy.
15 Ave.
Centre St. A
Centre St.
14 Ave.
14 Ave.
Russell Rd.
Arena
1 St.
2 St.
13 Ave.
13 Ave.
Randor Ave.
7 St.
12 Ave.
Edmonton Tr.
Regal Crescent
Regal Crescent
4 St.
5 St.
6 St.
11 Ave.
RENFREW
Remington Rd.
Rundle Cres.
10 Ave.
100 m
9 Ave.
Radford Rd.
9 St.
8 Ave.
8 Ave.
4 St.
4A St.
5 St.
7 Ave.
7 Ave.
7 Ave.
6 Ave.

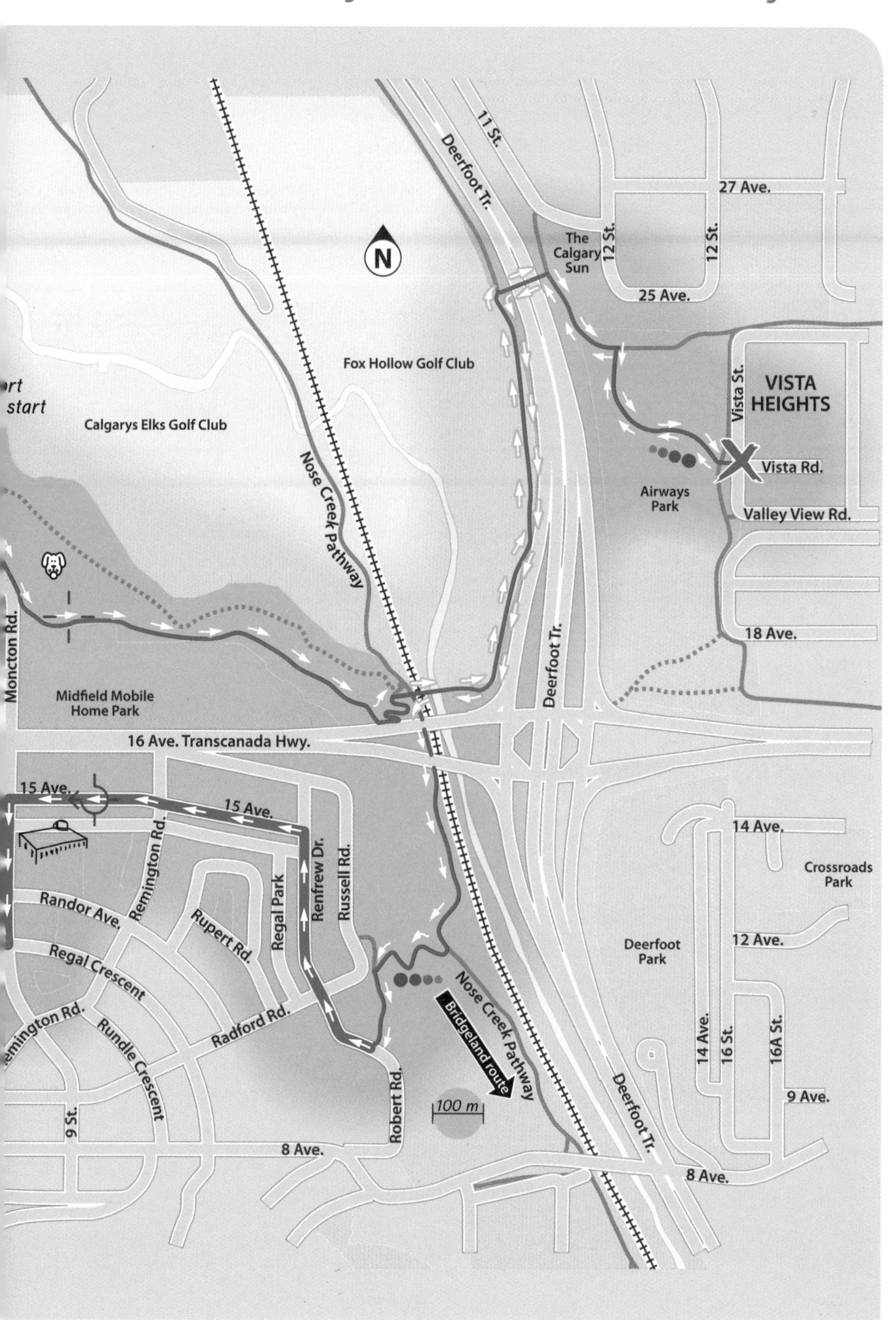
11 St.
Deerfoot Tr.
27 Ave.
The Calgary Sun
12 St.
12 St.
25 Ave.
N
Fox Hollow Golf Club
Vista St.
VISTA HEIGHTS
rt
start
Calgarys Elks Golf Club
Nose Creek Pathway
Vista Rd.
Airways Park
Valley View Rd.
18 Ave.
Deerfoot Tr.
Moncton Rd.
Midfield Mobile Home Park
16 Ave. Transcanada Hwy.
15 Ave.
15 Ave.
14 Ave.
Crossroads Park
Remington Rd.
Renfrew Dr.
Russell Rd.
Regal Park
Randor Ave.
Rupert Rd.
12 Ave.
Regal Crescent
Deerfoot Park
Nose Creek Pathway
Bridgeland route
emington Rd.
Rundle Crescent
Radford Rd.
14 Ave.
16 St.
16A St.
Deerfoot Tr.
Robert Rd.
100 m
9 Ave.
9 St.
8 Ave.
8 Ave.

Bridgeland–Bow River–Nose Creek

NE

Walk at a Glance:

Bridgeland, a community in transition, has a character that comes partly from its immigrant history and partly from rejuvenation. Germans and Russians who moved to Canada in the 1880s and decided to make their start in Calgary were the first people to settle in Bridgeland (then Riverside), where land was cheap. The area became known as Germantown, then, at the beginning of the twentieth century, Little Italy–a name that still resonates–when the immigrant population in the area included many Italians, as well as Ukrainians.

Today, the community is a mix of homes that date back to the early 1900s and modern abodes. This inner-city neighbourhood that was historically inexpensive,

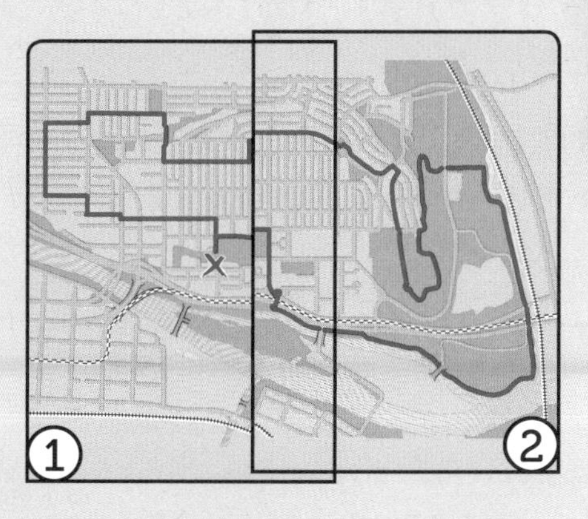

Route Details

Categories: C-Train, Café, Dog Friendly, Hilly, Historic, Home and Gardens, Nature, Neighbourhoods and Parks, People Watching and Shopping, River, Stroller, Vistas.

Starting-Point Parking: Street parking at 7A Street and Centre Avenue NE.

C-Train Start: Bridgeland Station.

Transit: Bus access at various points along the route. Check Calgary Transit at www.calgarytransit.com.

Facilities: Many cafés along or near the route.

Distance: 9.7 km

Degree of Difficulty: Moderate, with hills.

Seasonal Highlights/Cautions

Year-Round: Keep watch for a possible moose sighting while passing the Calgary Zoo.

Spring and Summer: Picnicking fun en route! Grab your grub along 1 Avenue.

a working-class community, is now settled by young families who love the central location and by urban executives who want a short commute to their downtown offices.

Shop and Eat: First Avenue and Edmonton Trail

Would you like Italian or Lebanese? Or perhaps a scrumptious, deluxe burger from Burger 320 topped with home-made aioli and optional rhubarb chutney, fresh cut fries, and homemade ice cream or gelato? Walk east along 1 Avenue and enjoy some tasty Lebanese food at Tazza or grab an ice-cream cone at the Bridgeland Market. Locally made ice cream, Made by Marcus, is indulgent, with flavours like cardamom raspberry, lemon curd, and wild blueberry. Enjoy your meal outdoors on the escarpment on a warm summer evening, and you'll soak up the leafy green carpet of treed streets below, backdropped by Calgary's towering core rising higher and higher each year. Look beyond those the city lights to the Rocky Mountains stretching across the horizon.

Walk the length of the increasingly compact First Avenue between Seventh and Eleventh Streets to find these tasty stops. Slow your pace at Edmonton Trail and stop for diner food, Mexican tacos, or sushi.

Because the neighbourhood is conveniently situated along the C-Train line as well as the Bow River Pathway, its residents take advantage of public transit and self-propelled travel. Our route follows the Bow River Pathway east, past the Canadian Wilds enclosure at the Calgary Zoo, which is visible from the main pathway. As you pass by, keep an eye out for the moose and grizzly bears that live in the enclosure. The pathway turns north and becomes the quieter Nose Creek Pathway. At Telus Spark (the science centre), walk up to the top of Tom Campbell's Hill, an off-leash natural park. The hill's name originates from a large sign that stood for many years advertising Tom Campbell's Hats. Soak up the views and pat a few pooches before continuing into the neighbourhood. A pathway along the edge of the escarpment offers a bird's eye view of the leafy streets of Bridgeland. Look for the landmark, copper-domed, Ukrainian Orthodox Church, St. Vladimir's. The church marks the set of stairs that you'll climb to the next viewpoint.

As condo towers rise up and Bridgeland and surrounding communities become more compact, independent shops and restaurants enjoy success along First Avenue and Edmonton Trail. Density brings variety, followed by life on the streets. Bridgeland is on its way to becoming bustling, a place to see and be seen. Grab a freshly roasted coffee or a picnic supper and soak up the sights in this wonderful inner-city neighbourhood.

Biophilic Bridgeland: The Urban Forest

From the escarpment trail above Bridgeland, it is hard to see the streets and houses for all the trees. Researchers call this a "biophilic community" or "green streets," where nature is integrated into the community from the ground up. Urban forests that canopy streets and include pocket-sized green spaces are the norm in Calgary's older neighbourhoods thanks to William Pearce and William Reader, two of Calgary's early parks superintendents. William Pearce envisioned a city of trees, and he devoted a lot of time and effort to develop the early boulevard plantings and parks that make the inner-city neighbourhoods great places to walk. You can thank him for the boulevard of trees along Memorial Drive. William Reader was also responsible for planting hundreds of trees, despite tough economic times in the early 1900s, a lack of water, harsh winters, and dehydrating Chinook winds.

Studies have shown that green streets lead to positive health outcomes; residents are healthier, more productive, and more generous. Nature is good for us, and a canopy of green is the one reason that walking in these areas is so pleasing, so enjoyable. Biophilic Bridgeland, from sidewalk to treetop, is a natural urban oasis.

Bridgeland–Bow River–Nose Creek - Start

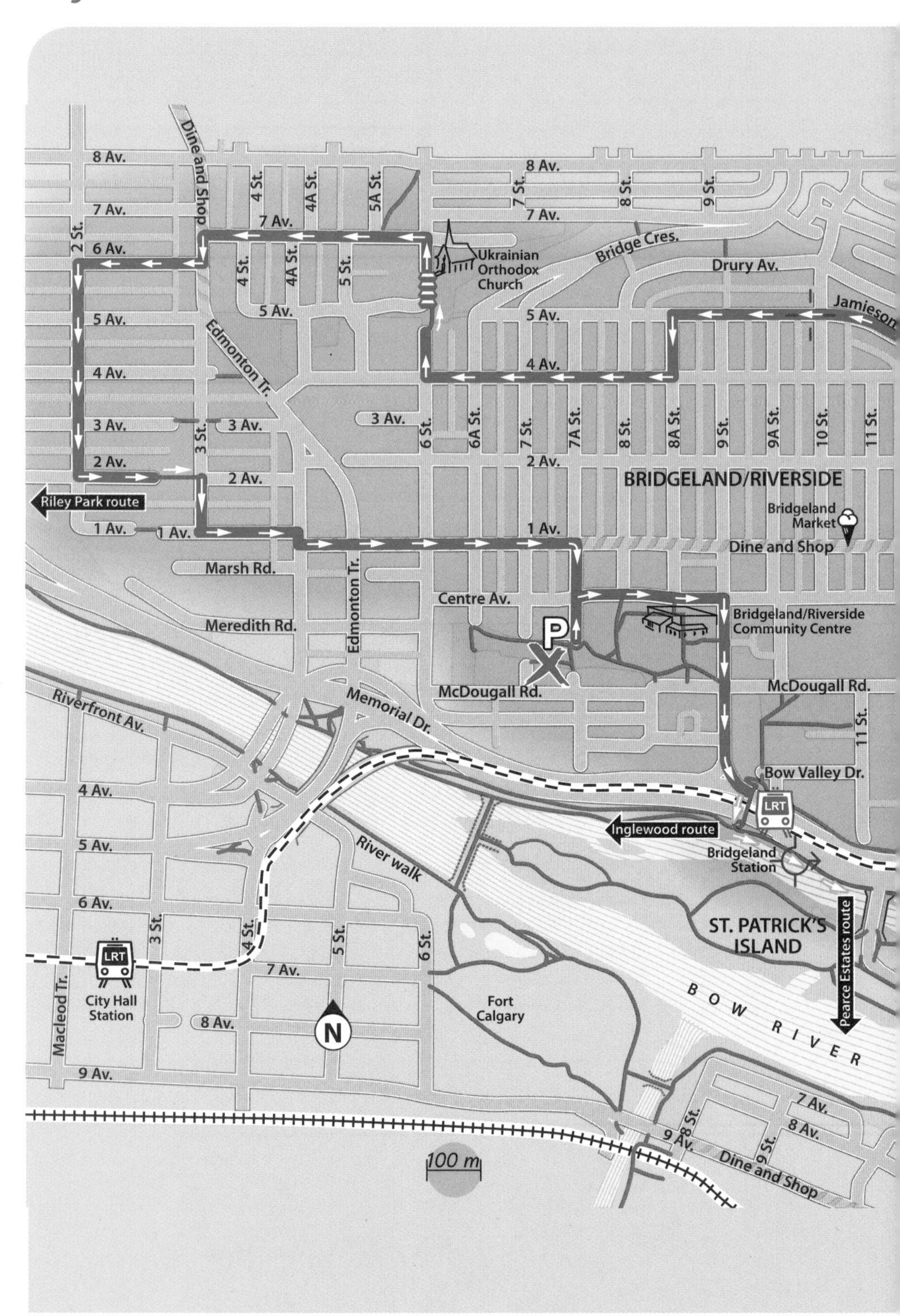

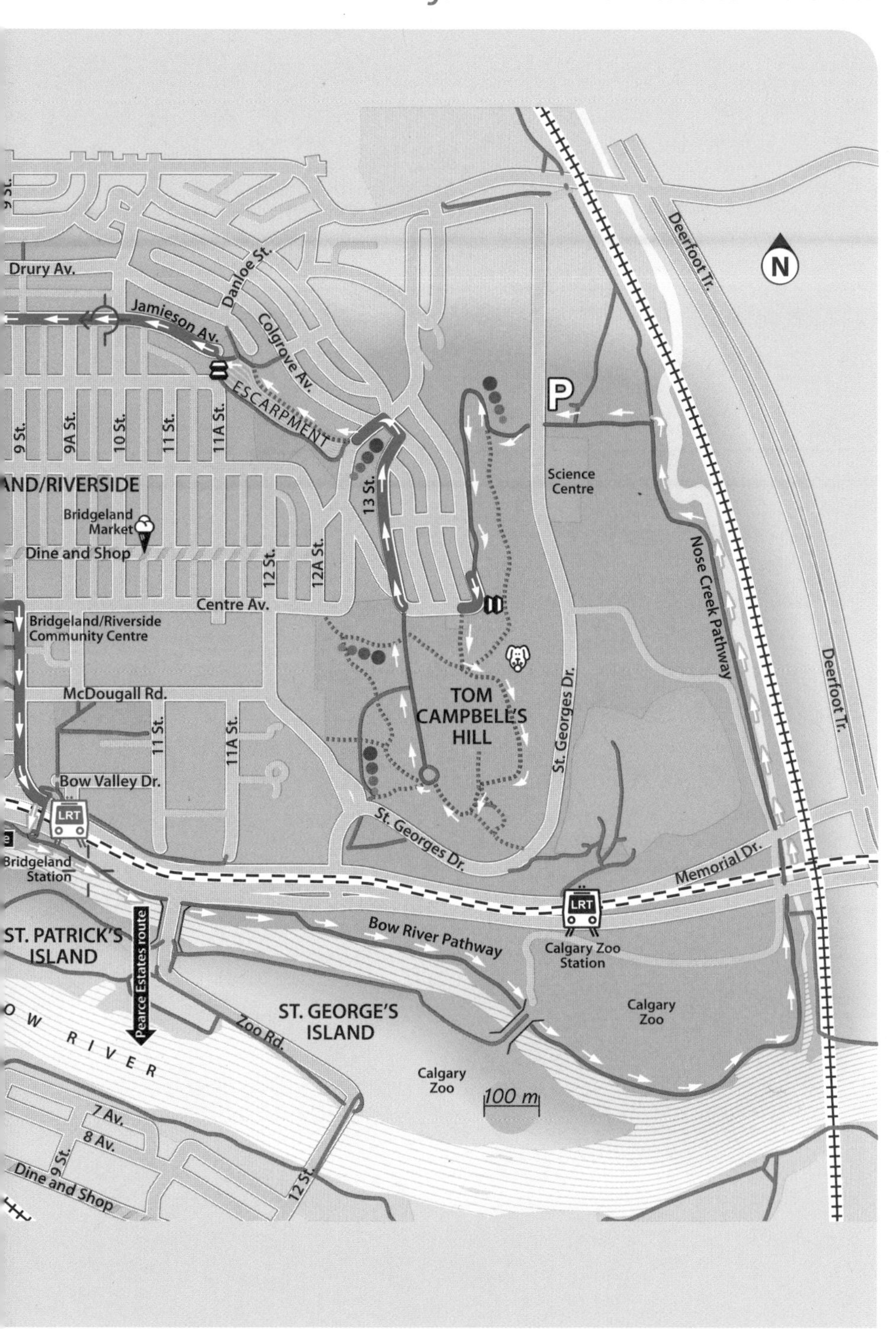

Drury Av.
Jamieson Av.
Danloe St.
Colgrove Av.
ESCARPMENT
9 St.
9A St.
10 St.
11 St.
11A St.
13 St.
AND/RIVERSIDE
Bridgeland Market
Dine and Shop
12 St.
12A St.
Centre Av.
Bridgeland/Riverside Community Centre
McDougall Rd.
11 St.
11A St.
Bow Valley Dr.
LRT
Bridgeland Station
P
Science Centre
TOM CAMPBELL'S HILL
St. Georges Dr.
St. Georges Dr.
Deerfoot Tr.
N
Nose Creek Pathway
Deerfoot Tr.
Memorial Dr.
LRT
Calgary Zoo Station
ST. PATRICK'S ISLAND
Pearce Estates route
Bow River Pathway
ST. GEORGE'S ISLAND
Zoo Rd.
Calgary Zoo
Calgary Zoo
BOW RIVER
100 m
7 Av.
8 Av.
9 St.
Dine and Shop
12 St.

Confederation Park–Capitol Hill–Mount Pleasant

NW

Walk at a Glance:

Serene, peaceful, and pleasant, Confederation Park is a break from the city's bustle and a wonderful place to walk and recharge. Once known as the North Hill Coulee, Confederation Park became a more manicured recreational park in 1967. The paved pathway that runs through the park parallels a stream and managed wetland.

Creekside balsam poplars thrive, and shrubs like water birch, red-osier dogwood, and several species of willow provide habitat for a variety of ducks, geese, and gulls along with muskrats and many winged invertebrates like butterflies and dragonflies.

Route Details

Categories: Café, Dog Friendly, Home and Gardens, Nature, Neighbourhoods and Parks, Stroller.

Starting-Point Parking: The Thirtieth Avenue parking lot, just south of Seventh Street.

Transit: Bus access at various points along the route. Check Calgary Transit at www.calgarytransit.com.

Facilities: Year-round bathrooms at the parks building near the trailhead. There are picnic spots and playgrounds at various spots.

Distance: Main route: 7.8 km

Degree of Difficulty: Easy and mostly flat, with small gradual hills.

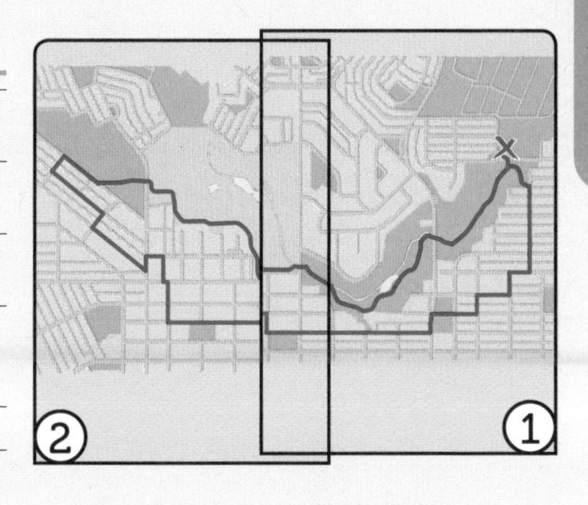

Seasonal Highlights/Cautions

Winter: Christmas lights are brilliant in December at the Lion's Festival of Lights in Confederation Park Golf Course along Fourteenth Street. Bring your cross-country skis and your toboggan. Ski trails are track-set by Foothills Nordic Ski Club in Confederation Park Golf Course when snow is abundant. Check www.skierbob.ca for trail and track-setting updates. Tobogganers should use the hill at the Tenth Street NW parking lot, on the north side of park immediately west of Rosemont Community Centre.

Summer: Bring your swim gear and drop by the Mount Pleasant outdoor pool in July and August, located at Twenty-Third Avenue and Sixth Street NW.

Post-park walk, traverse the side streets in Capitol Hill. At this writing, Capitol Hill is a 1950s bungalow community, but it is moving toward greater density by bringing Boston-style row houses into the mix. As of 2014, The City of Calgary was starting to rezone older neighbourhoods to allow for row-house developments, a middle ground between infills, duplexes, and condo-style apartment blocks. For community residents and visiting urban walkers, increased density means more services. And if you are like me and enjoy having an independent café, a bakery, or a sandwich shop to visit along your walking route, then you must support well done urban density increases. Local shops need a certain volume of sales to stay afloat.

Continue east, across Fourteenth Street and into the community of Mount Pleasant. Zigzag the through the neighbourhood until you are back in the green of Confederation Park.

Edelweiss Imports: The Kaffee Stube

Authentic European cuisine, that's what you'll find at Edelweiss. Perogies, cabbage rolls, schnitzel, bratwurst, sandwiches, and many tasty pastries, muffins, and desserts–all made fresh daily. After you fill up, be sure to look around the store for imported foods and local European-style breads and pretzels. And if you are a liquorice lover, the bulk section hosts a vast range of salty and sweet treats. Marzipan figures, chocolate sprinkles for your toast, along with many other European favourites can be found here. And if you need kitchen supplies, look no further. Now that you've had a great walk, eaten, picked up some groceries, jewellery, and a new cake tin, you can go home happy.

Location: 1921 Twentieth Avenue NW, www.edelweissimports.com
Phone: 403-282-6600
Hours: 9 am–7 pm (weekdays), 9 am–6 pm (Saturdays–closed Sundays and holidays)

Early Riser by Mandy Budan

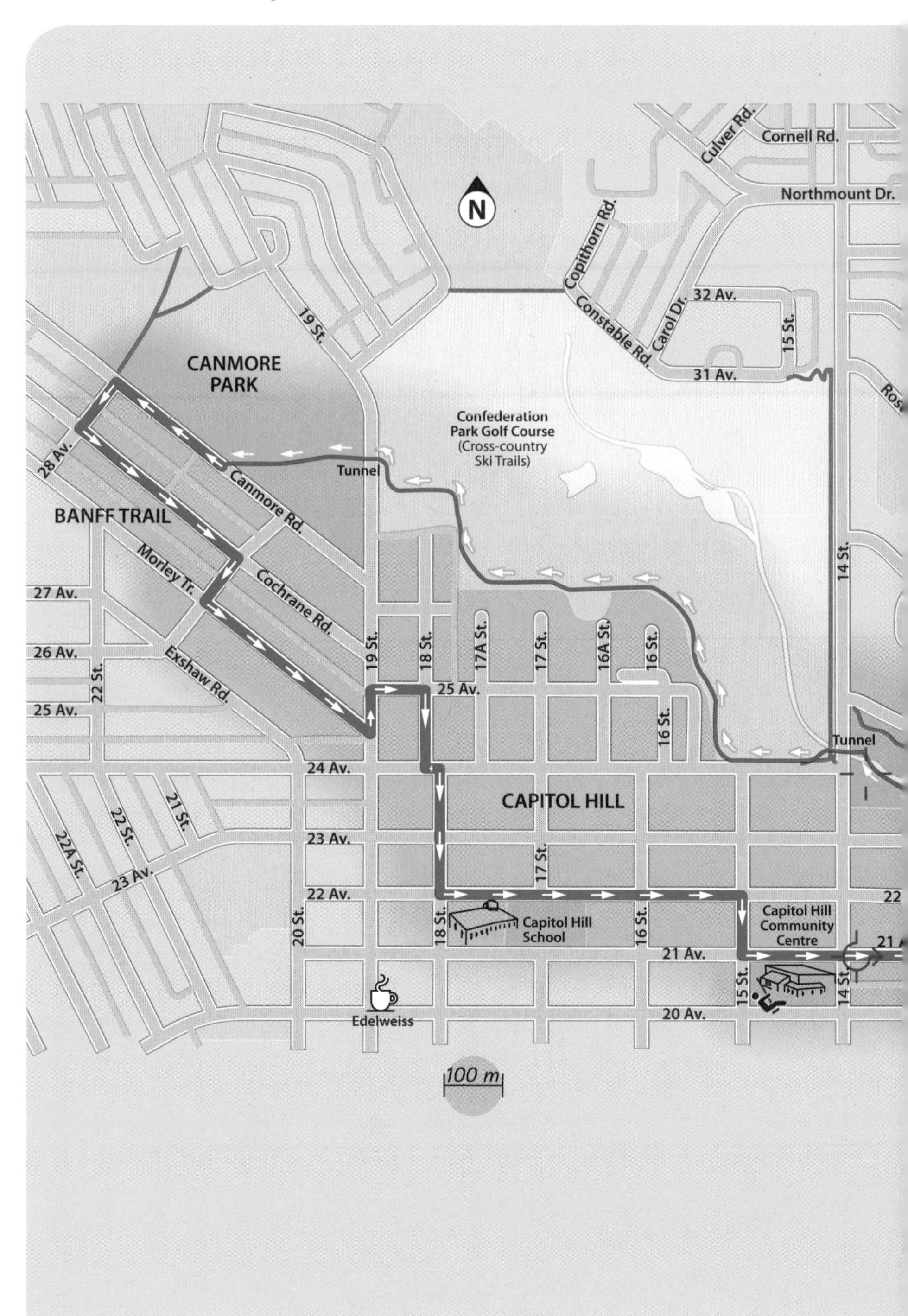
N
Culver Rd.
Cornell Rd.
Northmount Dr.
Copithorn Rd.
Constable Rd.
Carol Dr.
32 Av.
15 St.
31 Av.
CANMORE PARK
19 St.
Confederation Park Golf Course
(Cross-country Ski Trails)
Tunnel
28 Av.
Canmore Rd.
BANFF TRAIL
Morley Tr.
Cochrane Rd.
14 St.
27 Av.
26 Av.
22 St.
Exshaw Rd.
19 St.
18 St.
17A St.
17 St.
16A St.
16 St.
25 Av.
25 Av.
16 St.
Tunnel
24 Av.
CAPITOL HILL
22A St.
22 St.
21 St.
23 Av.
17 St.
23 Av.
22 Av.
20 St.
18 St.
Capitol Hill School
16 St.
Capitol Hill Community Centre
21 Av.
15 St.
14 St.
Edelweiss
20 Av.
100 m

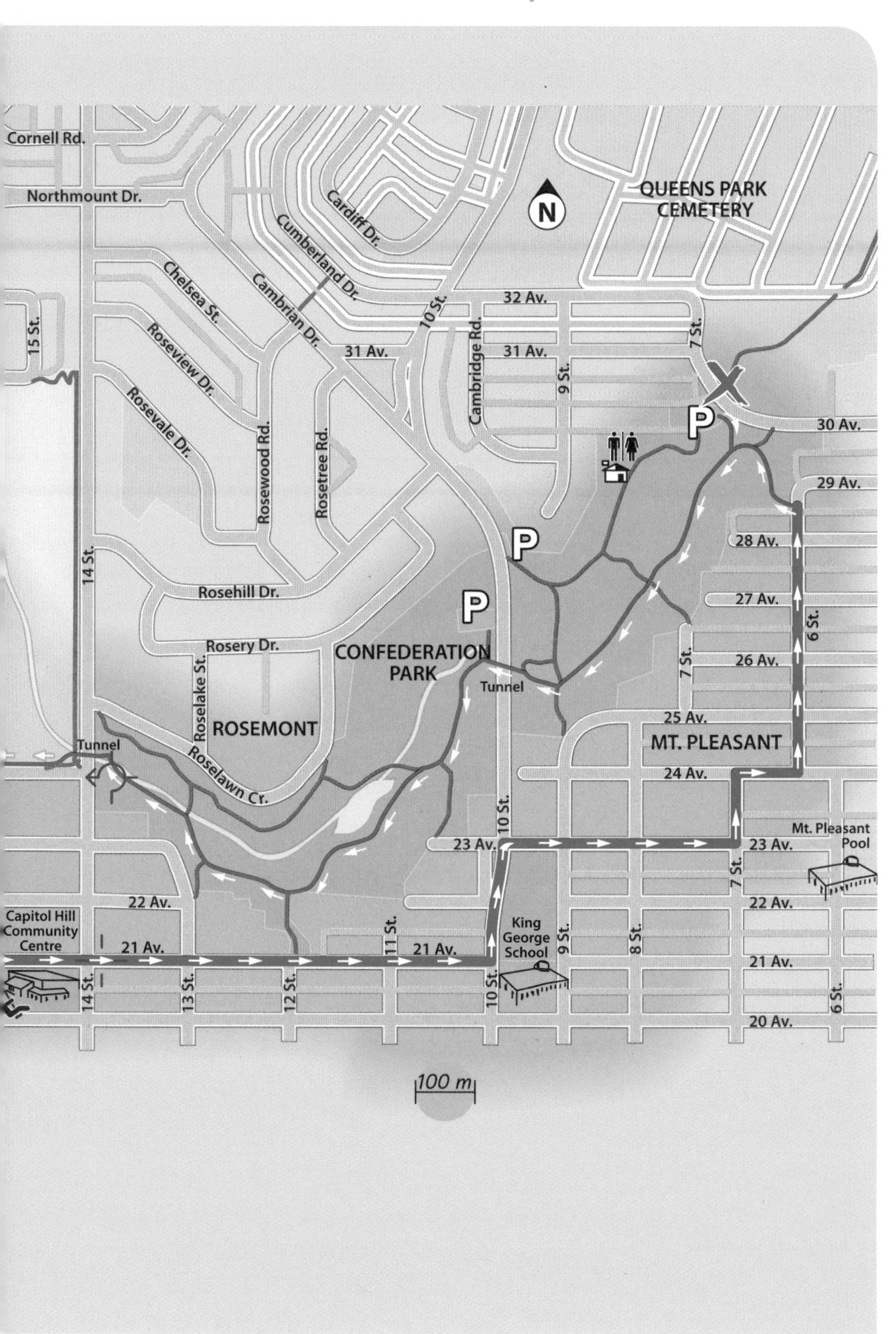

Cornell Rd.
Northmount Dr.
Cardiff Dr.
Cumberland Dr.
Chelsea St.
Cambrian Dr.
Roseview Dr.
Rosevale Dr.
Rosewood Rd.
Rosetree Rd.
15 St.
14 St.
10 St.
Cambridge Rd.
32 Av.
31 Av.
9 St.
7 St.
QUEENS PARK CEMETERY
30 Av.
29 Av.
28 Av.
27 Av.
26 Av.
25 Av.
24 Av.
23 Av.
22 Av.
21 Av.
20 Av.
6 St.
Rosehill Dr.
Rosery Dr.
Roselake St.
ROSEMONT
Roselawn Cr.
CONFEDERATION PARK
Tunnel
MT. PLEASANT
Mt. Pleasant Pool
Capitol Hill Community Centre
13 St.
12 St.
11 St.
King George School
8 St.
100 m

Riley Park–Kensington–McHugh Bluff

NW

Walk at a Glance:

This downtown urban hike criss-crosses the escarpment on the north side of the Bow River. Views of the Bow River Valley, the Rocky Mountains, and city-centre skyscrapers that reach up and out of the concrete are constant.

Riley Park is a hive of activity in the summer, with its playground, impressive wading pool, open park space for playing Frisbee or picnicking, and colourful flower beds. And for those wanting to watch some cricket matches, visit the east end of the park where cricket has been played since 1919. Ezra Hounsfield Riley donated the park land to the city in 1910 and then secured a permit from parks superintendent William Reader to create the still-popular cricket pitch.

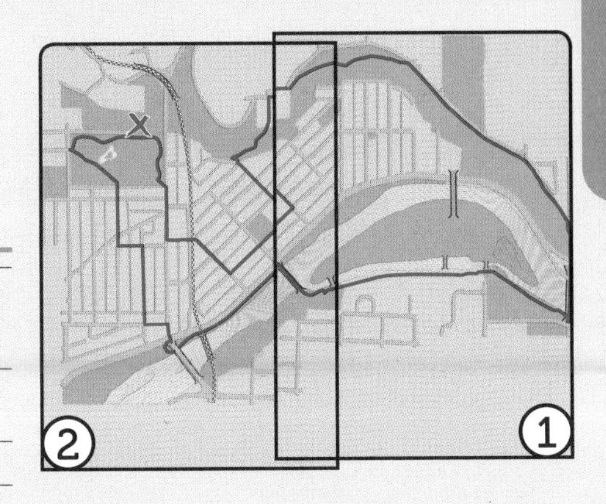

Route Details

Categories: C-Train, Café, Dog Friendly, Hilly, Home and Gardens, Neighbourhoods and Parks, People Watching and Shopping, River, Stroller, Vistas.

Starting-Point Parking: Park in the official three-hour, free, Riley Park parking area. 800 Twelfth Street NW.

C-Train Start: Sunnyside.

Transit: Bus access at various points along the route. Check Calgary Transit at www.calgarytransit.com.

Distance: 7 km

Degree of Difficulty: Moderate, with some challenging hills and stairs.

Seasonal Highlights/Cautions

Year-Round: Climb the Crescent Heights stairs to city and mountain views–and while you're at it, get a fine workout.

Winter: Bring your skates and enjoy free outdoor skating on the lagoon in Prince's Island Park.

Summer: Enjoy the spectacular flower gardens in Burns Memorial Park and Riley Park.

From Riley Park, continue your walk onto the streets of vibrant colourful Sunnyside, a community with character. Older renovated homes painted in primary colours line the side streets. Some handyman delights still exist for those hoping to find a somewhat-affordable inner-city home, but most of the area has been rejuvenated and renovated already. Travel along Kensington Road,

Vendome Café

Kensington and Sunnyside have no shortage of restaurants and cafés. Vendome Cafe is off the beaten path and is my favourite for its scrumptious, made-from-scratch food and cozy warm atmosphere. Tucked into an old brick two-storey, the walls are red-brick warm, and the food made on site is simply delicious. The café specializes in unique takes on the classic dishes; try the French toast that is chunked and piled up, or, at lunch, order my favourite lunch plate, the duck confit panini with apple sauce side. After the stairs and hills on this hike, you'll appreciate the extra calories and won't feel an ounce of guilt.

Location: 940 Second Avenue NW

a hotbed of shops and restaurants. Grab a pre-hike coffee and then walk to the impressive Poppy Plaza war memorial at the intersection of 10 Street and Memorial Drive. A dynamic public space, the plaza is perfect place at which to sit, reflect, and watch the river flow by.

Continue east along the Bow River Pathway. If you walk here during Calgary's commute–at 7:30 am or 5 pm–be prepared for an onslaught of cyclists peddling into or out of the downtown core. Cross the tubular Peace Bridge, a pedestrian bridge that accommodates both walkers and cyclists in harmony. Designed by Spanish architect Santiago Calatrava, the bridge was built to

Training on the Crescent Heights Stairs

The Crescent Heights stairs on McHugh Bluff have become a year-round freeway full of Calgarians in training. Climbing stairs can make your muscles burn. When the intensity of an activity increases and you stop breathing comfortably, your cells start to rely on anaerobic (oxygen-free) respiration to function. A by-product of anaerobic exercise is an accumulation of lactic acid in your muscles. That burn you feel is caused by this accumulation; slow down or stop when you feel the burn. Fitness levels determine lactate thresholds so the fitter you are the more you can climb before your legs burn. If you want an alternative to the Crescent Heights stairs, try the paved path that gradually climbs the escarpment. Gradual hills are perfect for quadriceps training. Those big muscles in at the front of your legs are used constantly when alpine skiing or climbing a hill on a bike. Build quad strength by walking uphill backward for twenty steps and then forward for twenty steps. Keep alternating until you reach the top. The bigger the step you take, the tougher the workout.

accommodate the six thousand–plus per day users who walk and bike for recreation and transport. Functional and artistic, it is a testament to the city's commitment to increasing its residents' pleasure in walking and cycling. Well lit for twenty-four-hour, year-round use, its red and white colours represent the Canadian flag.

Continue past Prince's Island, or take a side trip onto the island and follow one of the many trails. In the winter, the frozen pond in Prince's Island is cleared and maintained for skating.

Onward past China Town, cross the Bow River and climb up the McHugh Bluff escarpment. Named after Felix McHugh, who homesteaded this property and was a prominent early entrepreneur, the bluff host views extending downtown west to the mountains. On a winter evening, the sights are dramatic and impressive. With every step up the hillside, the downtown skyscrapers rise into view, bright, compact, and towering. In December the colourful light displays on the houses makes this area the perfect spot for a Christmas lights hike. Follow the pathway to the popular Crescent Heights stairs, where a hotbed of sweaty Calgarians regularly keep fit. Across from Prince's Island Park, these stairs are easy access for downtown office workers–or visitors staying at downtown hotels–needing a quick, outdoor, training session.

Continue to the hillside trails and walk into the trees: willows, ashes, balsam poplar, and white spruce. This is a popular dog-walking area, so you'll likely meet a furry friend or two while following these treed escarpment trails. Or, if you choose to stay on top of the slope, you'll continue to enjoy the Rocky Mountain and Bow River vistas before descending to Sunnyside and deciding where to go for a nice meal or a social drink.

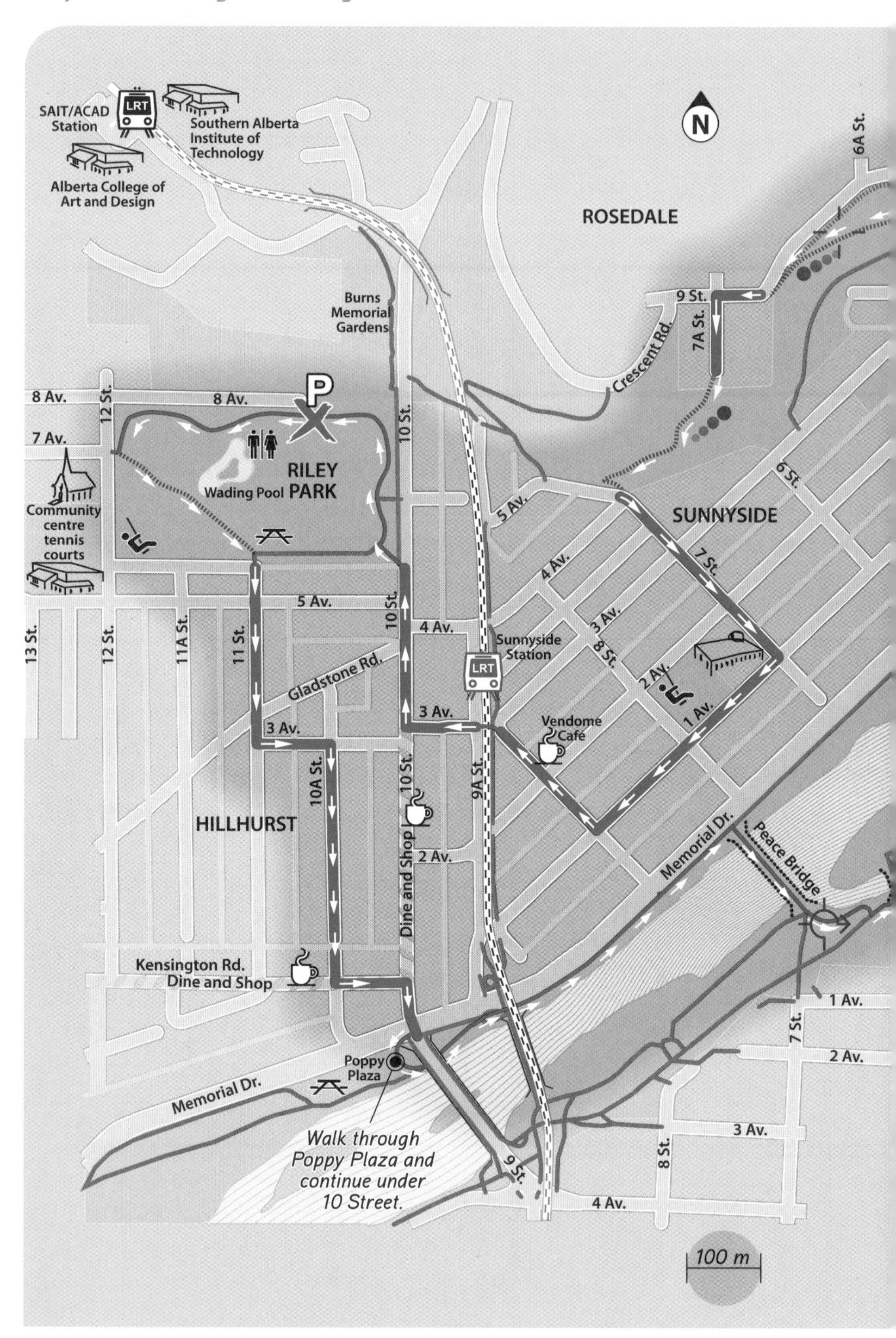
SAIT/ACAD Station
LRT
Southern Alberta Institute of Technology
Alberta College of Art and Design
ROSEDALE
N
6A St.
9 St.
7A St.
Crescent Rd.
Burns Memorial Gardens
8 Av.
12 St.
8 Av.
7 Av.
10 St.
RILEY PARK
Wading Pool
Community centre tennis courts
5 Av.
SUNNYSIDE
6 St.
7 St.
4 Av.
13 St.
12 St.
11A St.
11 St.
5 Av.
10 St.
4 Av.
Sunnyside Station
3 Av.
8 St.
2 Av.
1 Av.
Gladstone Rd.
3 Av.
3 Av.
Vendome Café
10A St.
10 St.
9A St.
HILLHURST
Dine and Shop
2 Av.
Memorial Dr.
Peace Bridge
Kensington Rd.
Dine and Shop
1 Av.
7 St.
2 Av.
Poppy Plaza
Memorial Dr.
Walk through Poppy Plaza and continue under 10 Street.
9 St.
3 Av.
8 St.
4 Av.
100 m

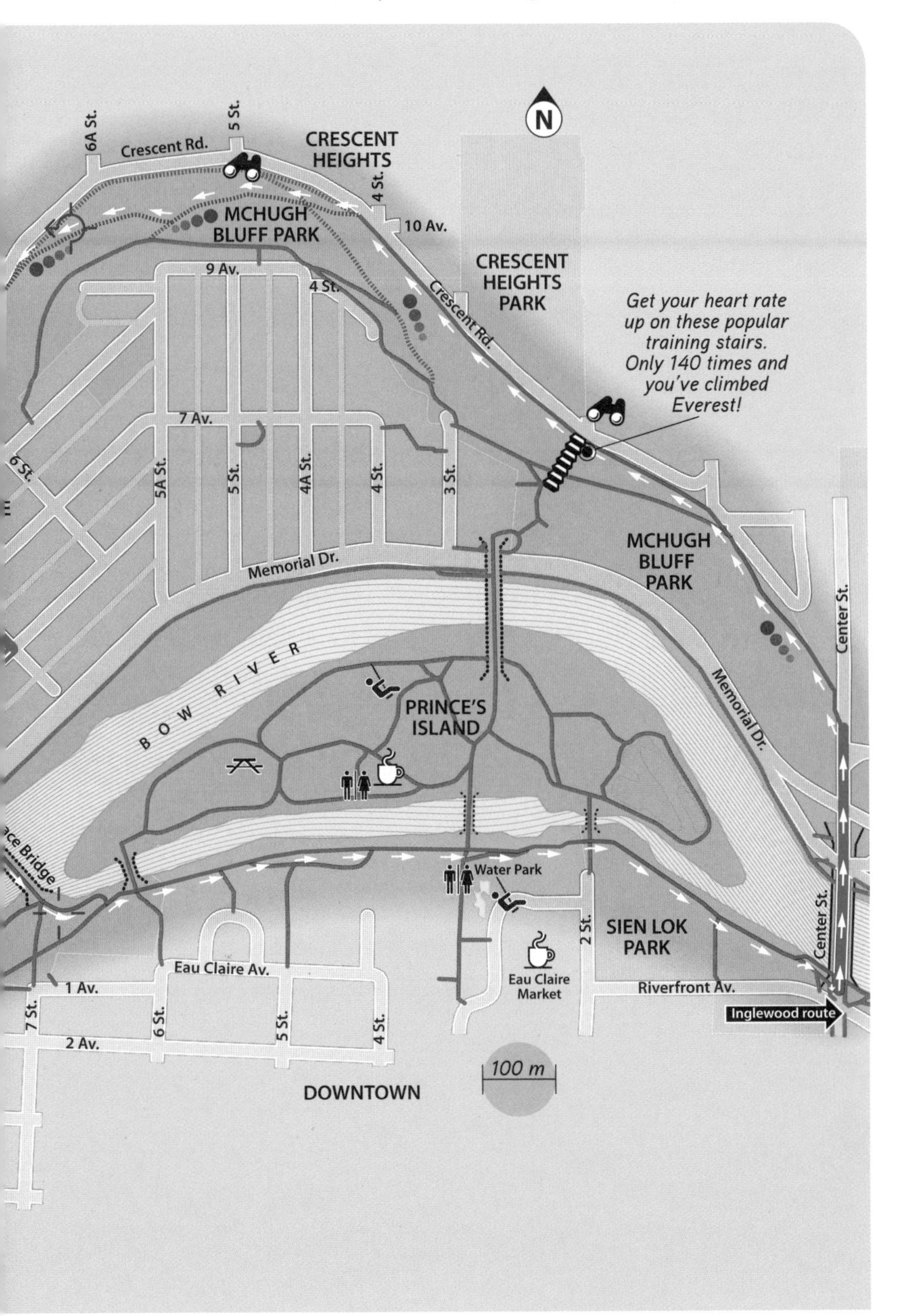
CRESCENT HEIGHTS
Crescent Rd.
6A St.
5 St.
4 St.
10 Av.
MCHUGH BLUFF PARK
9 Av.
4 St.
CRESCENT HEIGHTS PARK
Crescent Rd.
Get your heart rate up on these popular training stairs. Only 140 times and you've climbed Everest!
7 Av.
6 St.
5A St.
5 St.
4A St.
4 St.
3 St.
Memorial Dr.
MCHUGH BLUFF PARK
Center St.
BOW RIVER
PRINCE'S ISLAND
Memorial Dr.
Water Park
2 St.
SIEN LOK PARK
Center St.
Eau Claire Av.
1 Av.
Eau Claire Market
Riverfront Av.
Inglewood route
7 St.
6 St.
5 St.
4 St.
2 Av.
100 m
DOWNTOWN

Briar Hill–Houghton Heights–West Hillhurst–Westmount

NW

Walk at a Glance:

Grasshopper Hill, as the bluff was once known, leads you to the first of many wide-open views of the downtown skyline and the communities below. Briar Hill soon becomes Houghton Heights, Calgary's north-side Mount Royal. A quick walk south of the Lion's Park C-Train Station, Houghton Heights is an awe-inspiring neighbourhood perched on the bluffs. The modest bungalows are slowly being transformed into palaces with boulder-terraced yards that host multitudes of flowers, waterfalls, and ponds.

Skirt the bluff to enjoy constant skyline views, picking a single-track trail across the green space to descend into Hillhurst, or follow the quiet side streets to view the homes and the impressive landscaping.

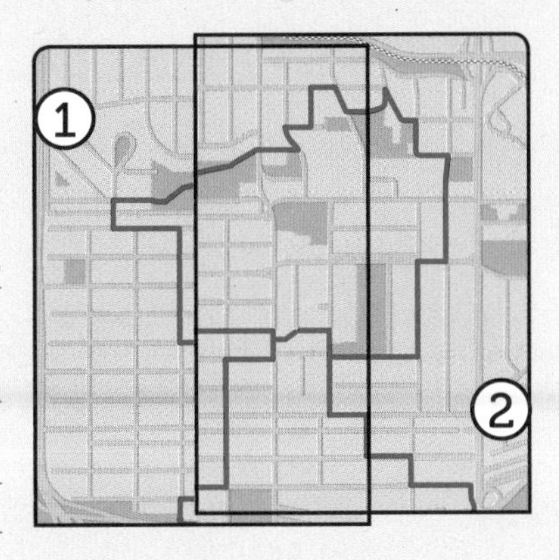

Route Details

Categories: C-Train, Café, Dog Friendly, Hilly, Historic, Home and Gardens, Neighbourhoods and Parks, People Watching and Shopping, River, Stroller, Vistas.

Starting-Point Parking: Park along Ninth Avenue, just east of Twenty-Second Street NW.

C-Train Start: Lions Park.

Transit: Bus access at various points along the route. Check Calgary Transit at www.calgarytransit.com.

Facilities: Cafés, restaurants, and ice cream shop en route.

Distance: 7.5 km

Degree of Difficulty: Moderate, with one hill climb.

Seasonal Highlights/Cautions

Winter: The Christmas lights are wonderful in December. Be prepared for icy and/or snowy pathways and sidewalks. Bring traction devices for your footwear, or wear cleats.

Spring, Summer, and Fall: Creative gardens abound.

First Settlers

Lawlessness and whisky trading in the late 1800s marked this area before the North-West Mounted Police arrived in 1875, built Fort Calgary, and helped bring some order to the chaos. The Canadian Pacific Railway arrived in 1884, and that meant Calgary had "arrived" as an urban centre.

Hounsfield Lodge Farm, owned by Thomas E. Riley and Georgina Jane Hounsfield, was the original settlement in the Briar Hill and Hillhurst area. In 1890 the property extended from Sunnyside to Parkdale in the west, and from the Bow River to Sixteenth Avenue in the north. Calgary's growth by 40,000 people between 1900 and 1910 meant that this land was in demand, and the family decided to subdivide and sell.

On June 10, 1910, the *Morning Albertan* featured the following headline, "Hounsfield Heights; All View Lots – An Ideal Location for an Ideal Home," accompanied by a view of the subdivision of Hillhurst from the top of the bluff. Instructions on how to get there included a walk "through the park donated by Mr. E. Riley," now known as Riley Park. At substantial price tag of $800 to $1000 per 50-ft (15-m) lot meant that only the moneyed could afford to live there. Hounsfield Heights was to be the "Mount Royal of the North." In 1913 a recession hit, along with threats of war and increased unemployment. The overheated economy came to a crashing halt. When you walk through Hounsfield Heights today, you will see that it did in fact become a mini-Mount Royal of the North, one hundred years after the fact.

Walk through Hillhurst, an inner-city community with a mix of fixer-upper rental houses and new homes. A close walk, bike, or transit ride to the Alberta College of Art and Design (ACAD), Southern Alberta Institute of Technology (SAIT), and the University of Calgary, Hillhurst is a popular community for students sharing houses and for professionals working downtown. Take a detour to pedestrian-populated Kensington Road and walk east to shop, eat, and people watch. Or, continue along the route and pass one of Calgary's more unique homes at the corner of 16a Street and Second Avenue. Watch for a distinct yellow house with a boulder field flowing across the front yard. A short cut through the houses is the option for those wanting a shorter walk or a direct path to some tasty stops along Nineteenth Street. For the longer route, keep on trekking south and explore Westmount.

Tucked in between Kensington Road and the Bow River, Westmount is easily overlooked, unless you live here, or you are visiting the CBC's Calgary studio. The main road in the community, Bowness

Road, is incredibility wide, parts of it with a tree-lined median. Impressive properties with character share the street with older homes and well-built new ones. The architectural variety keeps things interesting and attractive. Cross the Bow River and follow the Bow River Pathway. The city zips along Memorial Drive as you walk beneath the poplar trees. Calgary's well-used 800-km+ pathway system–the most extensive urban pathway and bikeway in North America–is such a wonderful way to link communities. And even in the winter these paths are well used since the city of Calgary clears the snow off 300 km of trail so Calgarians can walk and bike year-round. Bravo Calgary!

Continue over the pedestrian overpass and walk back through the community. On a hot day, make a motivational stop for some gelato on Kensington Road or warm up in the colder months with a coffee and diner meal along Nineteenth Street before zigzagging back to your starting point.

When The Days Turn by Sheila Kernan

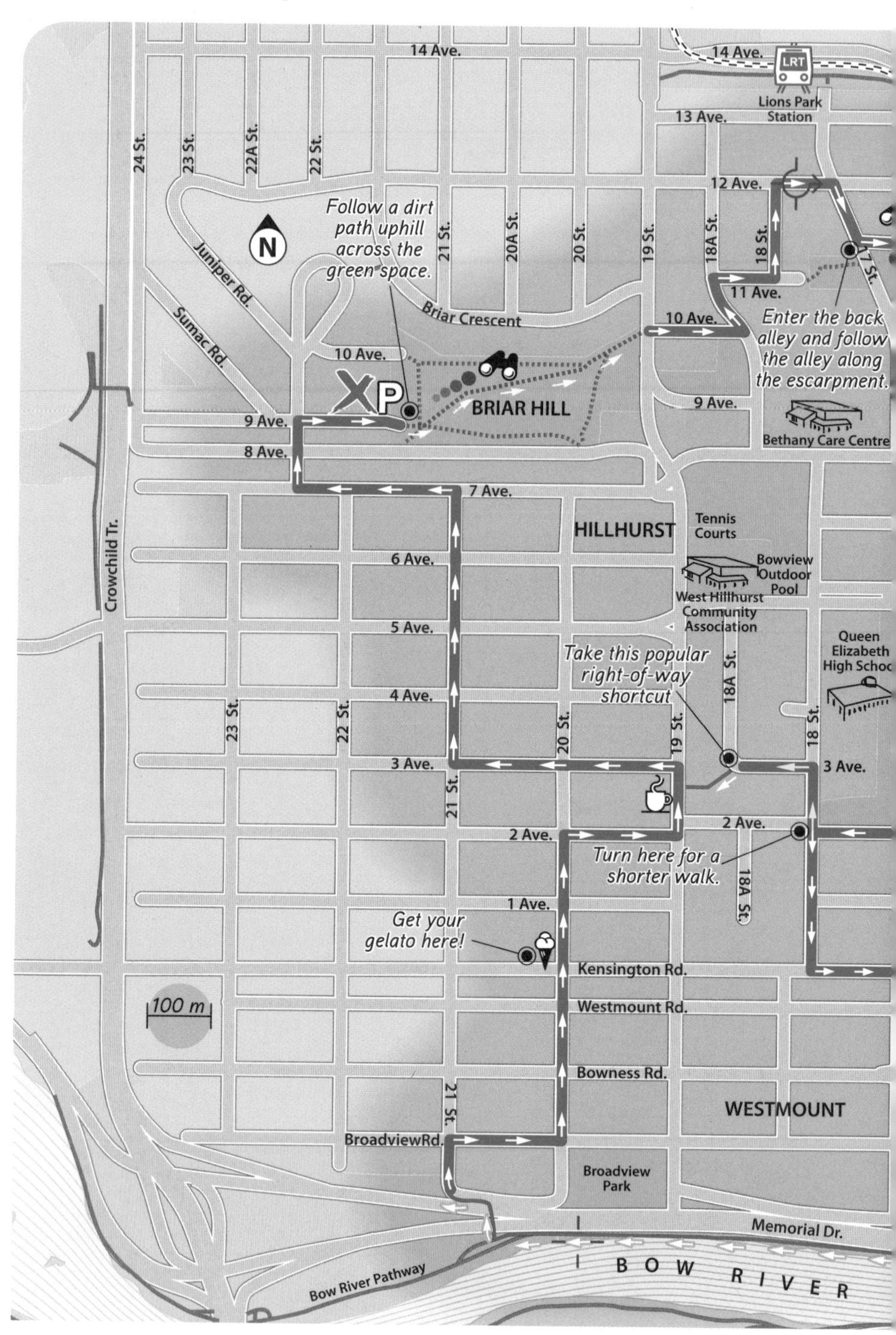
14 Ave.
14 Ave.
LRT
Lions Park Station
13 Ave.
12 Ave.
24 St.
23 St.
22A St.
22 St.
Follow a dirt path uphill across the green space.
21 St.
20A St.
20 St.
19 St.
18A St.
18 St.
17 St.
N
Juniper Rd.
Sumac Rd.
Briar Crescent
11 Ave.
10 Ave.
10 Ave.
Enter the back alley and follow the alley along the escarpment.
BRIAR HILL
9 Ave.
9 Ave.
8 Ave.
Bethany Care Centre
7 Ave.
HILLHURST
Tennis Courts
Bowview Outdoor Pool
West Hillhurst Community Association
6 Ave.
5 Ave.
Crowchild Tr.
Queen Elizabeth High Schoo
Take this popular right-of-way shortcut
4 Ave.
23 St.
22 St.
20 St.
18A St.
19 St.
18 St.
3 Ave.
3 Ave.
21 St.
2 Ave.
2 Ave.
Turn here for a shorter walk.
18A St.
1 Ave.
Get your gelato here!
Kensington Rd.
Westmount Rd.
100 m
Bowness Rd.
21 St.
WESTMOUNT
BroadviewRd.
Broadview Park
Memorial Dr.
BOW RIVER
Bow River Pathway

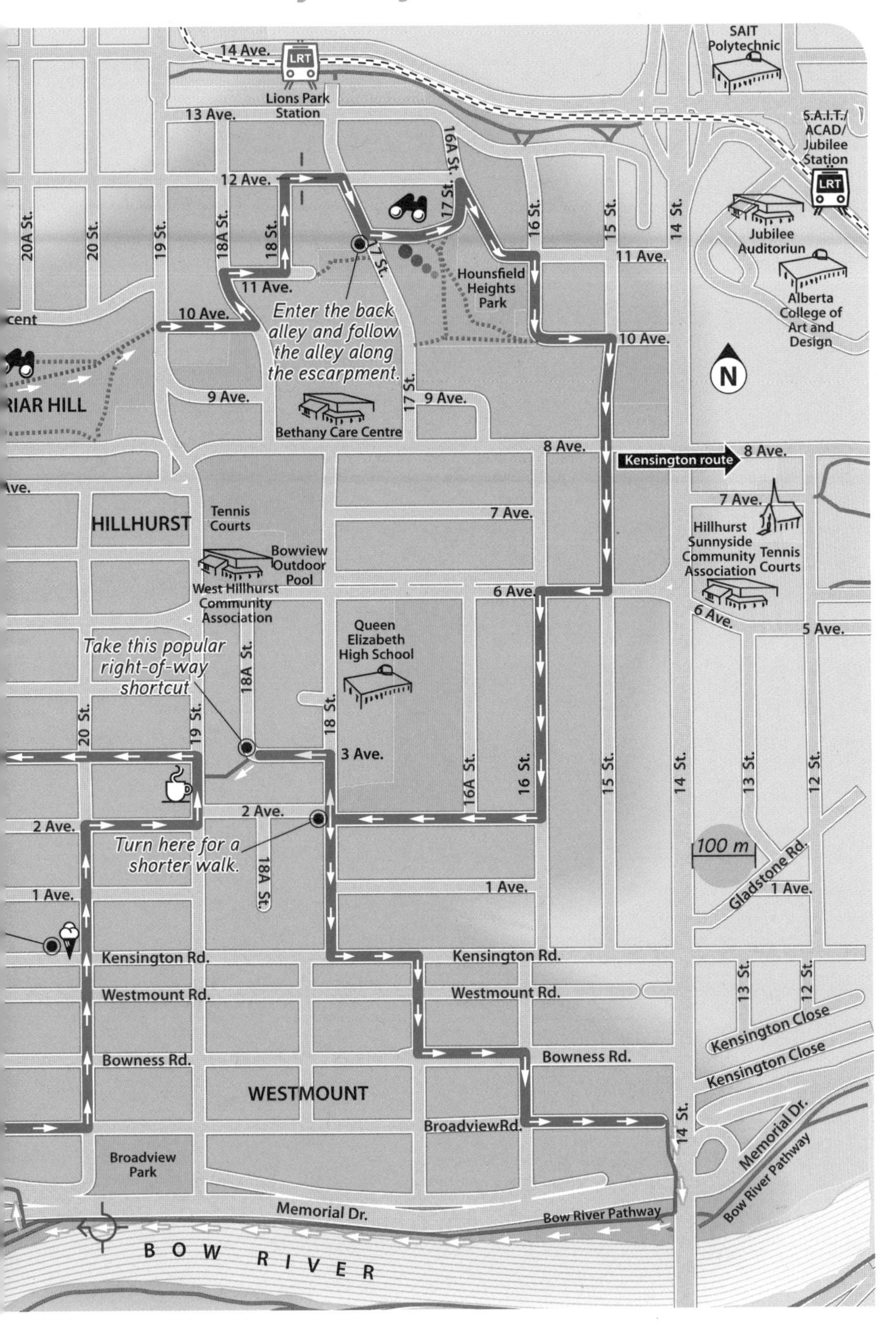

14 Ave.
LRT
Lions Park Station
13 Ave.
SAIT Polytechnic
S.A.I.T./ ACAD/ Jubilee Station
LRT
12 Ave.
16A St.
17 St.
16 St.
15 St.
14 St.
20A St.
20 St.
19 St.
18A St.
18 St.
11 Ave.
17 St.
Jubilee Auditoriun
Alberta College of Art and Design
Hounsfield Heights Park
10 Ave.
Enter the back alley and follow the alley along the escarpment.
10 Ave.
N
9 Ave.
9 Ave.
Bethany Care Centre
8 Ave.
Kensington route
8 Ave.
7 Ave.
7 Ave.
HILLHURST
Tennis Courts
Bowview Outdoor Pool
West Hillhurst Community Association
Hillhurst Sunnyside Community Association
Tennis Courts
6 Ave.
6 Ave.
5 Ave.
Queen Elizabeth High School
Take this popular right-of-way shortcut
18A St.
20 St.
19 St.
18 St.
3 Ave.
16A St.
16 St.
15 St.
14 St.
13 St.
12 St.
2 Ave.
2 Ave.
Turn here for a shorter walk.
100 m
18A St.
1 Ave.
1 Ave.
Gladstone Rd.
1 Ave.
Kensington Rd.
Kensington Rd.
13 St.
12 St.
Westmount Rd.
Westmount Rd.
Kensington Close
Bowness Rd.
Bowness Rd.
Kensington Close
WESTMOUNT
BroadviewRd.
14 St.
Memorial Dr.
Broadview Park
Bow River Pathway
Memorial Dr.
Bow River Pathway
BOW RIVER

Bow River–Parkdale–St. Andrews Heights

NW

Walk at a Glance:

It is interesting to explore neighbourhoods that border some of our popular parks. This walkabout leads you from Edworthy Park, along the Bow River Pathway, past the community of Point McKay and then north into Parkdale. This modest neighbourhood is alive with community spirit. Developed in the mid nineteen hundreds, Parkdale was once considered a suburb, but now is a central location for Calgarians who want shorter commutes and especially for those who work at one of the two hospitals up the hill.

Route Details

Categories: Café, Dog Friendly, Hilly, Home and Gardens, Neighbourhoods and Parks, River, Stroller, Vistas.

Starting-Point Parking–North Side: At the intersection of Bowness Road and Shaganappi Trail, turn onto Montgomery View and continue to the parking areas.

Starting-Point Parking–South Side: Follow Forty-Fifth Street north of Bow Trail to Spruce Drive. Turn west and follow signs and winding gravel road to south-side parking lot.

Transit: Bus access at various points along the route. Check Calgary Transit at www.calgarytransit.com.

Facilities: Year-round bathrooms on the north side; seasonal bathrooms on the south side (May–October); café en route.

Distance: 8.3 km

Degree of Difficulty: Moderate, with hills.

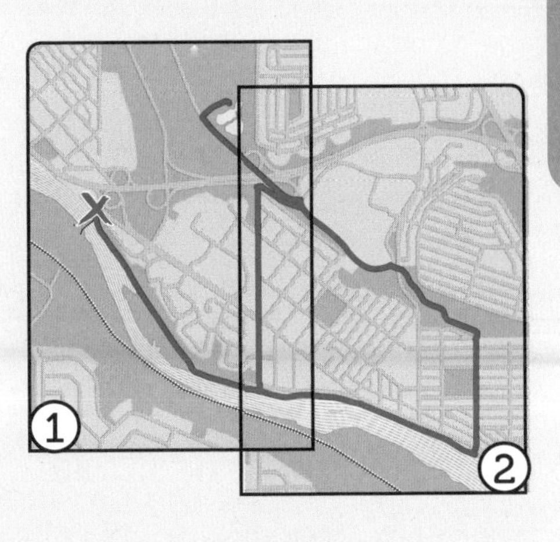

Seasonal Highlights/Cautions

Winter: This is the perfect alternate route to Edworthy Park when south-side Edworthy trails are packed with snow and slippery.

Spring, Summer, and Fall: Homes and gardens and Rocky Mountain views.

Pass by the very popular, "Helicopter Park", a playground that is always packed with families, no matter what time of the year. Climb through the escarpment green space along shaded pathways. Enjoy the views from the hilltop as you venture west, skirting the escarpment, past the Foothills Medical Centre. Along with views of the Rockies, the colourful Alberta Children's Hospital stands out. Children were asked how they would like the hospital to look, inside and out, and with their input; the multi-coloured, Lego-like structure was built. The building's colourful design, the multitude of windows bringing natural light to all rooms, and beds for family members, is meant to help reduce stress and promote healing.

Continuing along the paved pathway to the wetlands. Listen for the red-winged blackbirds and watch for the abundance hawks; they swoop, sometimes too close, to cyclists and walkers.

Return along the familiar path until just east of Sixteenth Avenue. Start the escarpment descent along the paved path and continue through the neighbourhood all the way to the Bow River. If lunch or a coffee or lunch is on your agenda, walk east or west along the pathway to find some tasty treats. Or hike back to Edworthy for a peaceful picnic along the Bow River.

Coffee, Lunch, and Ice Cream

The Lazy Loaf and Kettle Café is a great place to replenish lost calories with home-baked goods and hearty lunches. Substantial serving sizes, like cinnamon buns as big as your head, ensure you won't be short on calories. While you're there, buy a loaf of kettle bread for home. It's delicious and healthy.

Leavitt's Ice Cream Shop is in the same cul-de-sac as the Lazy Loaf. It's a local favourite in hot weather. Drive (or walk) east on Memorial Drive and turn left (north) into Parkdale Crescent (a cul-de-sac).

Angel's Café is also a convenient option for a hot drink, some lunch, or some ice cream. It is located at the route's north-side parking lot. On a hot summer's day, take your food and sit on the banks of the Bow River. Watch the world flow by.

Location:
Lazy Loaf and Kettle Café: 8 Parkdale Crescent NW, www.lazyloafandkettle.com
Leavitt's Ice Cream Shop: 3410 Third Ave NW, www.lics.ca
Angel's Café: Edworthy Park, north-side parking lot, Shaganappi Trail and Bowness Road NW, www.pathwayangels.ca
Hours:
Lazy Loaf and Kettle Café: 7 am–9 pm (weekdays), 8 am–9 pm (Saturdays), 8 am–8 pm (Sundays and holidays)
Leavitt's Ice Cream Shop: Hours change with the seasons
Angel's Café: 10 am–9 pm (late spring and summer; weather and staff permitting), 10 am–5 pm (fall and winter; closed when temperatures fall below -10°C)

The Jester by Mandy Budan

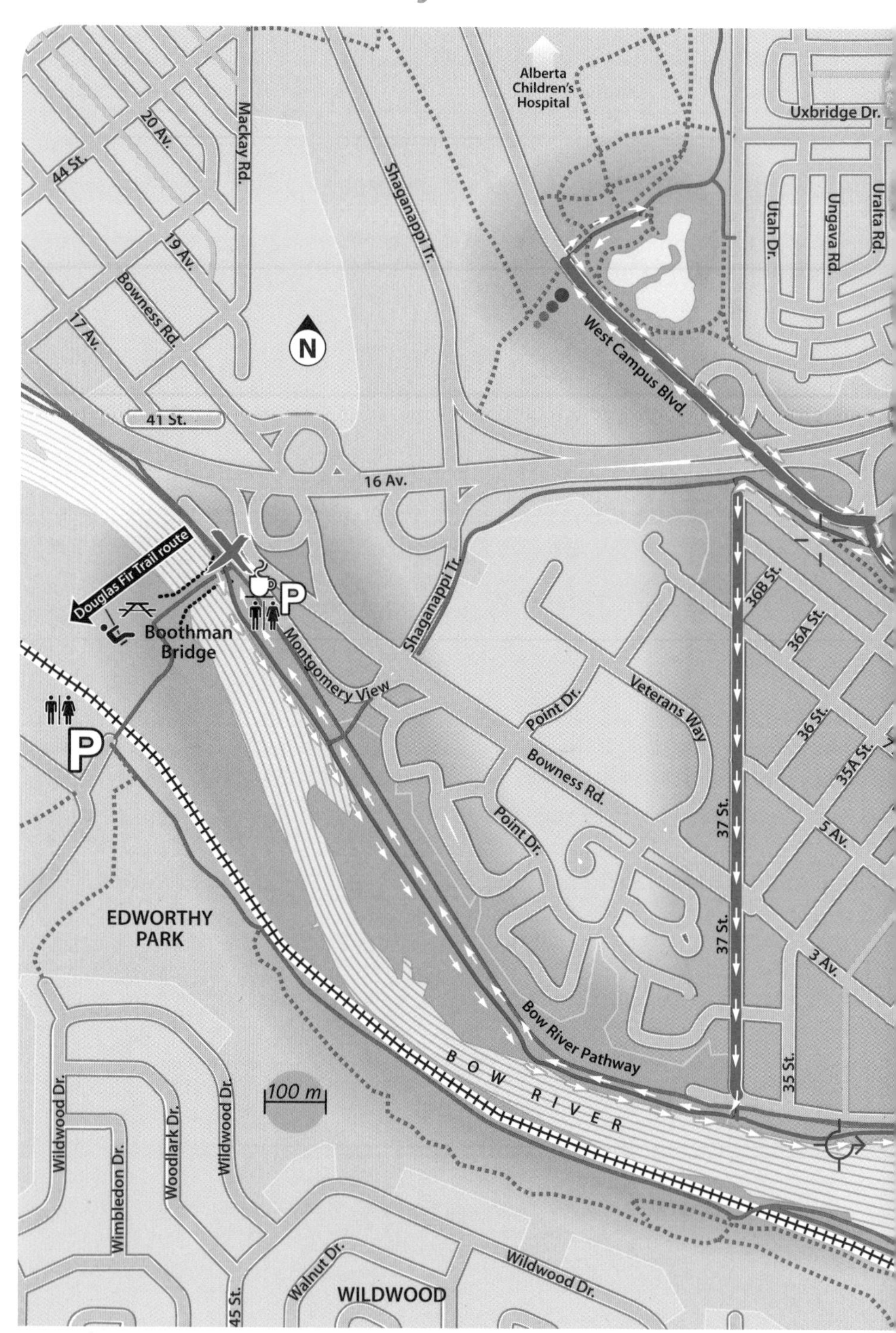
Alberta Children's Hospital
Uxbridge Dr.
Utah Dr.
Ungava Rd.
Uralta Rd.
Mackay Rd.
20 Av.
44 St.
19 Av.
Bowness Rd.
17 Av.
Shaganappi Tr.
West Campus Blvd.
N
41 St.
16 Av.
Douglas Fir Trail route
Boothman Bridge
Shaganappi Tr.
Montgomery View
36B St.
36A St.
Veterans Way
Point Dr.
36 St.
35A St.
Bowness Rd.
Point Dr.
37 St.
5 Av.
37 St.
3 Av.
EDWORTHY PARK
Bow River Pathway
35 St.
BOW RIVER
100 m
Wildwood Dr.
Wimbledon Dr.
Woodlark Dr.
Wildwood Dr.
Walnut Dr.
Wildwood Dr.
WILDWOOD
45 St.

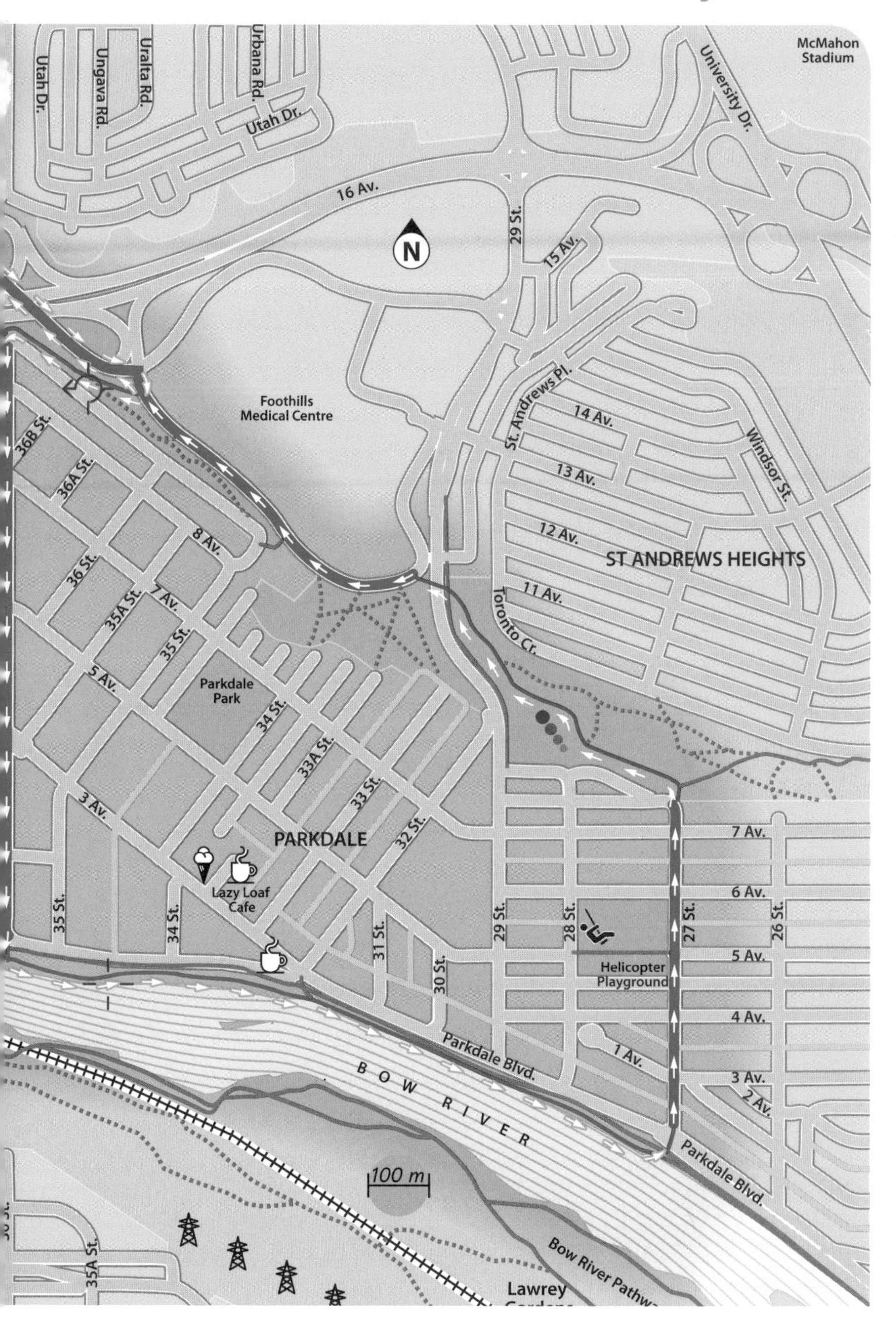
McMahon Stadium
University Dr.
Utah Dr.
Ungava Rd.
Uralta Rd.
Urbana Rd.
Utah Dr.
16 Av.
29 St.
15 Av.
N
Foothills Medical Centre
St. Andrews Pl.
14 Av.
Windsor St.
13 Av.
12 Av.
ST ANDREWS HEIGHTS
11 Av.
Toronto Cr.
36B St.
36A St.
8 Av.
36 St.
35A St.
7 Av.
35 St.
5 Av.
Parkdale Park
34 St.
33A St.
3 Av.
33 St.
32 St.
PARKDALE
Lazy Loaf Cafe
35 St.
34 St.
31 St.
30 St.
29 St.
28 St.
27 St.
26 St.
7 Av.
6 Av.
5 Av.
Helicopter Playground
4 Av.
1 Av.
3 Av.
2 Av.
Parkdale Blvd.
B O W R I V E R
Parkdale Blvd.
100 m
35A St.
Bow River Pathway
Lawrey

Douglas Fir Trail and Wildwood

NW

Walk at a Glance:

Hidden amongst the most easterly stand of Douglas fir trees that tower above the Bow River is the Douglas Fir Trail. Stairs, bridges, creeks, and narrow winding paths dip and climb 60 m from the river valley to the lookout point. A fantastic trail for physical training, it is also a shaded wilderness oasis in the height of the summer. Trees, some more than 2 m in diameter, and multitudes of western Canada violets line the trail. Descend to the marsh trail along the railway and listen for the chorus of frogs. Move slowly in an attempt to sneak a peek before they stop croaking and dive for cover. At dusk, tip you head back and watch for the great horned owls on this same open flat stretch of the trail. These magnificent birds fly low over the open areas near the railway tracks when the natural light fades.

Route Details

Categories: Café, Dog Friendly, Hilly, Historic, Nature, Neighbourhoods and Parks, River, Trail Running, Vistas.

Starting-Point Parking–North Side: At the intersection of Bowness Road and Shaganappi Trail NW, turn onto Montgomery View and continue to the parking areas.

Starting-Point Parking–South Side: Follow Forty-Fifth Street SW, north of Bow Trail to Spruce Drive. Turn west and follow signs and winding gravel road to south-side parking lot.

Transit: Bus access to the surrounding communities. Check Calgary Transit at www.calgarytransit.com.

Facilities: Year-round bathrooms on the north side; seasonal bathrooms on the south side (May–October); café en route (see "Coffee, Lunch, and Ice Cream," in Walk 15 on page 110).

Distance: Both routes: 7.7 km

Degree of Difficulty: Challenging, with many stairs and hills.

Seasonal Highlights/Cautions

Year-Round: The escarpment has many springs that are causing the hillside to slide and the bridges to tip. Sometimes portions of the Douglas Fir Trail are closed at various times throughout the year. Check the City of Calgary website, www.calgary.ca, for pathway and trail updates.

Winter and Spring: An ice flow covers part of the Douglas Fir Trail from December through May. Bridges can be slippery with frost on late-fall and early-spring mornings. Bring your cleats (traction devices that attach to your footwear) and be prepared to take the alternate route into Wildwood.

Summer: The Douglas Fir Trail offers relief from the sun in the height of the summer.

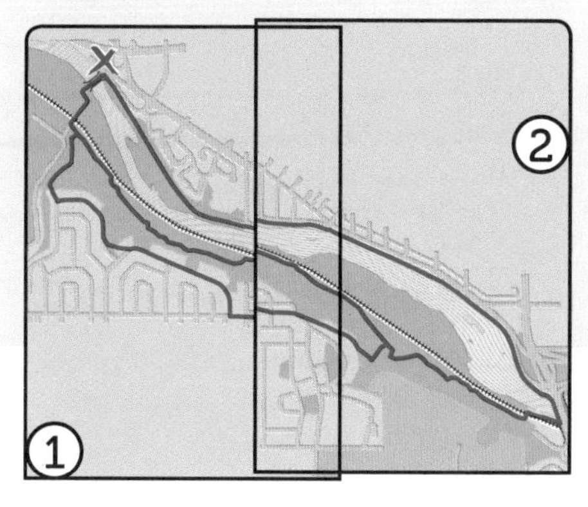

On winter and spring days when the Douglas Fir Trail is too slippery to navigate walk the alternate route through Wildwood and observe the magnificent homes perched on the escarpment. Travel off the beaten path through green-space trails tucked behind homes to reconnect with the Douglas Fir Trail and the Bow River Pathway below.

Pemmican

Archeological evidence shows that the Nitsitapii (Blackfoot) have been in the Bow Valley for over a thousand years, with Stoney, Cree, and Tsuu T'ina peoples arriving from the sixteenth century onward. The cliffs and steep slopes of the area made it a good spot for the Plains peoples to stampede buffalo. One bull might supply 500 lb (227 kg) of meat. This meat was dried and made into pemmican, a mixture of dried meat, berries, and bone marrow stored in buffalo-skin bags. Pemmican was the main for source of nutrients for the peoples of the plains throughout the winter. European explorers also used it as a nutritious and long-lasting food source.

Cross the Bow River on the pedestrian underpass under Crowchild Trail and follow the Bow River Pathway west. Keep your wallet ready for an ice-cream stop or a hot drink on a cold day. A few tasty eateries are en route or not far from the route. This wonderful wild walkabout has a very civilized café ending.

Edworthy West Trails: Trail Running and Hill Training

In the west end of Edworthy Park there are some single-track trails that are popular with trail runners. You can explore the area by making up a route that includes any number of the series of interconnecting pathways that parallel the train tracks. Connect to these trails from the south side of the Bow River. Start your walk from the off-leash dog park at the top of the hill or from the parking lot at the bottom of the hill. From the lower lot, walk west, past the bathrooms, and continue alongside the train tracks. This flat trail warms you up before a dirt path leads you uphill into the trees. At trail intersections, take the western route and continue on a combination of rolling wide and narrow dirt paths along the escarpment all the way to Sarcee Trail. Retrace your steps on the return route, or drop down to the path along the train tracks for a flat walk.

Once back in the south parking lot, join other Calgarians in training on the steep hill that climbs to the Edworthy off-leash park. The views from the top are worth a stop, so enjoy a much-needed rest break before tackling the hill once again.

Standing Room Only by Mandy Budan

Wildwood Slide

A sign that reads "Slide Area No Stopping" marks the spot where a landslide swept twenty-eight rail cars off the tracks in 1956. The instability of the slope is due partly to the number of springs in the area. Slide activity also increased with the development of the communities of Spruce Cliff and Wildwood. There are safety measures in place to prevent another slide in those areas, however, these have no effect on other parts of the slope. In 2013 Calgary had heavy rains that resulted in a hundred-year flood. The runoff caused the Douglas Fir Trail's slope to slump and slide. The trail continues to be monitored and repaired, but Mother Nature is powerful. As you hike the trail, watch for trees that show signs of tilting and bridges and stairs that are being displaced.

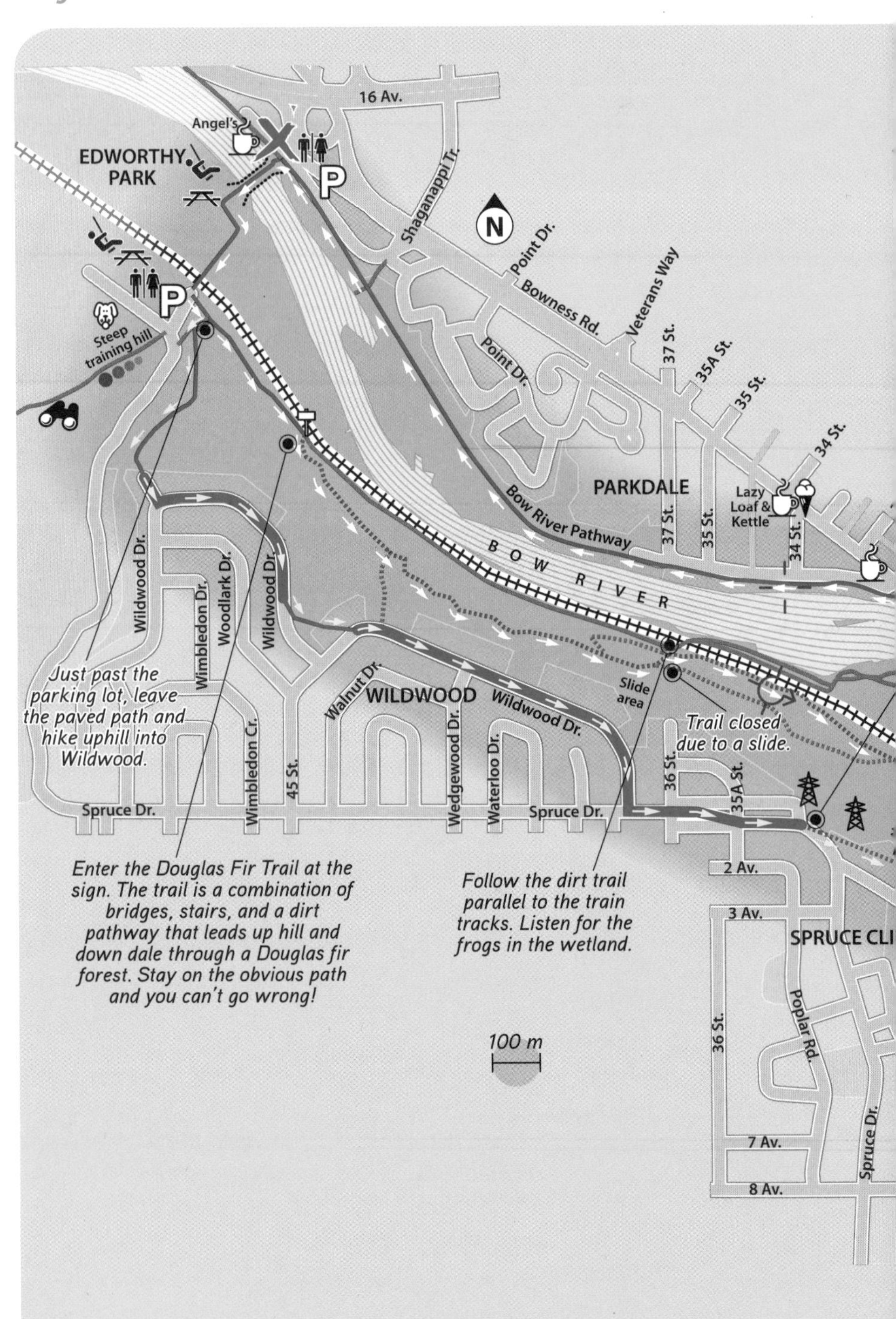
16 Av.
Angel's
EDWORTHY PARK
Shaganappi Tr.
Point Dr.
Bowness Rd.
Veterans Way
Steep training hill
Point Dr.
37 St.
35A St.
35 St.
34 St.
PARKDALE
Lazy Loaf & Kettle
Bow River Pathway
37 St.
35 St.
34 St.
BOW RIVER
Wildwood Dr.
Wimbledon Dr.
Woodlark Dr.
Wildwood Dr.
Just past the parking lot, leave the paved path and hike uphill into Wildwood.
Walnut Dr.
WILDWOOD
Wildwood Dr.
Slide area
Trail closed due to a slide.
Wimbledon Cr.
45 St.
Wedgewood Dr.
Waterloo Dr.
36 St.
35A St.
Spruce Dr.
Spruce Dr.
Enter the Douglas Fir Trail at the sign. The trail is a combination of bridges, stairs, and a dirt pathway that leads up hill and down dale through a Douglas fir forest. Stay on the obvious path and you can't go wrong!
Follow the dirt trail parallel to the train tracks. Listen for the frogs in the wetland.
2 Av.
3 Av.
SPRUCE CLI
Poplar Rd.
36 St.
100 m
7 Av.
8 Av.
Spruce Dr.

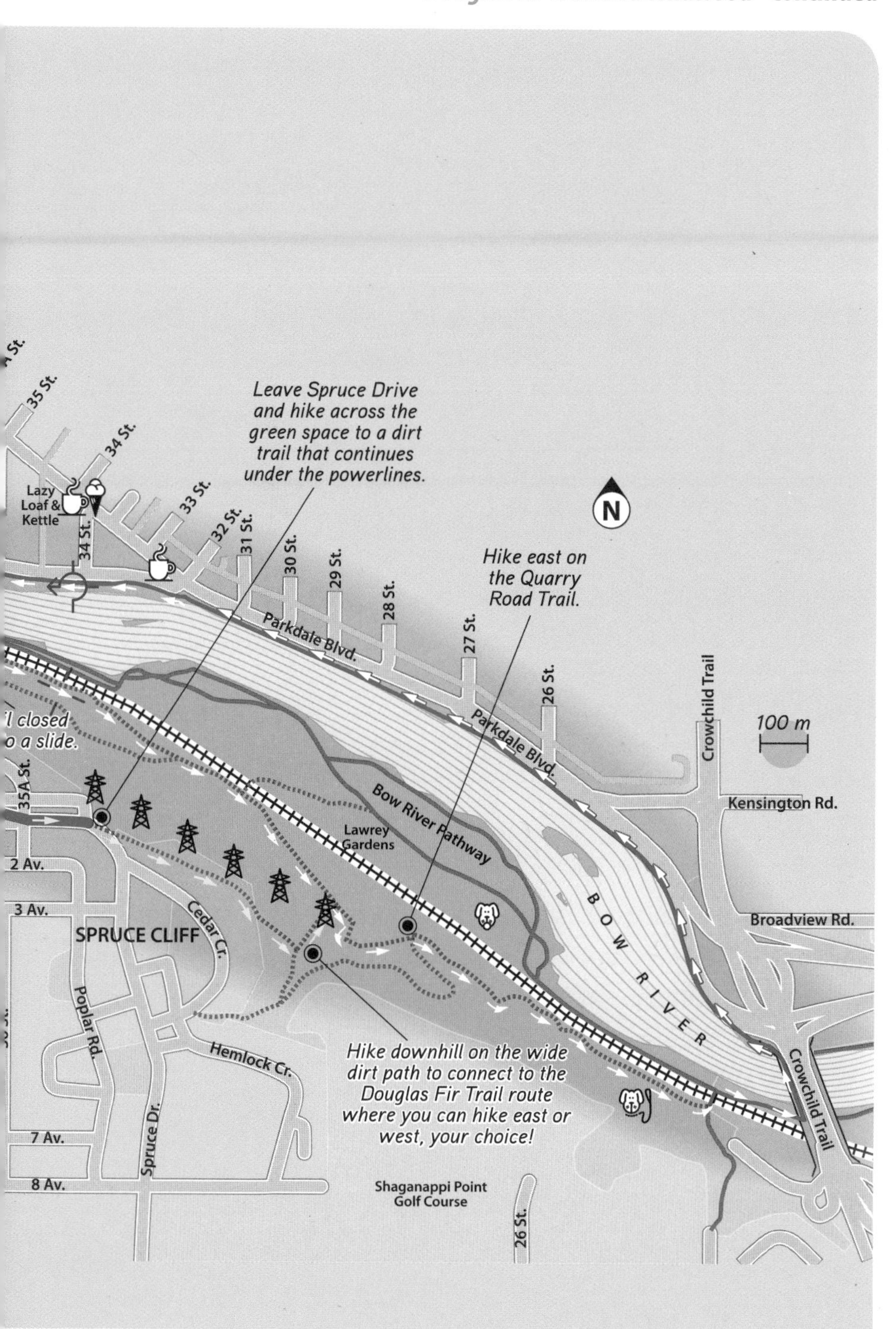
Leave Spruce Drive and hike across the green space to a dirt trail that continues under the powerlines.
Hike east on the Quarry Road Trail.
Hike downhill on the wide dirt path to connect to the Douglas Fir Trail route where you can hike east or west, your choice!
Lazy Loaf & Kettle
35 St.
34 St.
33 St.
32 St.
31 St.
30 St.
29 St.
28 St.
27 St.
26 St.
35A St.
Parkdale Blvd.
Crowchild Trail
100 m
Kensington Rd.
Broadview Rd.
Bow River Pathway
Lawrey Gardens
BOW RIVER
2 Av.
3 Av.
SPRUCE CLIFF
Cedar Cr.
Poplar Rd.
Hemlock Cr.
Spruce Dr.
7 Av.
8 Av.
Shaganappi Point Golf Course
N

Strathcona and Aspen Ravines

SW

Walk at a Glance:

Tucked into the suburbs of Strathcona and Christie Park, Strathcona Ravines Park is an environmental reserve that offers an immersion in the wilds alongside the cul-de-sacs of suburban Calgary. The trail at the bottom of the narrow, steep-sided ravine offers a break from the energy of the city, giving walkers a chance to slow the pace amongst the poplars and trembling aspens.

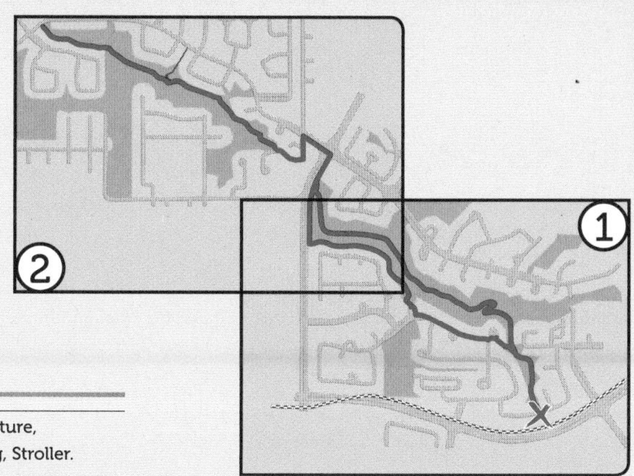

Route Details

Categories: C-Train, Café, Dog Friendly, Nature, Neighbourhoods and Parks, Trail Running, Stroller.

Starting-Point Parking: Park anywhere along Christie Park Hill.

C-Train Start: Sirocco Station, Sixty-Ninth Street line.

Transit: Bus access at various points along the route. Check Calgary Transit at www.calgarytransit.com.

Facilities: Seasonal bathrooms at trailhead, open from mid-May to mid-October; café; visitor centre.

Distance: 6.5 km

Degree of Difficulty: Easy.

Seasonal Highlights/Cautions

Winter: Bring your cleats because the ravine trails can be slippery after Chinooks.

A boardwalk at the west end of the ravine crosses a seasonal stream and wetland; it's an excellent area in which to look for birds such as flycatchers and waxwings. Birds of prey such as great horned and great gray owls have also been spotted in this park.

Due to the build-up in the surrounding communities, the ravines are now somewhat isolated, however, they were once part of a larger network of ravines that drained to the south shore of the Bow River. Continue west across Strathcona Boulevard and connect to the ravine in Aspen. This suburban wild walkabout refreshes the mind and body.

Good Earth Café in Aspen Landing

Aspen Landing is the shopping spot for all the communities along Seventeenth Avenue SW. It has all the services you could want, but best of all, it has one independent coffee shop. The Good Earth Café has a full range of baked goods and lunches, all made fresh daily. Grab a picnic lunch before your walk or stop by after your trek for a drink and some hearty comfort food.

Location: 332 Aspen Glen Landing, Seventeenth Avenue and Eighty-Fifth Street SW
Phone: 403-454-8711
Hours: 6:30 am–9 pm (weekdays), 7:30 am–8 pm (weekends). Beer and wine served after 3 pm.

Pine Sprites by Mandy Budan

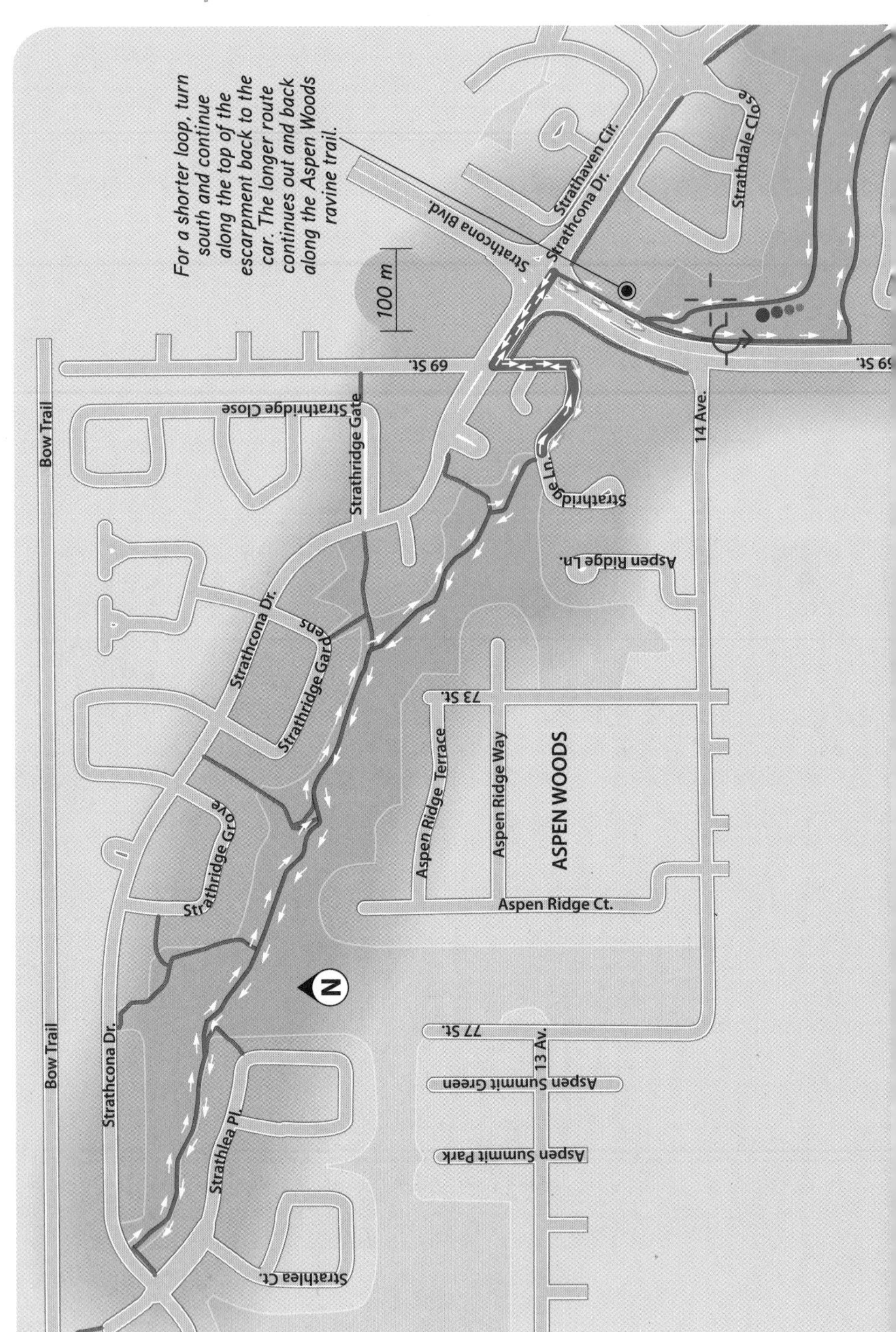
For a shorter loop, turn south and continue along the top of the escarpment back to the car. The longer route continues out and back along the Aspen Woods ravine trail.
100 m
Strathcona Blvd.
Strathaven Cir.
Strathcona Dr.
Strathdale Close
69 St.
14 Ave.
Strathridge Close
Strathridge Gate
Strathridge Ln.
Aspen Ridge Ln.
Bow Trail
Strathcona Dr.
Strathridge Gardens
73 St.
Aspen Ridge Terrace
Aspen Ridge Way
ASPEN WOODS
Strathridge Grove
Aspen Ridge Ct.
N
77 St.
13 Av.
Bow Trail
Strathcona Dr.
Aspen Summit Green
Strathlea Pl.
Aspen Summit Park
Strathlea Ct.

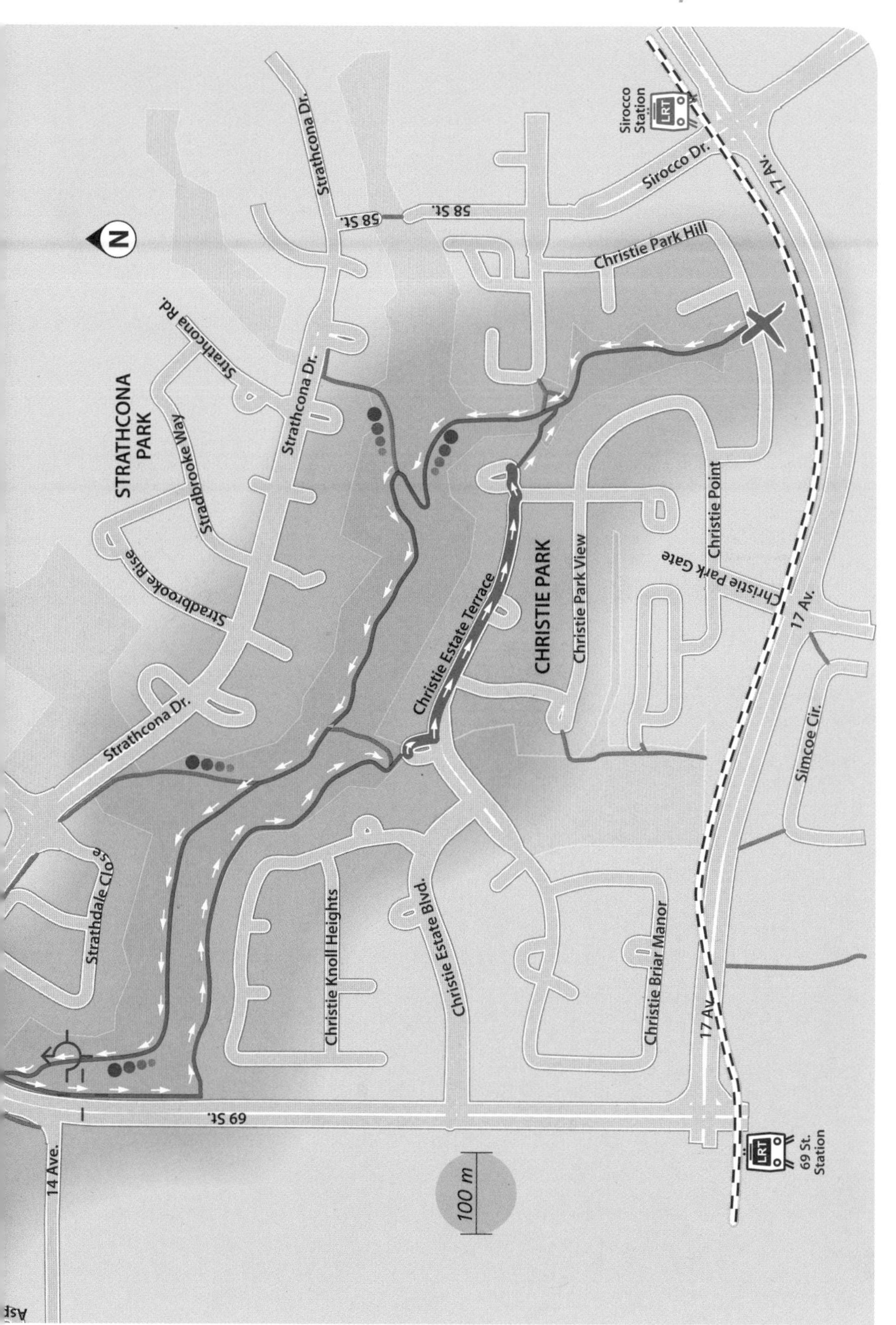

Sirocco Station
LRT
Sirocco Dr.
17 Av.
58 St.
Strathcona Dr.
Christie Park Hill
Strathcona Rd.
STRATHCONA PARK
Stradbrooke Way
Stradbrooke Rise
Christie Point
Christie Park Gate
CHRISTIE PARK
Christie Park View
Christie Estate Terrace
Simcoe Cir.
Strathdale Close
Christie Knoll Heights
Christie Estate Blvd.
Christie Briar Manor
69 St.
69 St. Station
14 Ave.
100 m

Bankview–Scarboro–Connaught

SW

Walk at a Glance:

Bankview is Calgary's mini-San Francisco with its steep streets and high density. The area has undergone many changes since its ranching beginnings in 1882. Now jam-packed with life, the neighbourhood's mix of apartment complexes, condos, 1900s bungalows, and new multi-million-dollar escarpment homes create a vibrant and varied community.

Continue north across Seventeenth Avenue and enter Scarboro, one of Calgary's more affluent neighbourhoods. Unlike most Calgary communities, Scarboro is not on a grid. The leafy streets curve, dip, and climb past well-kept homes with varying square

Route Details

Categories: C-Train, Café, Dog Friendly, Hilly, Historic, Home and Gardens, Neighbourhoods and Parks, People Watching and Shopping, Stroller, Vistas.

Starting-Point Parking: Street parking at the intersection of Thirteenth Avenue and Sixteenth Street SW.

C-Train Start: Sunalta Station.

Transit: Bus access at various points along the route. Check Calgary Transit at www.calgarytransit.com.

Facilities: Lots of cafés and restaurants along 17 Avenue.

Distance: 5.3 km

Degree of Difficulty: Mostly easy, with some challenging hills mixed in with long flat stretches.

Seasonal Highlights/Cautions

Winter: Christmas lights and a café or restaurant stop make for a nice evening walk in December.

Spring: People watching on Seventeenth Avenue is in full swing in April when spring-happy Calgarians stroll the streets, embracing the above-zero temperatures and sunlit evenings. In May and June the blossoming apple and cherry trees, as well as purple lilacs, are a feast for the senses.

Summer and Fall: In Calgary, gardens are in full bloom from mid-July through to October.

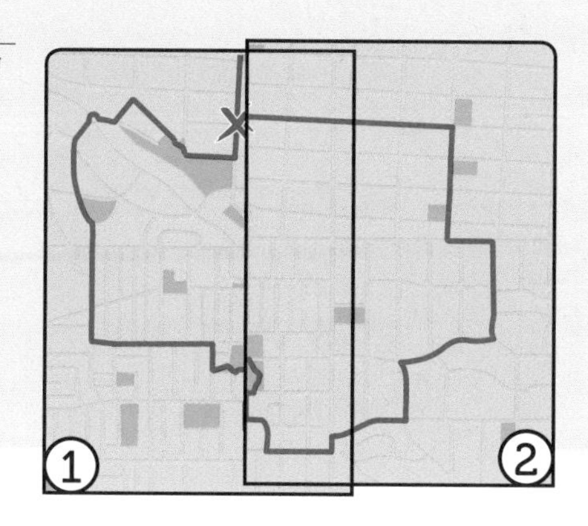

footage. Original mid-1900s houses, impressive in size and design in their day, look small beside the grandiose modern structures that are the current trend.

Continue through Sunalta, past well-placed pocket parks that increase the neighbourhood's green-space quotient. Density increases with every street as you move toward Fourteenth Street and the bustle of the city. Connaught is in the Beltline, a condo-populated inner-city area. No need for a car if you live here. All services and transit are just a walk away; this area is the perfect place to stop for lunch or a coffee. Take a detour and walk along Seventeenth Avenue, also known as the Red Mile, for a bit of people watching and window shopping. On warm April evenings, after a long Calgary winter, Seventeenth is abuzz with strolling Calgarians celebrating longer days and warmer weather.

Chinook Gardening

Snowstorms in the summer and patio days in the winter: this is normal in Calgary. While rapid changes in temperature make for great variety–and Calgarians do welcome those warm, dry, Chinook winds during the winter–these same temperature changes can make gardening a bit difficult. For example, warm January temperatures melt the snow and expose plants to the inevitable return of frigid days. Chinook-exposed plants may be tricked into beginning what are normally springtime processes, such as the growth of new root hairs, leaves, and flower buds, which then makes them vulnerable to injury from cold and frost. All of this said, Calgary gardeners are hardy and enjoy a good challenge. Despite the havoc a Chinook can wreak, Calgary gardens are beautiful from June into September.

Climb into the community of Mount Royal and soak up the city's wealth. Calgary is a city of entrepreneurs, risk takers, and mavericks. Some win and some lose. Mount Royal is home to the winners at this particular moment in time. The residents share their riches with the urban walker in the form of well-kept homes, varied in their design, and expansive gardens. On Halloween night, a home on Tenth Street hosts a great, big, open-to-everyone, zombie-filled party!

Seventeenth Avenue: Shops and Eats

As an urban walker, you may walk alone through green, lush, and peaceful landscapes, or amongst busy streets surrounded by other people. Seventeenth Avenue is a pedestrian-friendly shopping area that is worth a detour if you are in the mood for the latter. During the warm months, enjoy people watching on a patio while sipping a glass of wine and enjoying a meal.

Take a detour north off Seventeenth Avenue onto Eleventh Street and grab some olives, feta cheese, and baklava from Kalamata Grocery. A busy spot all day, every day, this shop is unassuming, just like its owners Gus and George Kukos. Shelves and rows are stacked full of Greek specialties, but it's the sixteen types of fresh olives, multiple varieties of feta, and the different kinds of sesame-based halva that will "make a Greek out of ya," as Gus once said after he handed me a spicy green olive to taste. Fresh pita bread is dropped off daily. Back on Seventeenth, continue east to Ninth Street and detour to Sixteenth Avenue to grab a hot drink and fresh sandwich at Caffe Beano. Sit on benches outside the café and watch the street life. The popular Analog Café, on the corner of Seventh Street and Seventeenth Avenue, is a nice place to warm up. The corner location with big windows is full of natural light and is perfect for people watching all year round. Grab some art supplies at Mona Lisa Artists' Materials, on Seventh Street, some funky new shoes at Gravity Pope, and then a pint at one the many pubs along the avenue. Seventeenth Avenue is a fun place to walk, watch, and soak up the urban energy.

Location:

Kalamata Grocery: 1421 Eleventh Street SW
Analog Café: 740 Seventeenth Avenue SW
Gravity Pope: 524 Seventeenth Avenue SW
Caffe Beano: 1613 Ninth Street SW
Mona Lisa Artists' Materials: 1518 Seventh Street SW

And The Beat Goes On by Sheila Kernan

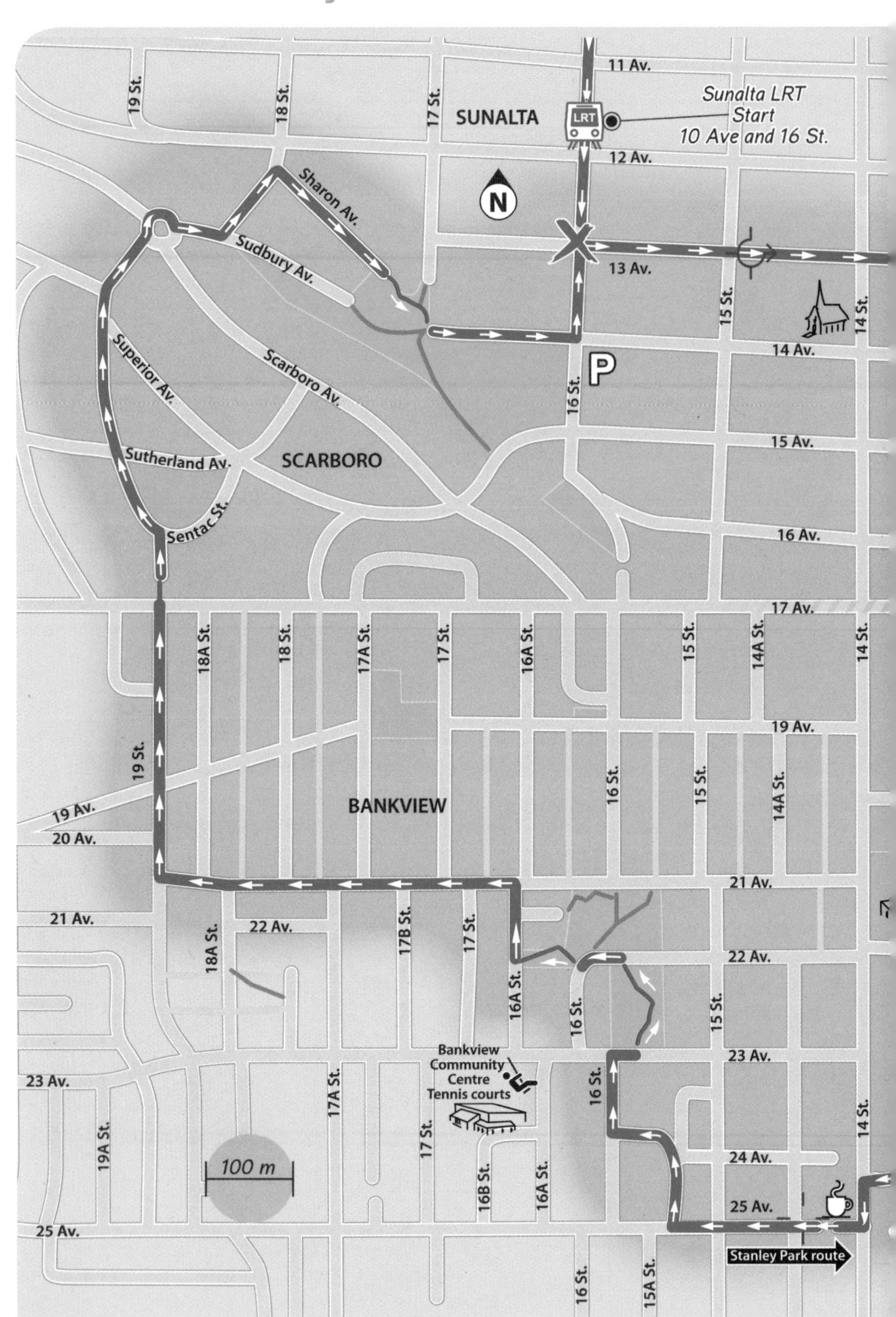
11 Av.
Sunalta LRT
Start
10 Ave and 16 St.
LRT
SUNALTA
19 St.
18 St.
17 St.
12 Av.
N
Sharon Av.
Sudbury Av.
13 Av.
15 St.
14 St.
14 Av.
P
16 St.
Superior Av.
Scarboro Av.
15 Av.
Sutherland Av.
SCARBORO
Sentac St.
16 Av.
17 Av.
18A St.
17A St.
16A St.
14A St.
19 Av.
BANKVIEW
20 Av.
21 Av.
22 Av.
17B St.
23 Av.
Bankview
Community
Centre
Tennis courts
19A St.
100 m
16B St.
24 Av.
25 Av.
Stanley Park route
15A St.

11 Av.
Sunalta LRT Start 10 Ave and 16 St.
13 St.
CONNAUGHT
12 Av.
N
Connaught School
15 St.
14 St.
12 St.
11 St.
10 St.
14 Av.
Kalmata Grocery
15 Av.
Good Earth Café
16 Av.
17 Av.
Dine and Shop
17 Av.
15 St.
14A St.
14 St.
13 St.
12 St.
11 St.
10 St.
9A St.
9 St.
19 Av.
Cameron Av.
15 St.
14A St.
LOWER MOUNT ROYAL
Mount Royal School
21 Av.
Colborne Cres.
9 St.
22 Av.
Carleton St.
Sydenham Rd.
10 St.
15 St.
23 Av.
14 St.
Prospect Av.
24 Av.
25 Av.
Carleton St.
100 m
Frontenac Av.
Montreal Av.
Stanley Park route
15A St.

Downtown Art Walk

SW

Walk at a Glance:

Engage in this public-art treasure hunt through the downtown core. Public art is always a surprise, a distraction from the business towers above you and the cars, people, and sidewalks surrounding you. Modern-day urban planners design streetscapes for the benefit of pedestrians, integrating the unexpected into the everyday built environment. The unpredictable is what makes walking in the city so enjoyable.

Route Details

Categories: C-Train, Café, Dog Friendly, Neighbourhoods and Parks, People Watching and Shopping, River, Stroller.

Starting-Point Parking–Downtown: Anywhere downtown.

Starting-Point Parking–North Side of River: City Parking Lot, Memorial Drive just east of Third Street NW.

Starting-Point Parking–South of Downtown: Anywhere between Tenth Avenue and Seventeenth Avenue, between Fourth Street SE and Ninth Street SW.

C-Train Start: Any downtown station between City Hall and Eleventh Street SW.

Transit: Bus access at various points along the route. Check Calgary Transit at www.calgarytransit.com.

Facilities: A variety of cafés and public buildings along the route.

Distance: No set route, no set distance.

Degree of Difficulty: Easy and flat.

Seasonal Highlights/Cautions

Winter: Christmas lights on Stephen Avenue Mall, Eighth Avenue, make this a festive walk from the end of November through Christmas. Bring your skates and enjoy the ice rink at Olympic Plaza. How about a night skate under the city lights? A Zamboni keeps the ice in perfect condition.

Spring, Summer, and Fall: Stephen Avenue Mall, Eighth Avenue, is upbeat with events and entertainment all summer. Stampede breakfasts abound in this area during Stampede week in early July.

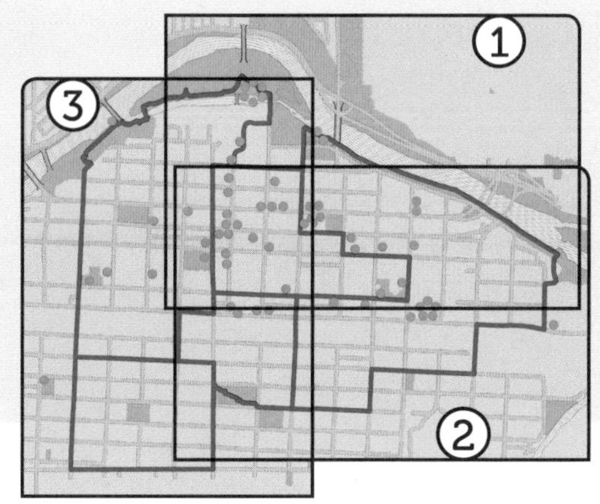

Slow your pace and appreciate walking for walking's sake, to simply experience the urban cityscape, alleyways, and hidden corners and surprises. Become a flâneur, which, according to the early nineteenth-century French, was a leisurely urban explorer who observed and contemplated as he or she sauntered.

Manuel Latruwe Belgian Bakery Café and Bread Shop

Make a detour, or a post-walk visit, to my favourite place to buy fresh bread. Real butter and real cream make the croissants, chocolate buns, and miniature dessert creations at Manuel Latruwe taste truly decadent. For lunch, try a quiche, and then grab a loaf of bread to enjoy later. If you would like to delay your gratification, buy a tub of homemade ice cream for a future indulgence.

Location: 1333 First Street SE (on Macleod Trail S, beside the Bernard Callebaut building), www.manuellatruwe.com
Hours: 7:30 am–5 pm (closed on Sundays)

For those who would like to pick up the pace and travel farther, follow the southerly route option provided that follows the people-populated streets of the Beltline, a community that is being rejuvenated with a pedestrian focus. Walk through the Memorial Park public space, grab a food truck lunch along Twelfth Avenue, and, on a blue-sky day, sit in

Some Stories behind the Art

There are many interesting pieces of art in downtown Calgary. Unfortunately, I don't have room in this book to provide details on each piece, however I feature six below.

"In Search of Gold Mountain" (11)
The central monument in Sien Lok Park in Calgary's Chinatown represents the proud history of Chinese settlement in Canada. The 15-ton granite stone was brought from Hoiping China and carved into a monument that pictorially describes the early Chinese gold miners of the 1850s and the railway workers of the 1860s who constituted the first wave of Chinese immigrants to Canada.

"Brotherhood of Mankind" (24)
In 1967 Calgarians were outraged! These elongated, abstract, and notably naked figures were seen as offensive, but over the years they have endured and are now a Calgary landmark and included in the logo of the Calgary Board of Education.

"Wonderland" (25)
This 3.5-m high, wire-frame sculpture of a giant girl's head stands guard on the outdoor plaza at The Bow building.

"Alberta's Dream" (26)
A bronze cast of a man embracing a live tree–a self-portrait of Spanish sculptor Jaume Plensa–is intimate and yet connected to the community: Alberta place names decorate the figure's body.

"Women are Persons" (29)
These "Famous Five" Alberta women fought to have Canadian women recognized constitutionally as "persons" in 1929. Emily Murphy led the battle along with Henrietta Muir Edwards, Nellie McClung, Louise McKinney, and Irene Parlby. The Supreme Court of Canada rejected their case in 1928, but the Judicial Committee of the British Privy Council decided in favour of the women on October 18, 1929.

"Chinook Arc" (60)
Interactive and illuminated, this Chinook arch–inspired sculpture provides an inviting internal glow that draws the eye. Park users become active participants in the sculpture experience by changing the lighting. The shape draws inspiration from the historic Beltline streetcar loop that once encircled the neighbourhood.

Life's Little Moments by Sheila Kernan

the sunshine at one of the many outdoor tables just outside Memorial Park Library. Stroll farther south to Seventeenth Avenue, the popular walking, shopping, and dining street, or walk west along the Thirteenth Avenue greenway followed by a visit to Barb Scott Park and an intriguing public sculpture called "Chinook Arc." It comes alive with colour at night.

The alternate loop takes you east to RiverWalk, which runs along the Bow River and hosts temporary and permanent art installations and murals. Designed to accommodate walkers and cyclists, there are two pathways, so you can relax and enjoy your chosen activity. Bring your lunch and get comfy on one of the many benches or lounge chairs. Sit back and watch the river, and the walkers and cyclists, flow by.

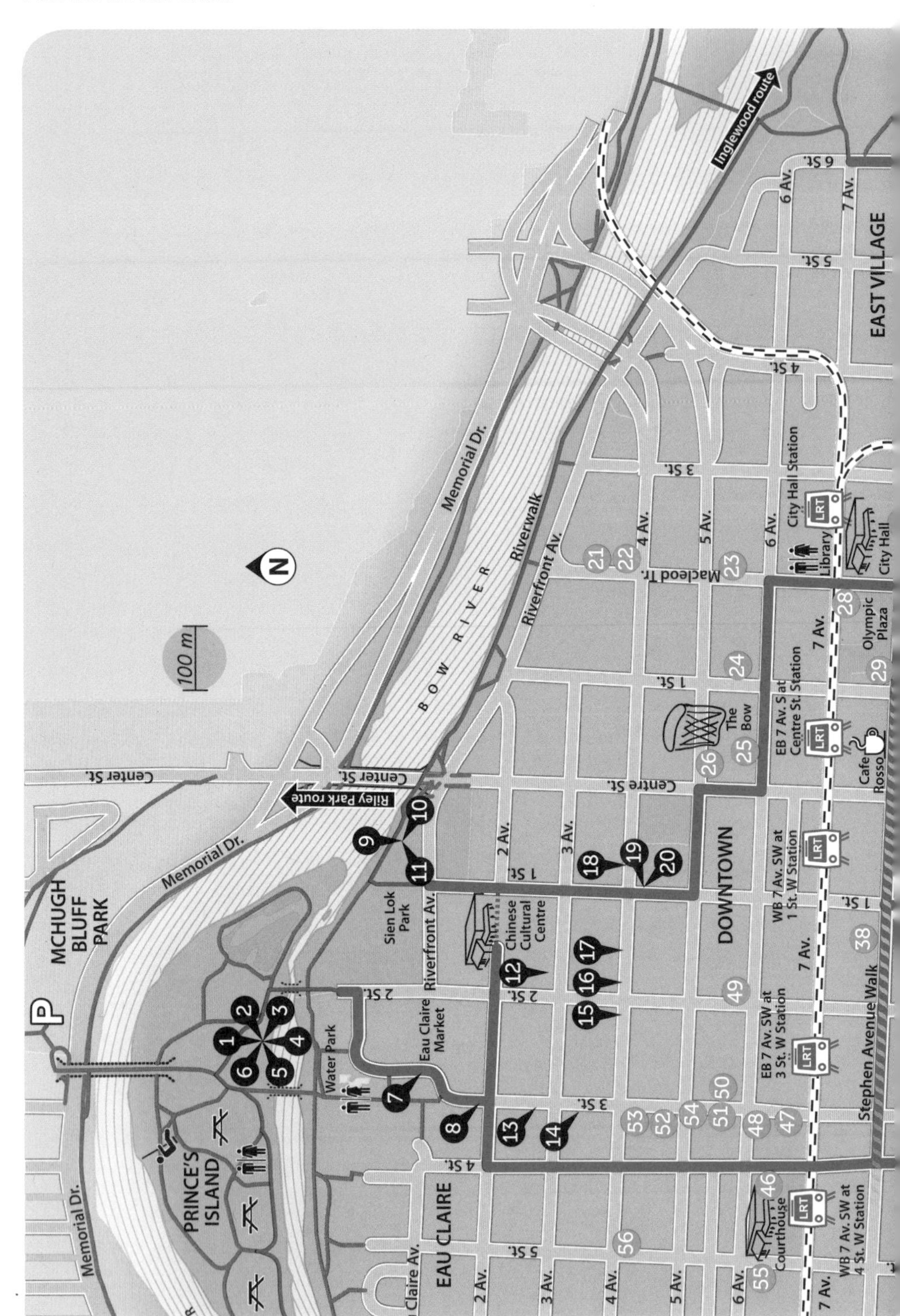
Inglewood route
6 St.
7 Av.
6 Av.
5 St.
EAST VILLAGE
4 St.
Memorial Dr.
Riverwalk
Riverfront Av.
3 St.
4 Av.
5 Av.
6 Av.
City Hall Station
City Hall
Library
Macleod Tr.
B O W R I V E R
100 m
N
Olympic Plaza
7 Av.
1 St.
The Bow
EB 7 Av. S at Centre St. Station
Cafe Rosso
Center St.
Centre St.
Riley Park route
2 Av.
3 Av.
DOWNTOWN
WB 7 Av. SW at 1 St. W Station
MCHUGH BLUFF PARK
Sien Lok Park
Riverfront Av.
Chinese Cultural Centre
Stephen Avenue Walk
2 St.
Water Park
Eau Claire Market
EB 7 Av. SW at 3 St. W Station
PRINCE'S ISLAND
EAU CLAIRE
Eau Claire Av.
Courthouse
WB 7 Av. SW at 4 St. W Station
Memorial Dr.
LRT

	1	2	3	4	5
Title	"Ducks"	"Prairie Collage"	"Cracked Pot Foundations"	"Buffalo Grass and Tumbleweed"	Untitled
Artist	Enzo DiPalma	Enzo DiPalma	Katie Ohe	Enzo DiPalma	Ben Mcleod
Year of Creation; Materials	1969	1969	1964; stone	1969	1987
Location	Prince's Island Park	Prince's Island Park	Prince's Island Park	Prince's Island Park	Prince's Island Park

	6	7	8	9	10
Title	"Copernicus (1473–1543)"	"An Auspicious Find"	"Cow Bench"	Sien Lok Lions	"Wall of Names Project"
Artist	Stanislaw Wyspianski	Lori Sobkowich	Gwen Hughes and Rick Barber	Unknown	Ferdinando Nichola Spina
Year of Creation; Materials	1975	2004; poured concrete and marbles	1993	Unknown	2001
Location	Prince's Island Park	Eau Claire	Second Av. and Third St. SW	Sien Lok Park	Sien Lok Park

	11	12	13	14	15
Title	"In Search of Gold Mountain"	"Outside Orion, Livingston Place Park"	"Friendship"	"Brown Trout Rising"	"Pathways to Everywhere"
Artist	Chu Honsun	Ken Macklin	Charles Hilton	Eric B. Peterson	Dennis Oppenheim
Year of Creation; Materials	1999; granite	2007	1980	1997	2009
Location	Sien Lok Park	Second Av. and Second St. SW (outside the Chinese Cultural Centre)	Third Av. and Third St. SW	Third Av. and Third St. SW	Fourth Av. and Second St. SW

	16	17	18	19	20
Title	"Porte Cocherie de la Lumiere"	"3Flames"	"River Fragments"	"Spine and Panels"	"Past, Present and Future"
Artist	Michael Hayden	Laszlo Szilvassy	Tony Bloom	Unknown	Gemot Kiefer
Year of Creation; Materials	1989	1990	Unknown	Unknown	1991
Location	240 Fourth Av. SW (BP Centre)	240 Fourth Av. SW (BP Centre)	144 Fourth Av. SW (Sun Life Plaza)	Fourth Av. and First St. SW (Trans Canada Building)	115 Fourth Av. SW (Trans Canada Building)

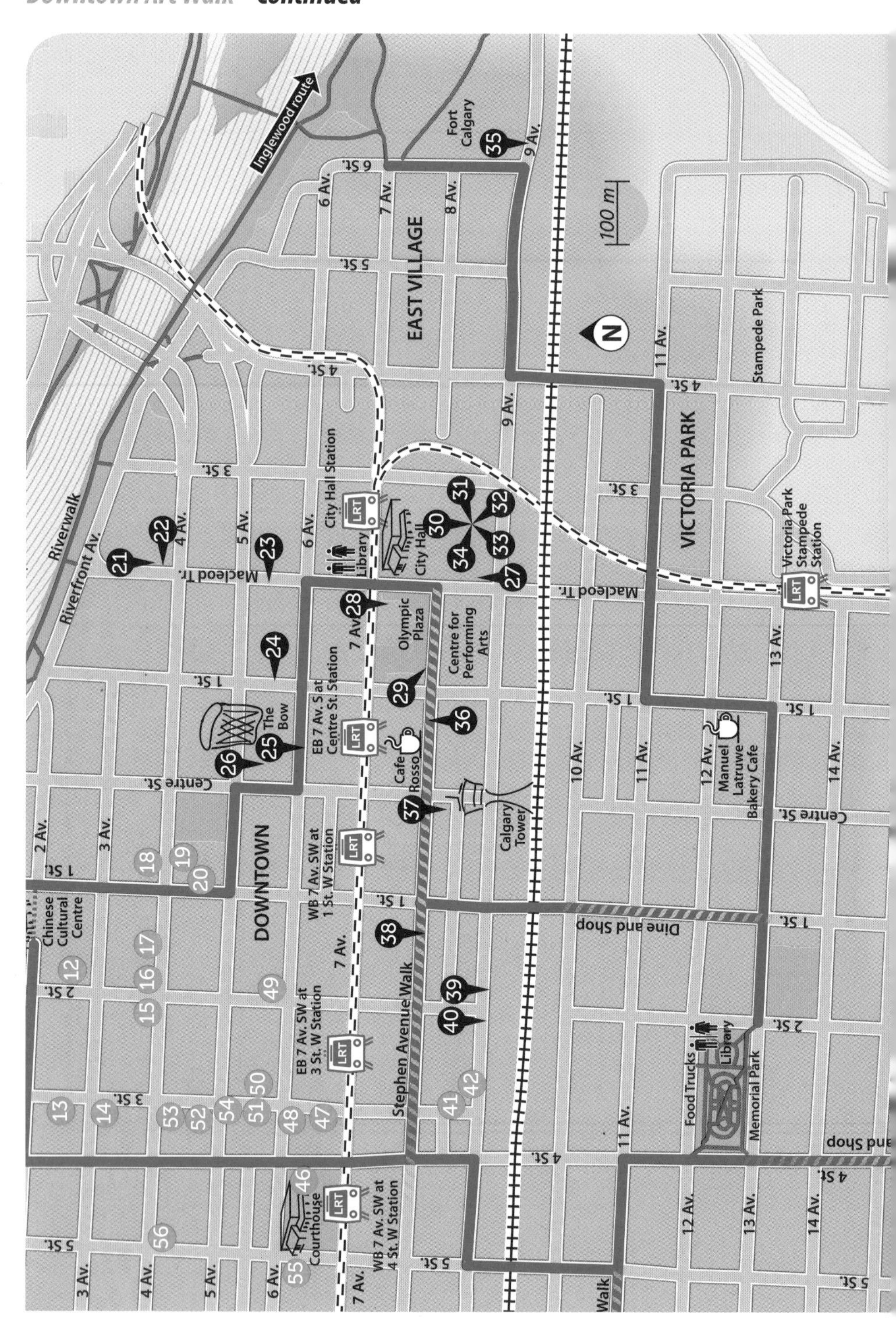
Inglewood route
Fort Calgary
EAST VILLAGE
100 m
N
Stampede Park
VICTORIA PARK
Victoria Park Stampede Station
City Hall Station
Library
City Hall
Olympic Plaza
Centre for Performing Arts
The Bow
EB 7 Av. S at Centre St. Station
Cafe Rosso
Calgary Tower
Manuel Latruwe Bakery Cafe
DOWNTOWN
WB 7 Av. SW at 1 St. W Station
Dine and Shop
Chinese Cultural Centre
Stephen Avenue Walk
EB 7 Av. SW at 3 St. W Station
Food Trucks
Memorial Park
Courthouse
WB 7 Av. SW at 4 St. W Station
Riverwalk
Riverfront Av.
Macleod Tr.
Centre St.
Walk

	21	22	23	24	25
Title	"Map of Canada / Coat of Arms"	"Untitled Aluminum"	"Children's Commemorative Obelisk"	"Brotherhood of Mankind"	"Wonderland"
Artist	Joe Chomistek	Doug Bentham	10,000 children	Mario Armengol	Jaume Plensa
Year of Creation; Materials	1986 / 1984	1981	Unknown; ceramic tiles set into building	1967	2013; wire
Location	First St. SE, between Third and Fourth Av.s (Harry Hays Building)	220 Fourth Av. SE (Harry Hays Building)	Fifth Av. and Macleod Trail SE	Sixth Av. and First St. SE	Sixth Av. and Centre St. SW (The Bow building)

	26	27	28	29	30
Title	"Alberta's Dream"	"Playful Cub"	"The Olympic Runner"	"Women are Persons"	"Family of Horses"
Artist	Jaume Plensa	Leo Mol	Unknown	Barbara Paterson	Harry O'Hanlon
Year of Creation; Materials	2013; bronze	1996	1987	1999; bronze	1989
Location	Fifth Av. and Centre St. SW, corner (The Bow building)	Seventh Av. and Third St. SE	222 Eighth Av. SE	Eighth Av. and Macleod Trail west side of Olympic Plaza)	800 Macleod Trail SE (Municipal Plaza)

	31	32	33	34	35
Title	"Lion"	"Balancing Act"	"Natural Engineer"	"Chief David Crowchild Memorial"	"Fort Calgary Sentinels"
Artist	James L. Thomson	Roy Leadbeater	Don Begg	Robert Stowell	Calgary's Heavy Industries
Year of Creation; Materials	1916	1989	1987	1988	2014
Location	800 Macleod Trail SE (Municipal Plaza)	800 Macleod Trail SE (Municipal Plaza)	800 Macleod Trail SE (Municipal Garden)	800 Macleod Trail SE (Municipal Atrium)	Ninth Av. and Sixth St. SE (east edge of East Village and Fort Calgary)

	36	37	38	39	40
Title	Glenbow Museum facade mural	Mechanical horse	"Conversation"	"Nuova Twist"	"Weather Vanes"
Artist	Bob Oldrich	Unknown	William McEicheran	Beverly Pepper	Colette Whiten and Paul Kipps
Year of Creation; Materials	1976; unpainted concrete relief	Unknown	1980; bronze	2010; corten steel	Unknown
Location	130 Ninth Av. SE (Glenbow Museum exterior)	Centre St. and Eighth Av. S	Eighth Av. and First St. SW (west side)	Ninth Av. and Second St. SW	Ninth Av. and Second St. SW

Vendome Café
Memorial Dr.
Peace Bridge
BOW RIVER
Water Park
Sien Lok Park
Eau Claire Av.
1 Av.
EAU CLAIRE
Eau Claire Market
Riverfront Av.
Riley Park route
2 Av.
Chinese Cultural Centre
3 Av.
4 Av.
5 Av.
6 Av.
WB 7 Av. SW at 7 St. W Station
Courthouse
EB 7 Av. SW at 3 St. W Station
6 St. W Station
7 Av.
WB 7 Av. SW at 4 St. W Station
8 Av.
Stephen Avenue Walk
9 Av.
Mountain Equipment Co-op
10 Av.
Bumpy's Cafe
11 Av.
Gallery Walk
12 Av.
Barb Scott Park
Food Trucks
Library
Memorial Park
13 Av.
BELTLINE
Lougheed House
14 Av.
15 Av.
Caffe Beano
Analog Cafe
16 Av.
17 Av.
Dine and Shop
100 m
9A St.
9 St.
8 St.
7 St.
6 St.
5 St.
4 St.
3 St.
2 St.
1 St.

	41	42	43
Title	"Between the Earth & the Sky Measuring the Immeasurable"	"Tribute to Land" (turtle)	"Swarm"
Artist	Jacqueline Metz and Nancy Chew	Irene F. Whittome	Stuart Keeler
Year of Creation; Materials	2000; rundle stone, bronze, fibre optics	1990	2009
Location	Ninth Av. and Third St. SW (northeast corner)	Ninth Av. and Third St. SW	Seventh Av. and Sixth St. SW (C-Train station)

	44	45	46
Title	"The Winner"	"Arrival Time, Departure Time"	"Do Re Mi Fa Sol La Si Do"
Artist	J. Seward Johnson	Living Lenses	Joe Fafard
Year of Creation; Materials	1986; bronze	2009	2010; steel
Location	Eighth Av. and Eighth St. SW	Seventh Av. and Seventh St. SW (C-train station)	Calgary Courts Park, Fourth St. between Sixth and Seventh Av. SW

	47	48	49
Title	"Eight Seconds to Glory"	"Ever Evolving Human"	"Saoko/Kabuki"
Artist	Shane R.L. Sutherland	Shane R.L. Sutherland	Sorel Etrog
Year of Creation; Materials	2000	1999	1975
Location	444 Seventh Av. SW	Sixth Av. and Third St. SW	Sixth Av. and Second St. SW

	50	51	52
Title	"Big Daddy"	"Brothers"	"Spirit Dance
Artist	Anton Perzinger	James R. Galts-Goldsmith	Bicki Yvon Smith
Year of Creation; Materials	1998	1997	1998
Location	333 Fifth Av. SW	505 Third St. SW	400 Fifth Av. SW

	53	54	55
Title	"Millennium Beetle"	"Peter's & Co. Bell"	"Calgary's Original Courthouse Doors"
Artist	James R. Galts-Goldsmith	Unknown	James R. Galts-Goldsmith
Year of Creation; Materials	2000	2002	1971
Location	407 Third St. SW	505 Third St. SW	601 Fifth St. SW

	56	57	58
Title	"Mating Dance"	"Peace Bridge"	The Pandrol Clip-Strength and Endurance
Artist	Kevan Leycraft	Santiago Calatrava	Unknown
Year of Creation; Materials	1991	2012	Unknown
Location	Fourth Av. and Fifth St. SW	Bow River Pathway, north end of Seventh St. SW	Corner of 9 St. and 4 Av., SW

	59	60
Title	Incipio Modo	"Chinook Arc"
Artist	Ascension	Joe O'Connell and Blessing Hancock, fabricated by Creative Machines (Arizona)
Year of Creation; Materials	Year of Creation: 2012	2014
Location	Location: 9 St. between 4 Av. and 5 Av., SW	Twelfth Av. and Ninth St. SW (Barb Scott Park)

Roxboro–Erlton–Ramsay

SW

Walk at a Glance:

Connecting five communities, this route sheds light on the kind of diversity Calgary can pack into a 5-km radius. Climb the dirt path into Roxboro Natural Park, an escarpment green space. The views from the top of the bluff are expansive, taking in the tree-canopied streets of Roxboro and the money-making business core beyond.

Continue south along the trail, keeping an eye out for a large cross marking the cut-off route into St. Mary's Cemetery. Welcome to Erlton, where fluffy cottontail tulip eaters roam free. Domestic rabbits expelled from residents' homes have multiplied and are driving local gardeners mad. Many a resident can now relate to Looney Tunes' Elmer Fudd when he cries out, "Kill the wabbit."

Route Details

Categories: C-Train, Café, Dog Friendly, Hilly, Historic, Home and Gardens, Neighbourhoods and Parks, People Watching and Shopping, River, Vistas.

Starting-Point Parking: Park on Roxboro Glen Road SW.

C-Train Start: Erlton Station.

Transit: Bus access at various points along the route. Check Calgary Transit at www.calgarytransit.com.

Facilities: Cafés along Fourth Street SW (see Walk 21 on page 150); Talisman Centre Sports Complex in Lindsay Park.

Distance: Main route: 7.5 km
Alternate route via Fourth Street SW: 8 km

Degree of Difficulty: Moderate, with a few hill and stair climbs.

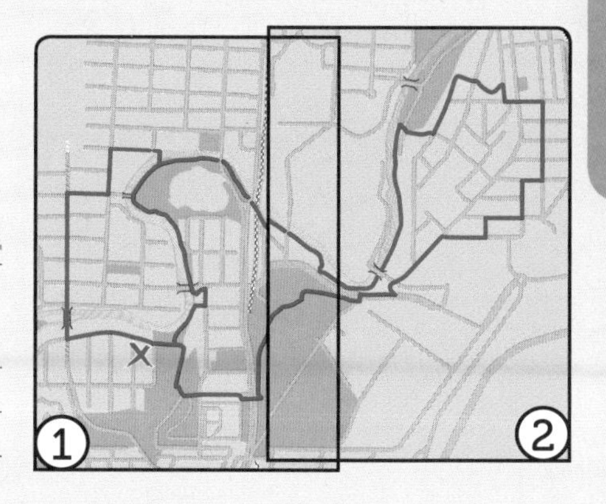

Seasonal Highlights/Cautions

Winter and Spring: The Roxboro/Erlton Natural Park trail climb can be slippery with ice or mud.

Summer and Fall: Plan to do this walk during Stampede week in early July to help you wind down and burn off the mini-doughnuts and deep-fried Mars bars.

Continue up and over Macleod Trail and get a glimpse of the treadmill of life, the cars whizzing below, before you descend into the calm of Queen's Park Cemetery. Reader Rock Garden is the next detour, a wonderful, inner-city, perennial garden that sits below the cemetery, on the south side of the Stampede grounds. It is the

Reader Rock Garden

As you walk through Reader Rock Garden, imagine that in 1913 the site was nothing more than a dusty barren bit of land. Thanks to William Reader, an Englishman who brought his love of gardening to Calgary in 1908, the site was transformed. In April 1913 Reader became the parks superintendent for Calgary, and during his twenty-nine-year career, he helped develop many of Calgary's parks, cemeteries, and civic nurseries. Between 1922 and 1929, thousands of tons of boulders, originating from Banff to Drumheller, were brought to the garden site to create an alpine rock garden. Reader's passion for gardening led him to collect plants from around the world. He introduced many of these into the rock garden, and at one time, up to 850 varieties of seeds were documented in the Reader Rock Garden. Reader taught Calgarians that it is possible to have a beautiful garden in Calgary, despite our tough growing conditions.

perfect Stampede escape for those of you who crave a little nature with your corn dogs and mini-doughnuts. The garden is named after creator William Roland Reader, the City of Calgary parks superintendent from 1913 to 1942. In the early 1900s, Reader collected alpine plants while hiking in the mountains. He introduced them to this formerly bare hillside. Over thirty years he continued to develop his garden, testing the abilities of

Caffe Rosso Coffee Roasters

Tucked away in an industrial landscape is one fantastic coffee shop. Stop by Rosso and enjoy the on-site roasted coffee and freshly baked goods and lunches. The cappuccino makes my mouth water. This little café is one of three located in the city, and I can highly recommend them all. My daughter enjoyed the most impressive teddy-bear foam art on her hot chocolate at the Eighth Avenue, downtown, Rosso location. Impressive and tasty; don't miss it!

Location: Ramsay, Dominion Bridge, 803 Twenty-Fourth Avenue SW, www.rossocoffeeroasters.com
Phone: 403-971-1800
Hours: 7 am–5 pm (weekdays); 8 am–5 pm (weekends)

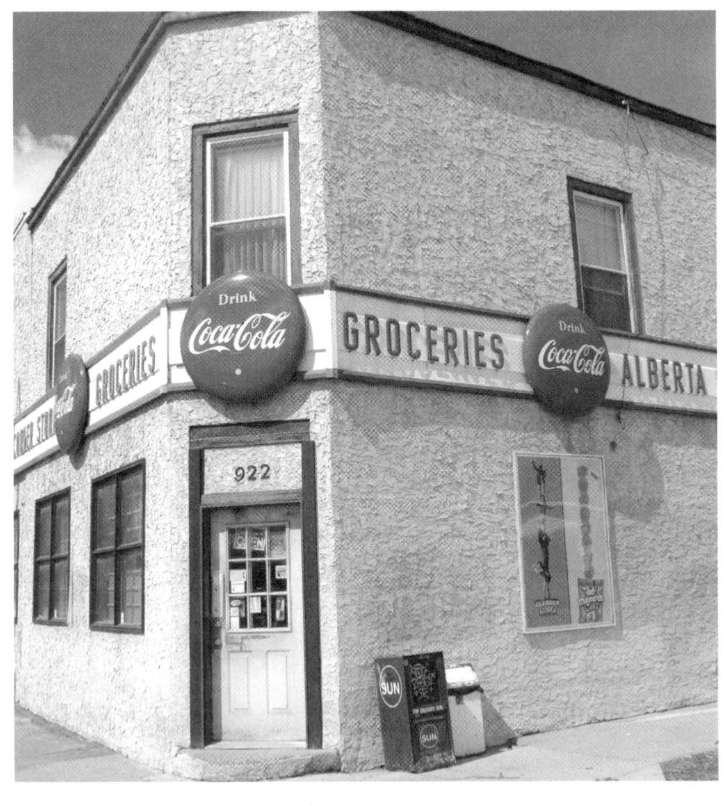

Only In My Imagination by Sheila Kernan

over four thousand plants in the prairie climate. The now-reconstructed garden blooms from mid-March through October. It is a mini oasis, a nice spot for a picnic or just a wander.

Walk east past the Reader house, now a restaurant and a popular spot for weddings, and set your sights on Ramsay and Inglewood, Calgary's first communities. Variety is the spice of life, and not knowing what you might find around the next corner is what makes for a fun urban walkabout. Ramsay is a neighbourhood wherein residents' interests, and thus their characters, are visible to all who pass by. An art installation, a colourful house, the Little Free Library (littlefreelibrary.org) on a front lawn; I always have my camera at the ready for the unexpected. Plan to graze as you walk. A warm microclimate and rich soil brings early blooms, as well as a multitude of pears and apples falling from trees throughout the fall.

Climb to Scotsman's Hill, the place to watch the Stampede fireworks in early July, and snap a photo of the iconic view over the Saddledome: city towers reach skyward and the Rocky Mountains stretch out across the horizon. Find the escarpment staircase and drop down to the newly developed RiverWalk pathway and Stampede extension. Follow the Elbow River Pathway south along the Stampede grounds to Lindsay Park. Walk through the side streets of Mission and along popular Fourth Street for a coffee or some shopping, or continue along the Elbow River Pathway to the hidden pathway that leads you back to your car.

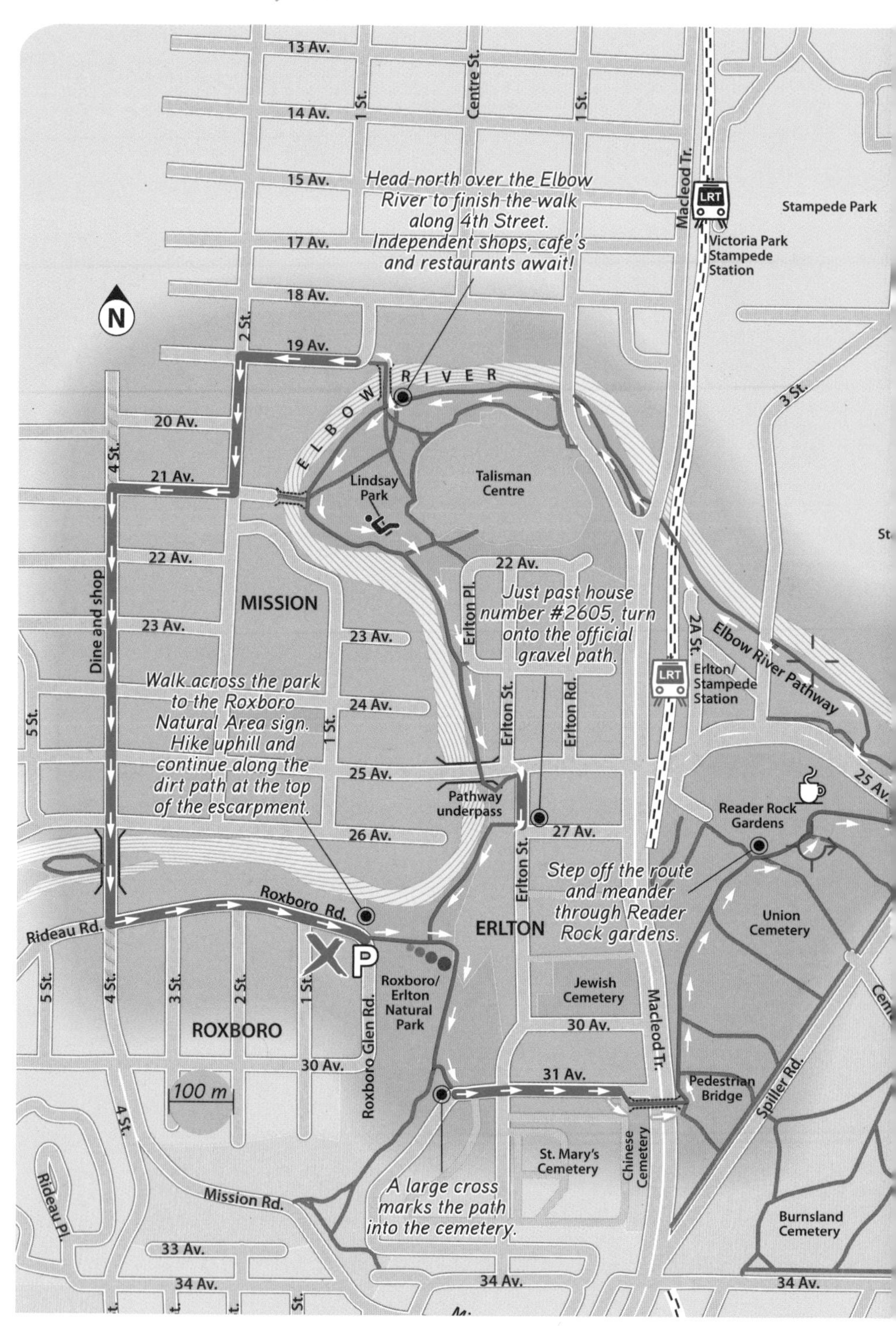
13 Av.
14 Av.
15 Av.
17 Av.
18 Av.
19 Av.
20 Av.
21 Av.
22 Av.
23 Av.
24 Av.
25 Av.
26 Av.
27 Av.
30 Av.
31 Av.
33 Av.
34 Av.
1 St.
Centre St.
2 St.
4 St.
5 St.
3 St.
2A St.
3 St.
Macleod Tr.
Head north over the Elbow River to finish the walk along 4th Street. Independent shops, cafe's and restaurants await!
LRT
Victoria Park Stampede Station
Stampede Park
ELBOW RIVER
Lindsay Park
Talisman Centre
Erlton Pl.
Erlton St.
Erlton Rd.
Just past house number #2605, turn onto the official gravel path.
Erlton/ Stampede Station
Elbow River Pathway
MISSION
Dine and shop
Walk across the park to the Roxboro Natural Area sign. Hike uphill and continue along the dirt path at the top of the escarpment.
Pathway underpass
Reader Rock Gardens
Step off the route and meander through Reader Rock gardens.
Union Cemetery
Roxboro Rd.
Rideau Rd.
ERLTON
Roxboro/ Erlton Natural Park
Roxboro Glen Rd.
Jewish Cemetery
ROXBORO
100 m
Pedestrian Bridge
Spiller Rd.
St. Mary's Cemetery
Chinese Cemetery
A large cross marks the path into the cemetery.
Mission Rd.
Rideau Pl.
Burnsland Cemetery

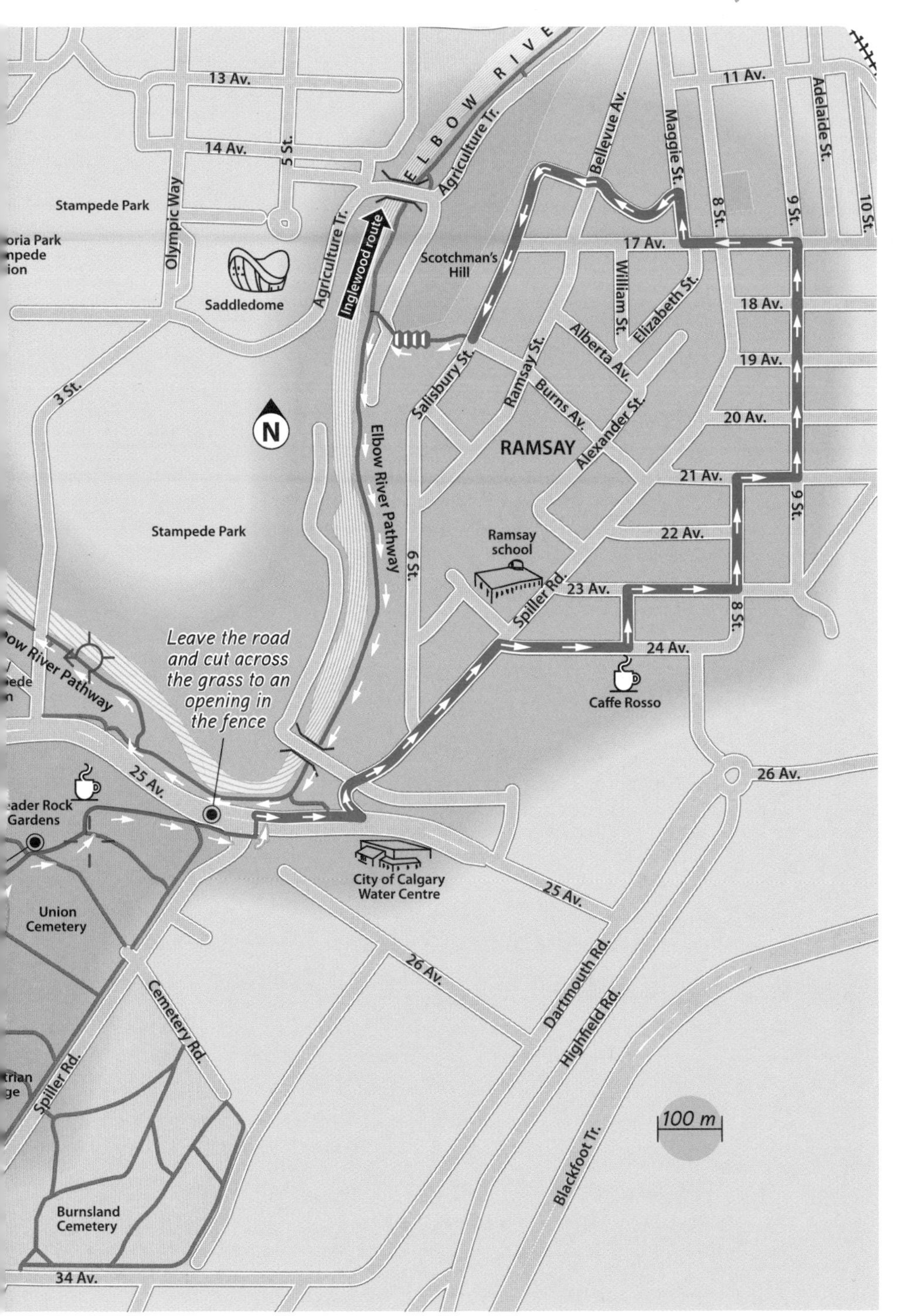
13 Av.
14 Av.
5 St.
ELBOW RIVER
Agriculture Tr.
Bellevue Av.
Maggie St.
11 Av.
Adelaide St.
8 St.
9 St.
10 St.
Stampede Park
Olympic Way
Agriculture Tr.
Inglewood route
Scotchman's Hill
17 Av.
William St.
Elizabeth St.
18 Av.
Saddledome
Alberta Av.
19 Av.
Ramsay St.
Salisbury St.
Burns Av.
Alexander St.
20 Av.
3 St.
N
Elbow River Pathway
RAMSAY
21 Av.
9 St.
Stampede Park
6 St.
Ramsay school
22 Av.
Spiller Rd.
23 Av.
8 St.
Leave the road and cut across the grass to an opening in the fence
24 Av.
Caffe Rosso
26 Av.
25 Av.
City of Calgary Water Centre
25 Av.
Union Cemetery
26 Av.
Dartmouth Rd.
Cemetery Rd.
Highfield Rd.
Spiller Rd.
100 m
Blackfoot Tr.
Burnsland Cemetery
34 Av.

Stanley Park–Roxboro–Mount Royal–East Elbow

SW

Walk at a Glance:

Walk from Stanley Park uphill to Parkhill, a neighbourhood with unique architecture, where contemporary houses are replacing the original modest homes. The elementary school–turned condos on Second Street mixes the old with the varied infill designs. Skirt the escarpment along grass paths and soak up big views of the Rockies beyond and the community of East Elbow below.

A set of stairs leads you to the next green-space gem: Roxboro/Erlton Natural Park. Calgary has an abundance of off-the-sidewalk trails that give the urban hiker the feeling she is walking in a remote wilderness area. Wolf willow shrubs are in full bloom in June as you climb from Mission Road into the park space. The scent of their yellow flowers is pungent–a prairie trademark. Descend the slope and travel through Roxboro and Rideau, two

Route Details

Categories: C-Train, Café, Dog Friendly, Hilly, Home and Gardens, Nature, Neighbourhoods and Parks, People Watching and Shopping, River, Stroller, Vistas.

Starting-Point Parking: Stanley Park official parking lot on Forty-Second Avenue just west of 1A Street SW.

C-Train Start: Thirty-Ninth Avenue Station (then a short walk).

Transit: Bus access at various points along the route. Check Calgary Transit at www.calgarytransit.com.

Facilities: Seasonal bathrooms in the park near the parking lot are open from mid-May to mid-October; outdoor pool and tennis courts.

Distance: 10.6 km

Degree of Difficulty: Moderate, with hills.

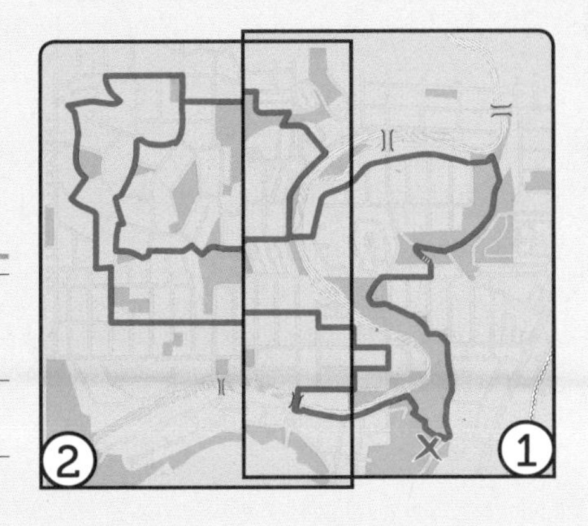

Seasonal Highlights/Cautions

Winter: Skating on the phenomenal outdoor rink and sledding at Stanley Park (4011 1A Street SW) from the first cold snap until the final melt–the perfect winter outing. The Christmas lights are wonderful in December. Be prepared for icy and/or snowy pathways and sidewalks.

Spring, Summer, and Fall: Plan a post-walk picnic or a summer swim at the outdoor pool in Stanley Park.

affluent communities that enjoy prime river real estate. The Bow River occasionally floods and when it does, Roxboro is the worst hit. The community is situated at a critical turn in the river, and high waters do not make the turn but rather flow easily through the streets, up to the main level on many homes during the flood of 2013.

Cross the Elbow River on one of the many pedestrian bridges that allow self-propelled folks to efficiently connect communities. Continue through the streets of Elbow Park before climbing up the green-space slopes that are covered in saskatoon shrubs. Stop for a saskatoon snack in August before continuing between houses on the cut-through pathway. Mount Royal is the next community on your urban hike bucket list. This neighbourhood is pleasant to walk through year-round, and at Christmastime, the colourful light displays are festive. A nighttime, full-moon, winter walk is fun in this community: the moon is bright enough to allow you to walk confidently through the quiet residential streets. Sometimes nighttime walks allow you to catch glimpses of the lit-up interiors giving walkers a chance to assess paint colours and enjoy some artwork.

Venturing onward, the route crosses Elbow Drive into East Elbow Park, a hidden gem tucked away in the heart of the inner city. Without reason to visit East Elbow, most people would just drive on by. The walker experiences a peaceful jaunt in this community, enjoying a landscape of well-tended gardens and a mix of older modest homes and grand new abodes. The new mansions are testament to Alberta's natural resource wealth.

Connect to the Elbow River Pathway once again and continue back to Stanley Park. A large leafy green space, this is the perfect stop for a post-hike picnic, a swim in the outdoor pool in the summer, or in the winter a skate at Calgary's nicest outdoor rink and a toboggan on the hill above. Enjoy a mini-skating oval, curling area, two hockey rinks, and bonfires to keep you warm.

Fourth Street Eats and Drinks

Take a detour north along Fourth Street SW to find a host of restaurants, cafés and shops. Yann Haute Patisserie occupies a yellow house tucked off Fourth Street. Pastries, a few breads and baguettes, and colourful macaroons are house specialties. My favourite is the almond croissant that melts in your mouth. There is no sit-down service at Yann's, so plan on packing your treat with you to enjoy post-walk at a picnic table along the river in Stanley Park.

Another top-notch stop is Mercato. This family-run Italian shop and restaurant has tasty sandwiches, soups, and desserts, all made on site. No need for table service, since Mercato encourages patrons to pull up a stool at the bar. My daughter's favourite is the fresh focaccia bread. Grab a loaf and plunk yourself at the bar where olive oil and balsamic vinegar is available for dipping. Mercato has a host of house-made pasta sauces, pizza dough, and a full deli to complement its bright upbeat restaurant.

Right beside Mercato is the Purple Perk Coffee Market, a local favourite for its full menu of comfort food and good coffee. It has a sidewalk sitting area that is perfect for summertime people watching. Bustling with energy, this a perfect stop after a neighbourhood walk.

Location:
Yann Patisserie: 329 Twenty-Third Avenue SW (the yellow house behind the Bank of Montreal)
Mercato: 2224 Fourth Street SW, www.mercatogourmet.com
Purple Perk Coffee Market: 2212 Fourth Street SW, www.purpleperk.com

Hours:
Yann Patisserie: 9 am–6 pm (Tuesday–Saturday), 9:30 am–6 pm (Sunday), closed on Monday
Mercato: market open daily 9:30 am–7 pm; restaurant open at 11:30 am
Purple Perk Coffee Market: 7 am–10 pm (Monday–Wednesday), 7 am–11 pm (Thursday–Saturday), 8 am–10 pm (Sunday)

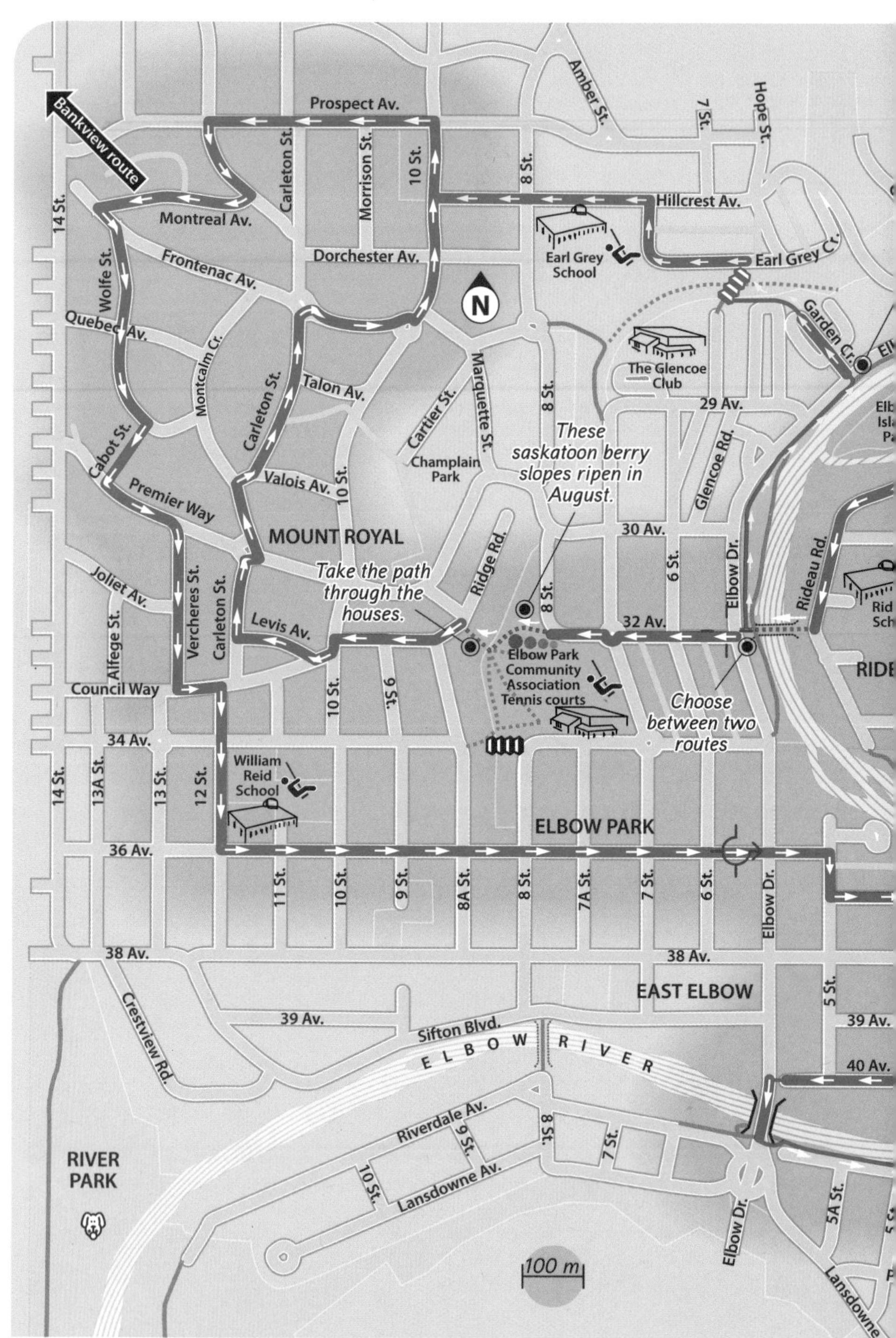

Bankview route
Prospect Av.
Carleton St.
Morrison St.
10 St.
Amber St.
7 St.
Hope St.
8 St.
Hillcrest Av.
14 St.
Montreal Av.
Dorchester Av.
Earl Grey School
Earl Grey Cr.
Frontenac Av.
Wolfe St.
Quebec Av.
N
Garden Cr.
Montcalm Cr.
Carleton St.
Talon Av.
Marquette St.
Cartier St.
The Glencoe Club
29 Av.
Cabot St.
Champlain Park
These saskatoon berry slopes ripen in August.
Glencoe Rd.
Valois Av.
Premier Way
MOUNT ROYAL
Ridge Rd.
30 Av.
Take the path through the houses.
Rideau Rd.
Joliet Av.
Vercheres St.
Carleton St.
Levis Av.
6 St.
Elbow Dr.
32 Av.
Alfege St.
Elbow Park Community Association Tennis courts
Council Way
9 St.
Choose between two routes
34 Av.
14 St.
13A St.
13 St.
12 St.
William Reid School
ELBOW PARK
36 Av.
11 St.
10 St.
9 St.
8A St.
8 St.
7A St.
7 St.
6 St.
Elbow Dr.
38 Av.
38 Av.
EAST ELBOW
5 St.
39 Av.
Crestview Rd.
Sifton Blvd.
39 Av.
E L B O W R I V E R
40 Av.
Riverdale Av.
9 St.
8 St.
7 St.
10 St.
Lansdowne Av.
RIVER PARK
Elbow Dr.
5A St.
100 m
Lansdowne

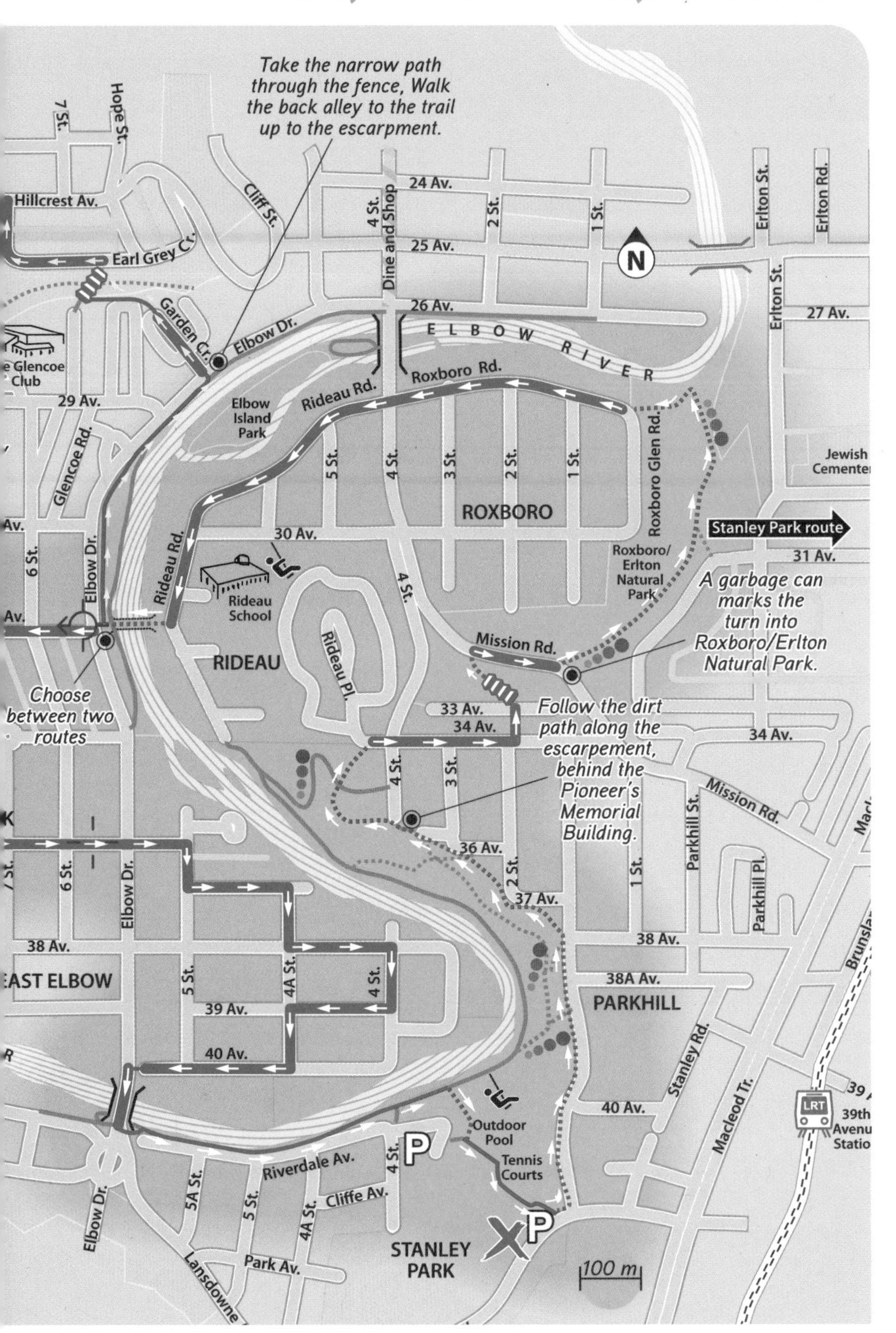

Take the narrow path through the fence, Walk the back alley to the trail up to the escarpment.
A garbage can marks the turn into Roxboro/Erlton Natural Park.
Choose between two routes
Follow the dirt path along the escarpment, behind the Pioneer's Memorial Building.
Stanley Park route
ROXBORO
RIDEAU
EAST ELBOW
PARKHILL
STANLEY PARK
ELBOW RIVER
Elbow Island Park
Rideau School
Roxboro/ Erlton Natural Park
Jewish Cementer
Glencoe Club
Outdoor Pool
Tennis Courts
39th Avenu Statio
LRT
100 m
N
24 Av.
25 Av.
26 Av.
27 Av.
29 Av.
30 Av.
31 Av.
33 Av.
34 Av.
36 Av.
37 Av.
38 Av.
38A Av.
39 Av.
40 Av.
Hillcrest Av.
Earl Grey Cr.
Garden Cr.
Elbow Dr.
Cliff St.
Hope St.
7 St.
4 St.
2 St.
1 St.
3 St.
5 St.
6 St.
4A St.
5A St.
Dine and Shop
Erlton St.
Erlton Rd.
Roxboro Rd.
Rideau Rd.
Roxboro Glen Rd.
Glencoe Rd.
Rideau Pl.
Mission Rd.
Parkhill St.
Parkhill Pl.
Stanley Rd.
Macleod Tr.
Riverdale Av.
Cliffe Av.
Park Av.
Lansdowne

Sandy Beach–Elbow Park–Britannia

SW

Walk at a Glance:

Connecting neighbourhoods on foot is my favourite way to get to know a city. This route travels across pedestrian bridges, along regional pathways, and then detours on short-cut community pathways and stairways tucked in between houses.

From Sandy Beach Park, an earthy stairway leads into the trees and exits into the River Park off-leash area, where breathtaking views of the Elbow River Valley and the downtown core are your reward. Chinook arches are a spectacular, and very welcome, sight from the River Park escarpment. The warm winds that blow in from the West Coast, over the Rocky Mountains, melt Calgarians' frosty faces.

Route Details

Categories: Café, Dog Friendly, Hilly, Home and Gardens, Nature, Neighbourhoods and Parks, River, Stroller, Vistas.

Starting-Point Parking: At the intersection of 14A Street and Fiftieth Avenue SW, follow Fiftieth Avenue east past River Park and the Emily Follensbee Centre, down the hill to the Sandy Beach parking lot.

Transit: Bus access at various points along the route. Check Calgary Transit at www.calgarytransit.com.

Facilities: Seasonal bathrooms at trailhead, open mid-May to mid-October.

Distance: 8 km

Degree of Difficulty: Moderate, with hills throughout.

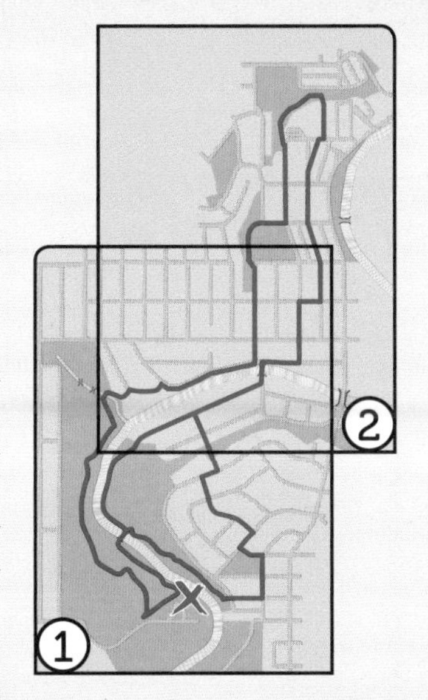

Seasonal Highlights/Cautions

Winter: Early-morning hoar frost covers trees surrounding the Elbow River on frigid days. Caution: The treed trail from Sandy Beach to River Park can be slippery in the winter and spring. An alternative is the paved path or the road up the hill to River Park.

Fall: Burnt orange and terracotta, vibrant yellows against rich blue skies: the escarpment slopes are covered in shrubs that are multi-coloured in late September.

Continuing through River Park, you'll cross a couple of small bridges and climb through the trees to the community of Elbow Park. One of Calgary's oldest communities, Elbow Park was an upper middle-class suburb of Calgary shortly before World War One. It is hard to believe that in 1909, Elbow Park was considered a suburb but it now sits in the heart of the inner city; a city that is now home to over one million people.

The pleasant tree-lined streets host some of Calgary's most impressive homes and gardens. Walking this route in May and June is guaranteed to lift winter-weary spirits as the neighbourhood comes alive with a palette of purple, pink, and white: blossoming lilac, apple, crab-apple, and cherry trees. The sweet smell of these blossoms is sure proof that summer is near.

A hidden staircase behind Christ Church takes you off the sidewalk and along shaded pathways. In August these trails are an urban foraging hotspot when the saskatoon berries are deep purple and plump. More dips and climbs lead to a Rocky Mountain viewpoint from the top of the Glencoe stairs in the community of Mount Royal.

Bell's Bookstore Café

Your cozy local coffee stop on this route is Bell's Bookstore Café. It's a great place to feed your soul with homemade baked goods, specialty coffees, and lunches. All the muffins are baked in small batches so they are fresh throughout the day. The rhubarb muffins are fantastic!

Location: 1515a Thirty-Fourth Avenue SW

If the sight of the mountains inspires you, then do a few sets of stairs to train your legs for the mountain hikes that beckon. Continue south through Elbow Park, back over the Elbow River, before climbing the tucked-away pathway into the community of Britannia, or stay low along the river pathway for a flat walk. The Britannia route is a zigzag along the quiet streets of one of Canada's wealthiest neighbourhoods. If you need a coffee, ice cream, or a picnic lunch, Britannia Plaza has it all. Grab your food and head to the escarpment, where you can sit on a bench and watch for birdlife high above or pet a few pooches at ground level. I often see bald eagles soaring low along the Elbow River from this vantage point. A brief walk downhill and then across the Elbow River leads you back to Sandy Beach. Dip your feet in the river, skip some rocks, and relax, or, on a very cold winter day, watch the steam rise from the river–a frigid, yet beautiful, sight.

Britannia Plaza: Grab a Picnic

Britannia Plaza is a great place to grab some food, a coffee, or some locally made ice cream. Sunterra Market has hot food to go, sandwiches, paninis and all sorts of baked goods and fresh produce. Stop by Village Ice Cream for an assortment of locally made ice cream, or grab a coffee at the Starbucks. If you have more time, be sure to stop by Owl's Nest Books, one of Calgary's few independent bookstores.

Location: Britannia Plaza, Elbow Drive and Forty-Ninth Avenue SW

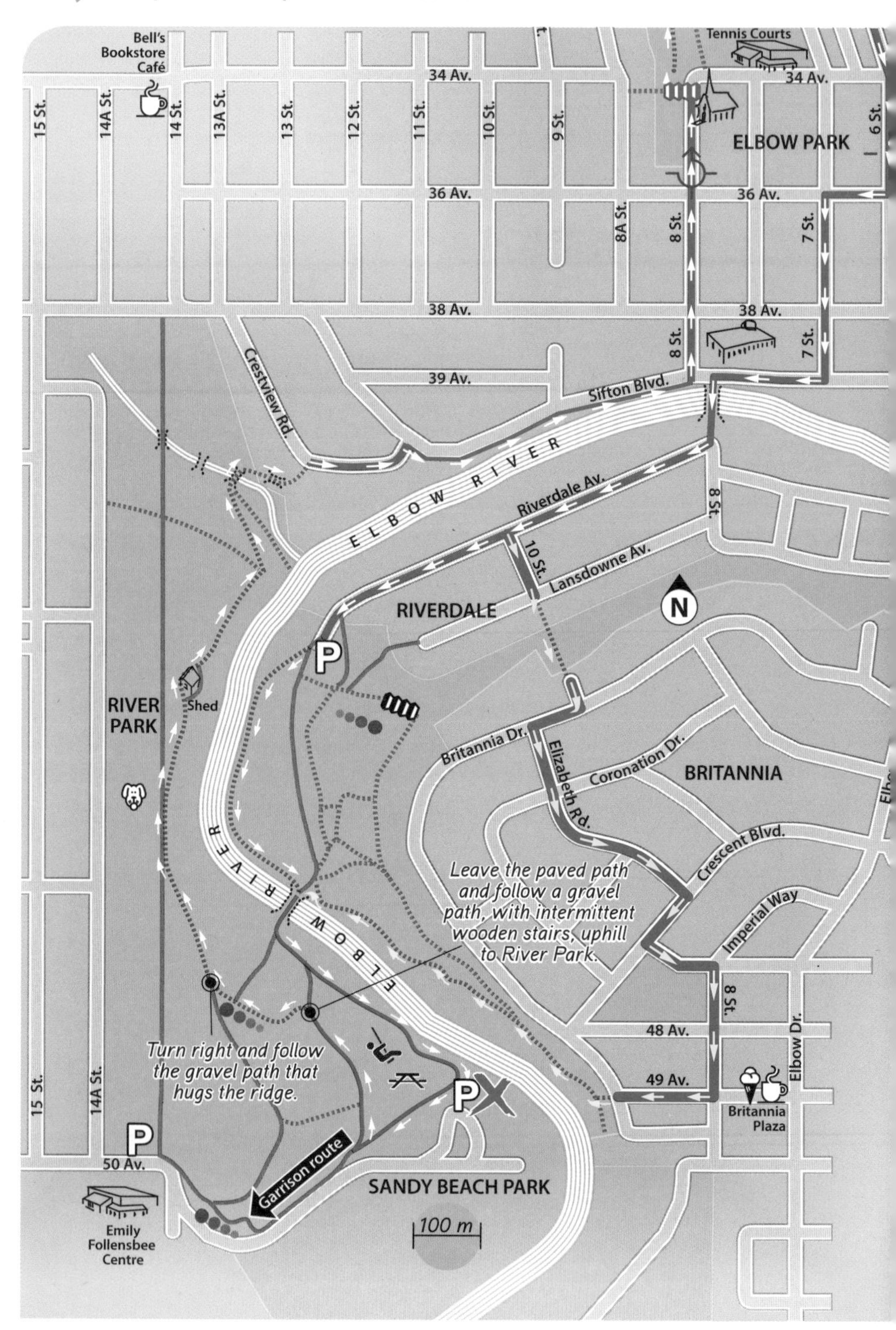
Bell's Bookstore Café
Tennis Courts
34 Av.
15 St.
14A St.
14 St.
13A St.
13 St.
12 St.
11 St.
10 St.
9 St.
6 St.
ELBOW PARK
36 Av.
8A St.
8 St.
7 St.
38 Av.
39 Av.
Crestview Rd.
Sifton Blvd.
ELBOW RIVER
Riverdale Av.
10 St.
Lansdowne Av.
RIVERDALE
N
RIVER PARK
Shed
Britannia Dr.
Elizabeth Rd.
Coronation Dr.
BRITANNIA
Crescent Blvd.
Imperial Way
Leave the paved path and follow a gravel path, with intermittent wooden stairs, uphill to River Park.
Turn right and follow the gravel path that hugs the ridge.
48 Av.
49 Av.
Elbow Dr.
Britannia Plaza
50 Av.
Garrison route
SANDY BEACH PARK
100 m
Emily Follensbee Centre

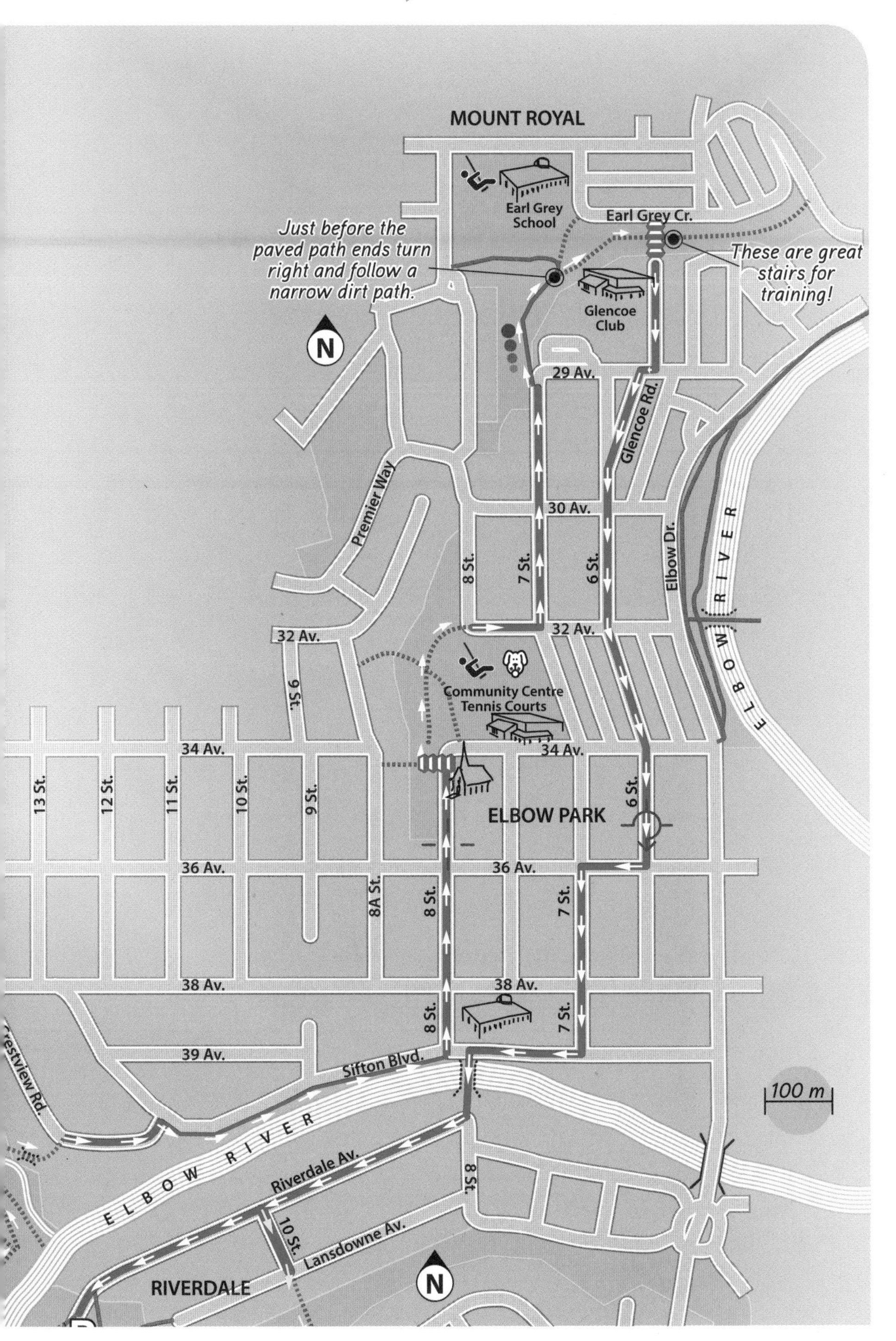
MOUNT ROYAL
Earl Grey School
Earl Grey Cr.
Just before the paved path ends turn right and follow a narrow dirt path.
These are great stairs for training!
Glencoe Club
29 Av.
Glencoe Rd.
Premier Way
30 Av.
8 St.
7 St.
6 St.
Elbow Dr.
ELBOW RIVER
32 Av.
32 Av.
9 St.
Community Centre Tennis Courts
34 Av.
34 Av.
13 St.
12 St.
11 St.
10 St.
9 St.
6 St.
ELBOW PARK
36 Av.
36 Av.
8A St.
8 St.
7 St.
38 Av.
38 Av.
8 St.
7 St.
39 Av.
Sifton Blvd.
Crestview Rd.
100 m
ELBOW RIVER
Riverdale Av.
8 St.
10 St.
Lansdowne Av.
RIVERDALE
N

Garrison Woods–Glenmore Dam–Altadore

SW

Walk at a Glance:

Neighbours coming and going, or, in the summer, sitting on porches while their children play in the streets or sell lemonade to passersby, that's Garrison Woods. A new neighbourhood with old roots, these friendly streets were originally part of the Currie Army Barracks. Built in the 1930s, the community experienced a complete overhaul when the base closed in 1998. The tidy, compact, army houses now share the streets with brick and multi-coloured row houses and sizable single-family homes. The military history is still alive here, with streets named Vimy Ridge and Passchendaele. The Military Museums of Calgary, with tanks and armoured vehicles, also calls this community home.

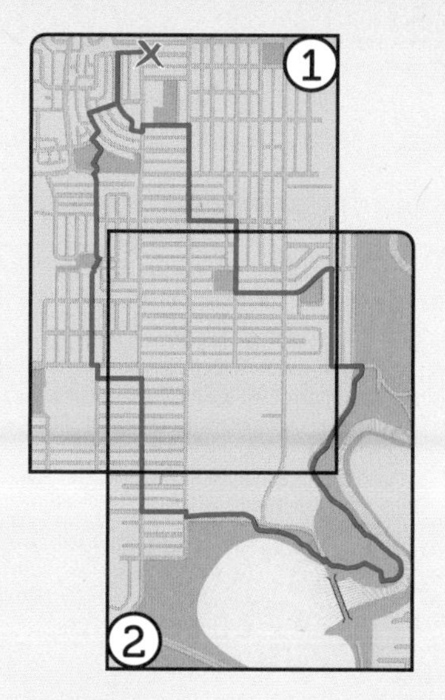

Route Details

Categories: Café, Dog Friendly, Home and Gardens, Nature, Neighbourhoods and Parks, River, Stroller, Vistas.

Starting-Point Parking: Park anywhere close to the intersection of Twentieth Street and Somme Avenue SW.

Transit: Bus access at various points along the route. Check Calgary Transit at www.calgarytransit.com.

Facilities: Coffee shops and restaurants along Thirty-Third Avenue in Marda Loop.

Distance: 7.22 km

Degree of Difficulty: Easy and mostly flat, with one hill.

Seasonal Highlights/Cautions

Year-Round: Most of this walk is accessible with a stroller with the exception of the off leash area near the dam. It is easy to park the stroller and explore on foot in this area or to bypass it and stay on the paved pathway above the river.

Garrison Woods–designed to move people on foot, bike, and with public transit–hosts people-friendly streets. The promenade start to the walk, as well as cut-through pathways that offer walkers and cyclists efficient and pleasant route options, make walking and cycling easy. With its people-populated porches and free-range kids, the community is a throwback to the days when everyone knew their neighbours and kids made their own fun, meeting in the middle of street and setting up the hockey nets. Listen for "Car!" and "Game on!" as you walk through the area. And Garrison Woods, with its dense housing and abundance of families, is the epicentre of the ultimate Halloween haul. If you live there, you must invest a sizeable portion of your income on mini-chocolate bars and chips come October. Be prepared.

A short walk away is the Elbow River and the Glenmore Dam. Leave the paved path along the escarpment and descend to the river valley, following a series of haphazard trails below the dam. Popular with dog walkers and fitness enthusiasts, this treed trail system boosts your chlorophyll quotient. With many route options, you can meander along the river or through the trees before climbing your way back to the paved path. Soak up the river-valley views while you catch your breath.

My favourite image of Calgary comes from Calgary-based author Will Ferguson, who described it as an "Etch A Sketch city." Buildings go up and they come down. Calgary is a young city, and it is always recreating itself, changing its look as it grows. There is always a crane on the horizon, and in the once suburban, now inner-city communities like Altadore, the 1960s bungalows are being erased in favour of the latest housing styles. Deviate from the grid, and walk the diagonal Acton Avenue. Look up, look way up, since this a street with ducks–dozens and dozens of them on the front yard of a feather-friendly resident who feeds them all winter long.

Calgary's older neighbourhoods are always growing and changing, like the city itself. Close-knit communities like Garrison Woods and Altadore, where neighbours don't just nod in acknowledgement, but become your friends, are the building blocks of a great city.

Neighbourhoods that Make You Fit

It turns out that the design of your community will impact your health. Walking and biking have been engineered out of most people's lives, contributing to increasing rates of obesity, heart disease, and diabetes.

Prior to the 1930s, all neighbourhoods were built on grids. With the advent of the car, this all changed. Le Corbusier, a Swiss-French architect and urban planner in the early to mid-1900s, believed that streets were no longer relevant in the era of cars and that we needed to kill the street. His work has been very influential in the creation of the suburban street design. Built with the car in mind, the suburban cul-de-sac street networks funnel traffic to main arterial and collector roads. This so-called "Garden City" design philosophy that become popular after the Second World War creates what researchers call an "inferior pedestrian environment." The popularity of the power centre–the big-box store development–is also to blame for more driving and less walking. Few people walk to Walmart.

In denser, more grid-like communities, like Altadore, where streets intersect and cul-de-sacs are rare, there are lower rates of obesity, diabetes, and high blood pressure. The take-home message? In communities where walking is easy and enjoyable, people walk more and their health benefits.

Garrison Woods–Glenmore Dam–Altadore - Start

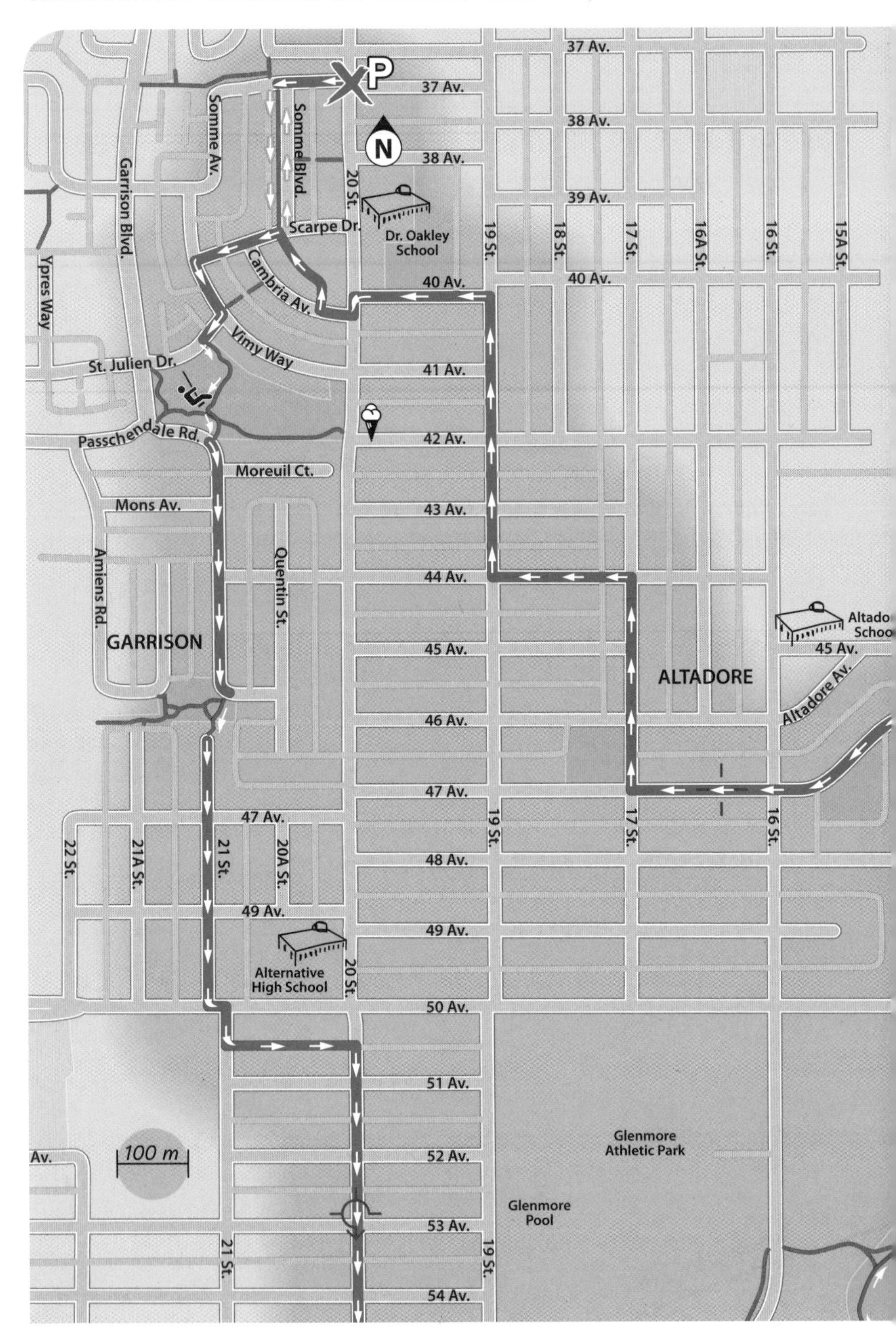

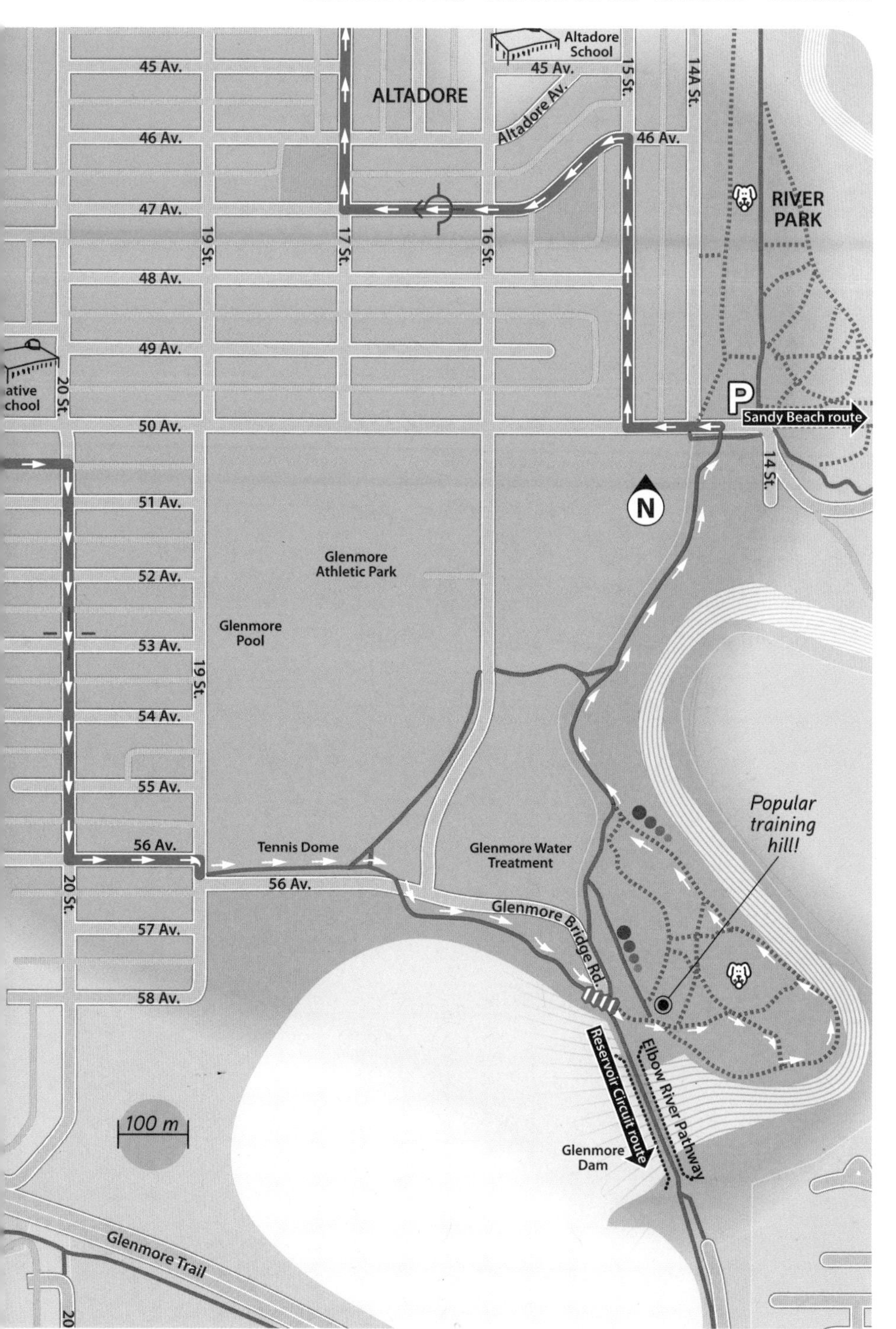

Altadore School
45 Av.
ALTADORE
Altadore Av.
15 St.
14A St.
46 Av.
47 Av.
19 St.
17 St.
16 St.
48 Av.
49 Av.
RIVER PARK
P
Sandy Beach route
ative
chool
20 St.
50 Av.
14 St.
N
51 Av.
52 Av.
Glenmore Athletic Park
Glenmore Pool
53 Av.
19 St.
54 Av.
55 Av.
Popular training hill!
56 Av.
Tennis Dome
Glenmore Water Treatment
56 Av.
20 St.
Glenmore Bridge Rd.
57 Av.
58 Av.
Reservoir Circuit route
Elbow River Pathway
100 m
Glenmore Dam
Glenmore Trail
20

Weaselhead Flats Park–North Glenmore Park

SW

Walk at a Glance:

Wilderness walks with no city noise are urban dwellers' respite, the antidote to constant connectivity. Disconnect from all devices and enjoy the solitude that you find in the Weaselhead.

Route Details

Categories: Nature, River, Stroller, Trail Running, Vistas.

Starting-Point Parking: Longer walk: parking lot F in North Glenmore Park.

Shorter walk: Weaselhead parking area, Sixty-Sixth Avenue and Thirty-Seventh Street SW.

Transit: Bus access to the Weaselhead parking lot in Lakeview. Check Calgary Transit at www.calgarytransit.com.

Facilities: Seasonal bathrooms in North Glenmore Park by the Snowy Owl picnic area, open mid-May to mid-October. Porta Potty at Weaselhead parking lot. Picnic spots can be reserved at www.calgary.ca.

Distance: 9 km (6.5 km from Weaselhead parking lot)

Degree of Difficulty: Easy and mostly flat, with one long hill.

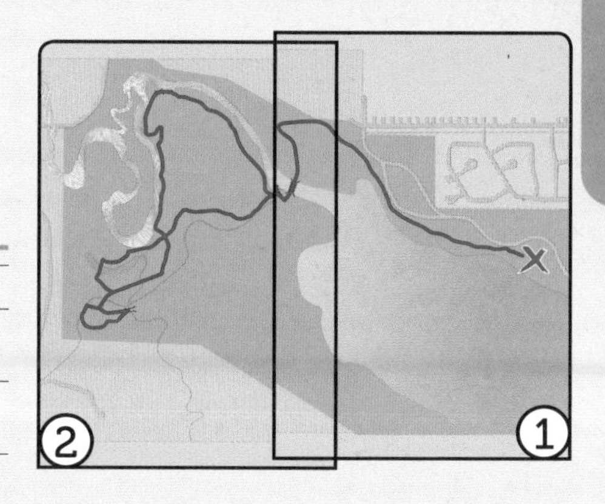

Seasonal Highlights/Cautions

Year-Round: The trails can be snow packed and slippery or muddy from November through May. Big-wheel strollers will be able to manage most of the trail, except for the add-on southern portion. No dogs or bikes are allowed on the Weaselhead trails, only on the paved regional pathway.

This relatively flat walk starts in North Glenmore Park and follows the paved path along the top of the escarpment, looking west to the Rockies. North Glenmore Park is picnic and barbecue hot spot from spring through fall. You can reserve a picnic spot from the City of Calgary before you arrive or just wing it and plunk yourself down on the grass if no tables are available. Following the paved pathway, past the Weaselhead parking lot, descend into tree cover immediately, soaking up the sounds of nature: birds chirping, ducks landing, and the unmistakable buzz of mosquitos in early summer. At times you will see activity on the water. Canoes and kayaks weave through Weaselhead waterways to the Elbow River, and cross-country skiers kick and glide along the same waterways when the temperature drops in January.

The untrained eye will spot bald eagles, all kinds of ducks, geese, and goslings (in the spring), and red-winged black birds. Those with binoculars and a birding book in hand will be very busy keeping watch for up to seventy bird species that frequent the park.

Enter the Weaselhead trail network, a mix of dirt trails and boardwalks. There are no bikes or dogs allowed on these trails, which makes for a peaceful stroll. Keep your map handy since navigating is challenging in this forested area. Interpretive signs marked on the map will keep you oriented and informed. The route follows the twists and turns of the Elbow River before turning inland on a marshy boardwalk trail over a wetland. Keep your eyes peeled. Deer, coyotes, rabbits, and the occasional black bear and moose (as well as school children on

Why is a Walk in the Woods so Good for You?

There is no Wi-Fi in the forest, but trust me, you will find a better connection. Walking in the woods offers a break from distractions. In Japan they call it *shinrin-yoku*, or "forest bathing." We call it a walk in the woods, and we know that it makes us feel good.

Scientists have studied the physical and mental benefits that come from a walk in nature. Many theories suggest various reasons why nature feels good: clean air, lack of noise pollution, and even the fine mist that comes off the trees, that fresh evergreen smell that makes us breathe deeply through our noses. But the most convincing argument for the peace we feel in nature is that the flowers and the birds never aggressively grab our attention. The voluntary attention we pay them is very different from the attention we are forced to pay to a car horn honking, for example.

Going for a walk in the park allows your mind to wander, which benefits your brain. Throughout the day, we are required to use voluntary attention repeatedly for cognitive tasks, like responding to texts and e-mail, or remembering our shopping list. Our brain grows tired and inefficient without a break. Going for a walk in the park or a quiet place without distractions gives voluntary attention a break, lets your mind wander, and allows you to be involuntarily engaged by your surroundings. The other benefits of walking in nature are the fresh smells, the clean air, and being surrounded by earthy hues. All of these factors contribute to why a walk in the woods makes you feel good.

My hunch, based on anecdotal on-the-trail research, is that the break from distractions plays a pivotal role in making the woodsy walker feel refreshed. Focusing on walking, one foot in front of the other, is therapeutic. Left, right, left, right. And don't forget to turn off that cell phone.

Sunshine Streaming Through by Sheila Kernan

midweek fieldtrips) are your hidden hiking companions. Listen for the pileated woodpecker that rocks his noggin making huge holes in dead trees.

Hit the refresh button on your busy city life with a walk in the Weaselhead's wilderness. A dose of nature, without electronic interruptions, calms the mind and engages the senses.

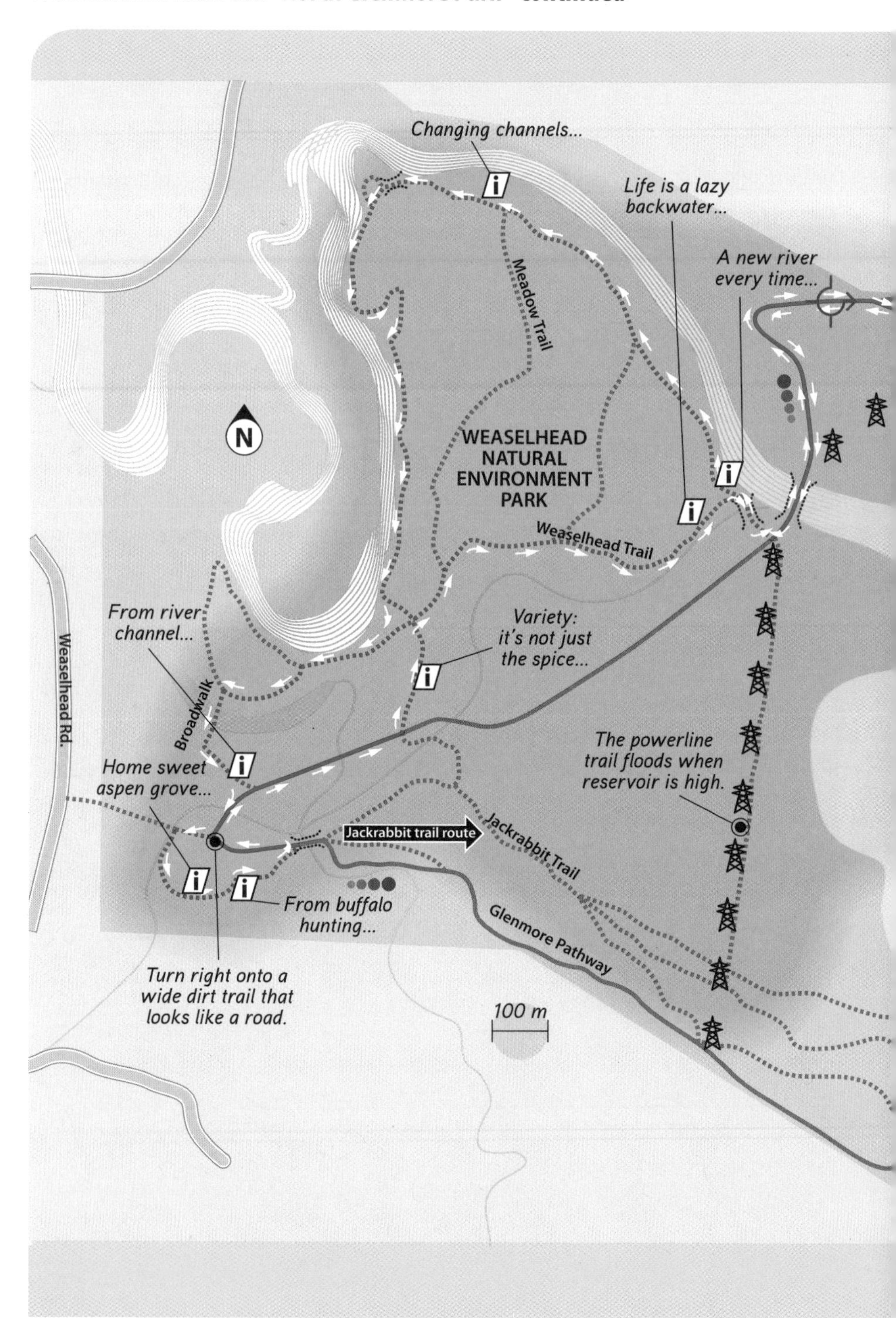
Changing channels...
Life is a lazy backwater...
A new river every time...
Meadow Trail
WEASELHEAD NATURAL ENVIRONMENT PARK
Weaselhead Trail
From river channel...
Variety: it's not just the spice...
Weaselhead Rd.
Broadwalk
Home sweet aspen grove...
The powerline trail floods when reservoir is high.
Jackrabbit trail route
Jackrabbit Trail
From buffalo hunting...
Glenmore Pathway
Turn right onto a wide dirt trail that looks like a road.
100 m

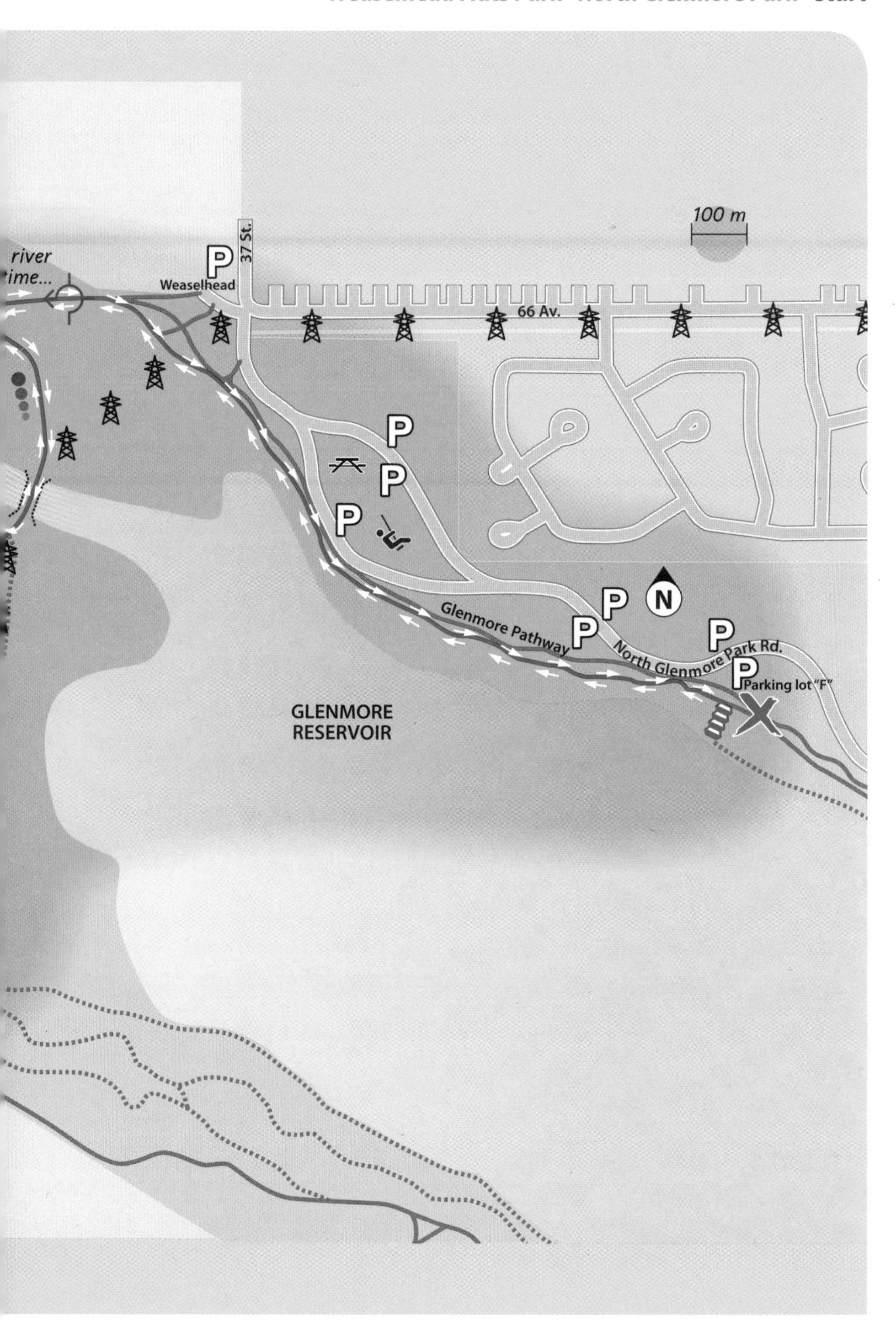
100 m
river
time...
Weaselhead
37 St.
66 Av.
Glenmore Pathway
North Glenmore Park Rd.
Parking lot "F"
GLENMORE
RESERVOIR
N

Jackrabbit Trail–South Glenmore Park

SW

Walk at a Glance:

Chickadees are your constant companions on this wilderness trail that dips and climbs through the forest just below the popular paved Glenmore Pathway. Within minutes of the trailhead, you leave the paved path and begin a shaded walk on a rolling, single-track, dirt trail. All along you enjoy intermittent views of the Glenmore Reservoir.

Route Details

Categories: Café, Hilly, Nature, River, Trail Running, Vistas.

Starting-Point Parking: Park at South Glenmore Park, at the intersection of Ninetieth Avenue and Twenty-Fourth Street SW.

Transit: Bus access along Ninetieth Avenue SW. Check Calgary Transit at www.calgarytransit.com.

Facilities: Seasonal bathrooms at trailhead, open mid-May to mid-October. Year-round bathrooms at the trailhead farther west.

Distance: 7 km

Degree of Difficulty: Moderate, with rolling hills on the way out. Easy, flat-paved path on the return.

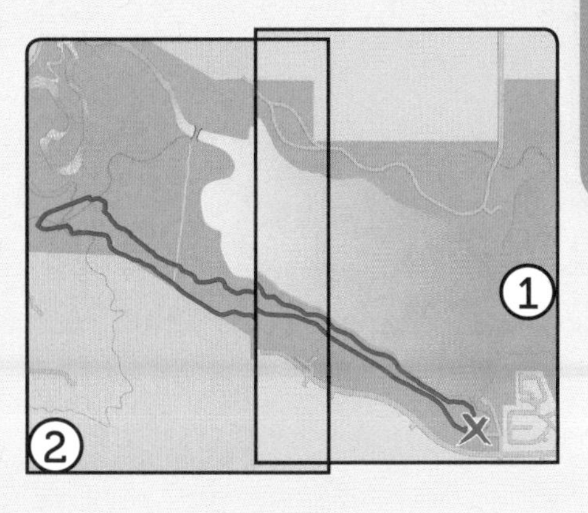

Seasonal Highlights/Cautions

Year-Round: Friendly chickadees along the trail.

Winter and Spring: Snow covered at times. Can be slippery after a Chinook and during the spring melt. Bring traction devices for your footwear.

Fed by the Elbow River, the reservoir is Calgary's largest body of water and is a friendly sight for all homesick East or West Coasters who crave large bodies of water. Just throw some salt in the air and this prairie walk becomes an imaginary seaside stroll.

Glenmore Landing Café and Lunch

Stop on the way to your walk and grab some picnic items, or, at the end of your walk, continue along the pathway east for another fifteen minutes until you arrive at Glenmore Landing. The shopping plaza has many options for food and a grocery store at which you can build picnic lunches. For a nice atmosphere and a good cup of freshly roasted coffee, stop at the Good Earth Café. You can also choose something tasty to eat from its full menu of baked goods, lunches, and desserts. I'm like a chickadee and go for their toasted seed buns that are covered with sunflowers, and sesame and pumpkin seeds. Take one of their sandwiches on your trek. They are tasty and tough, so they won't get squashed in your backpack.

Location: Glenmore Landing, Ninetieth Avenue and Fourteenth Street SW

The narrow path grows wider when you enter the Weaselhead trail system. Keep your eyes peeled for moose, bear, and bobcats. While moose and bear sightings are rare, these animals do, at times, follow the Elbow River Valley into the city. I once saw a moose along the Jackrabbit Trail, and the next day that same moose was on the news, walking north on Crowchild Trail before heading downtown and settling into a parking lot. Calgary is full of surprises.

When you need to recharge, get your heart rate up, or simply soak up the sights and sounds of nature, take a walk on the Jackrabbit Trail. It is a year-round gem.

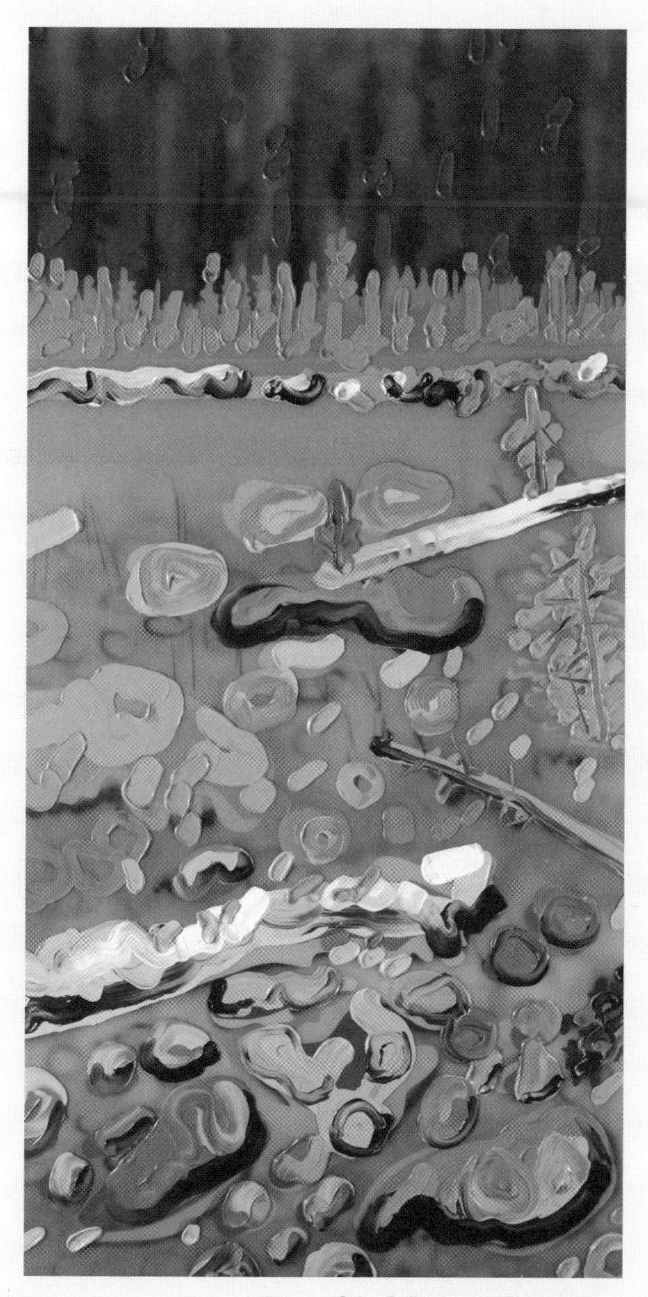

Calm Reflections by Sheila Kernan

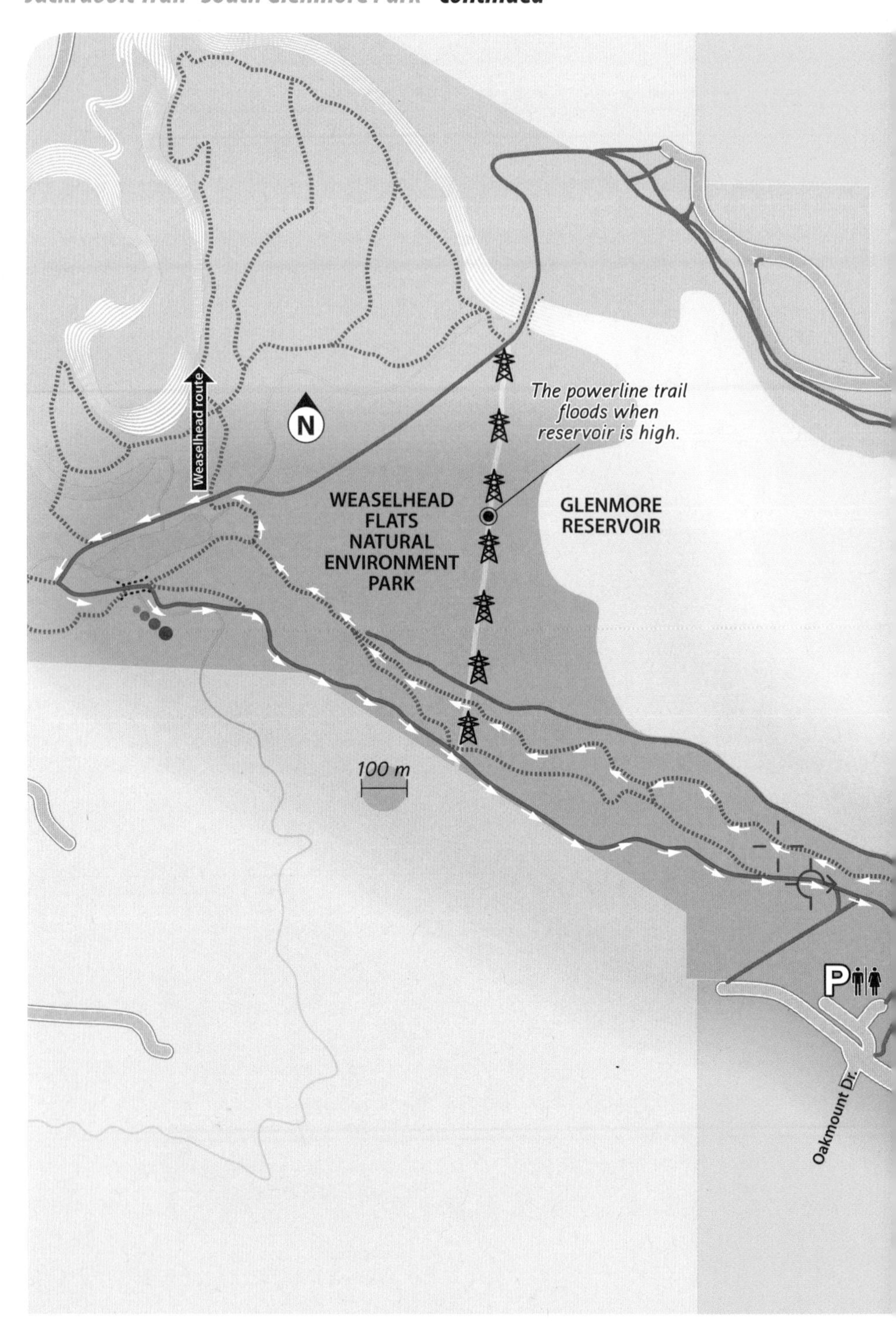
The powerline trail floods when reservoir is high.
Weaselhead route
N
WEASELHEAD FLATS NATURAL ENVIRONMENT PARK
GLENMORE RESERVOIR
100 m
Oakmount Dr.

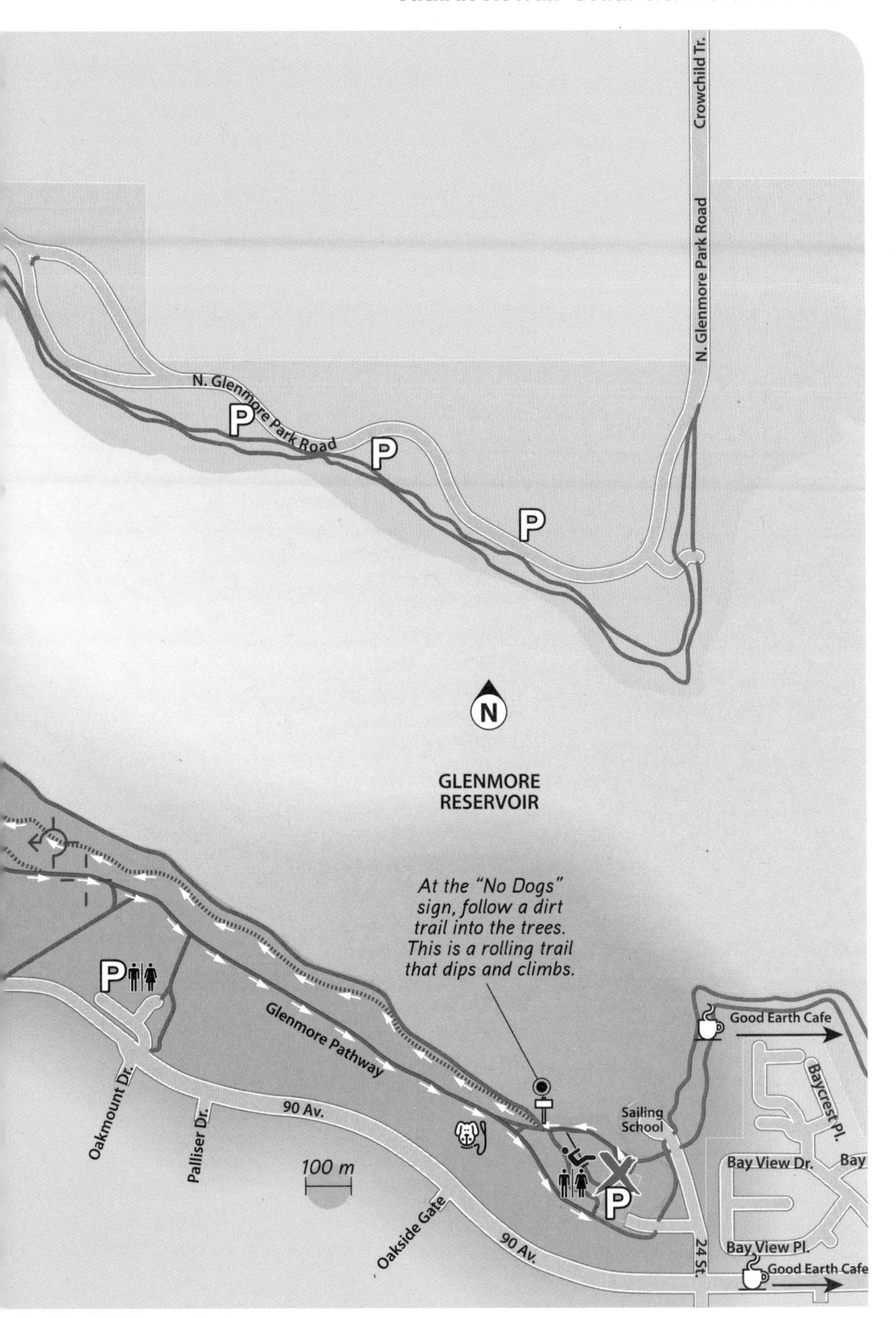
Crowchild Tr.
N. Glenmore Park Road
N. Glenmore Park Road
P
P
P
N
GLENMORE
RESERVOIR
At the "No Dogs" sign, follow a dirt trail into the trees. This is a rolling trail that dips and climbs.
Good Earth Cafe
Glenmore Pathway
Baycrest Pl.
Sailing School
Oakmount Dr.
Palliser Dr.
90 Av.
100 m
Bay View Dr.
Bay
P
Oakside Gate
90 Av.
24 St.
Bay View Pl.
Good Earth Cafe

Glenmore Reservoir Circumnavigation

SW

Walk at a Glance:

Views are immediate and constant as you follow the paved pathway at the top of the bluffs in North Glenmore Park. A popular spot for picnics and family reunions, this people-populated park is a hive of activity in the summer and a peaceful spot in the colder months, when Calgarians hunker down and hibernate. You can walk the reservoir loop on a straightforward paved path or a on some more exploratory side trails. I provide many off-trail options, popular paths that dip and climb closer to the water. You can switch it up and take your bike some days, run it on others, and simply stroll portions of the trail when you'd like a shorter outing.

Route Details

Categories: Café, Dog Friendly, Hilly, Nature, Neighbourhoods and Parks, River, Stroller, Trail Running, Vistas.

Starting-Point Parking: My starting-point parking is the Weaselhead parking lot, Thirty-Seventh Street and Sixty-Sixth Avenue SW. This walk is a loop and there are many parking options, check the map.

Transit: Bus access at various points along the route. Check Calgary Transit at www.calgarytransit.com.

Facilities: Porta Potty at the trailhead. Seasonal and year-round bathrooms in North and South Glenmore Park. Café, grocery store, and restaurant in Glenmore Landing. Restaurant and public washrooms at Gasoline Alley, Heritage Park.

Distance: Long route: 16.5 km
Short route: 15 km

Degree of Difficulty: Moderate, with two major hills. More hills possible when following the "off the beaten path" route options.

Seasonal Highlights/Cautions

Year-Round: Dogs and cyclists are only allowed on the regional paved Glenmore Pathway.

Winter and Spring: The paved Glenmore Pathway is cleared of snow from South Glenmore Park through to the Glenmore Dam. It is not cleared of snow on west side, in the Weaselhead valley. You can walk the trail, but be ready for slippery conditions in the spring melt and after a Chinook.

Summer and Fall: On warm summer and fall weekend afternoons, the Glenmore Pathway is a very popular cycling route. You can avoid the cyclists, and have the trail to yourself, by following the off-trail route options provided.

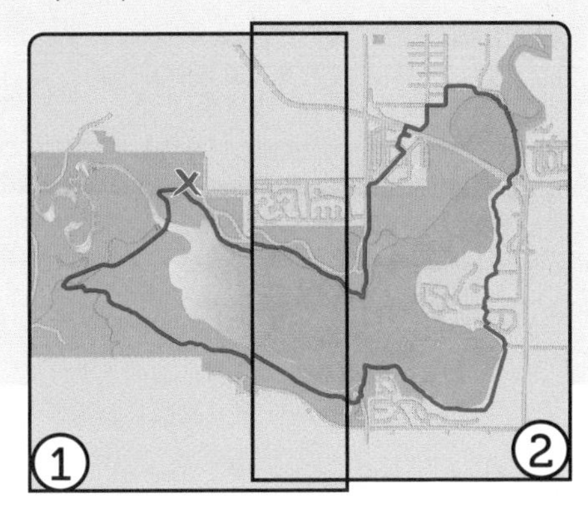

Once through North Glenmore Park, you pass by the canoe club, Lakeview Golf Course, and the community of Lakeview. Choose to take the very noisy path parallel to Glenmore Trail or walk the quieter, yet longer, route over Glenmore Trail, through the neighbourhood of North Glenmore, and over the dam. The two routes converge at the south end of the Glenmore Trail pedestrian overpass.

If you take the noisy route along Glenmore Trail, watch for a trail cut-off, an opening in the fence just before you wind uphill towards the pedestrian overpass. This narrow pathway leads you along the base of the escarpment overlooking the water. If you stay on the paved path, continue uphill and follow the winding shaded pathway south to a series of benches that perch on the edge of the bluffs. For the explorers out there, walk west of the bench toward to water and find a narrow dirt path that descends through the trees to the shoreline. This off-trail option will add some hills and adventure to your walk.

Once past the Rockyview Hospital, the paved path descends to the quiet side streets of affluent Eagle Ridge. After a brief side-street walk you return to the pathway and come upon the next attraction en route, Heritage Park Historical Village. A summertime place to visit, it hosts an extensive collection of period buildings and a circa 1890 replica of Calgary's CPR train station. Stop for a snack and bathroom break or continue onward, along the off-trail treed pathway that follows the water or along the paved path all the way to Glenmore Landing: the perfect halfway point at which you can recharge: lunch or a coffee and muffin. The pathway soon splits, and I suggest taking the lower route, along the paved path closest to the water. Boats are on the reservoir as soon as the ice breaks in May and continue sailing through October, if the weather holds. Binocular-clad birders are also a regular sight here, watching for the varieties of feathered friends that visit the reservoir, many en masse. The Glenmore Yacht Club and South Glenmore Park playground and waterpark soon appear.

For a complete immersion in nature, switch to my Jackrabbit Trail map (see page 176). This chickadee-intensive trail rolls along, offering a hilly workout and a more peaceful hike. After a winter Chinook, the trail can be slippery but spectacular. Whichever route you choose, the two trails reconnect at the beaver dam pond at the base of the long hill on the paved path. Now you must choose between the direct paved pathway route, or, for a more solitary outing, switch to the Weaselhead Flats map (see page 170). Bordering the Tsuu T'ina First Nation Reserve, the low-lying Weaselhead trails are a network of possibilities, so plan on taking extra time to explore. A hill climb ends the outing and leads you back to fantastic views of the reservoir and the Rockies.

Chinook: The Snow Eater

In the winter, when warm moist air from the West Coast hits the mountains, winds called Chinooks descend on Calgary. Chinook means "snow eater," but it could also mean "snow plow" in Calgary since we depend on it to clear snow-filled side streets. Calgarians love to brag to relatives and friends in eastern Canada or even in Edmonton about the huge temperature changes we experience during some Chinooks. "It went from −20°C to 20°C in one day," we report to snow-weary Canadian friends. However, Chinook thaws make gardening under the arch a challenge. Trees and plants can be tricked into budding by warm winds in January, only to be frozen during the next deep freeze. This is the price we pay for our trademark blue skies and warm winds.

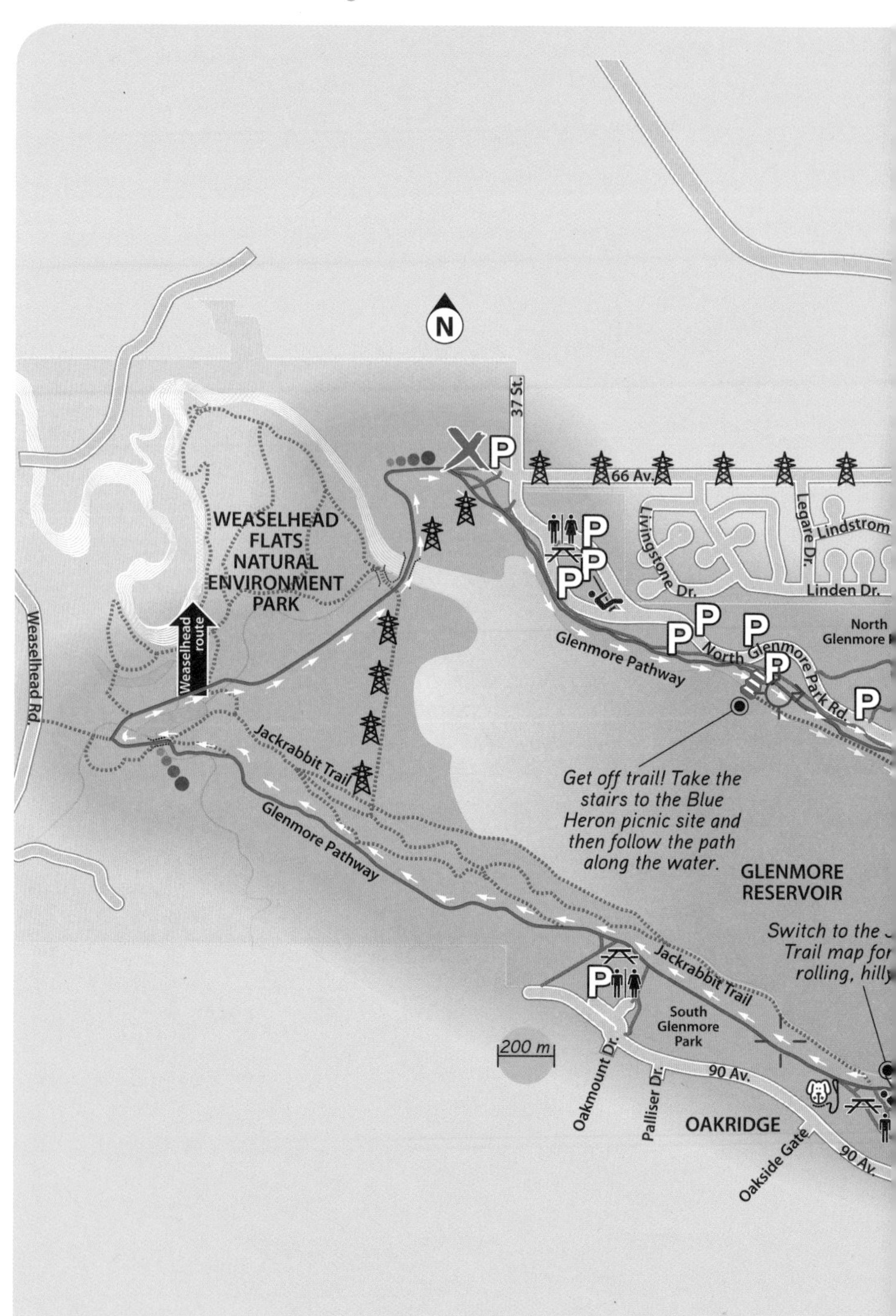

N
37 St.
66 Av.
WEASELHEAD
FLATS
NATURAL
ENVIRONMENT
PARK
Weaselhead route
Weaselhead Rd.
Livingstone Dr.
Legare Dr.
Lindstrom
Linden Dr.
North Glenmore
Glenmore Pathway
North Glenmore Park Rd.
Jackrabbit Trail
Glenmore Pathway
Get off trail! Take the stairs to the Blue Heron picnic site and then follow the path along the water.
GLENMORE RESERVOIR
Jackrabbit Trail
South Glenmore Park
200 m
Oakmount Dr.
Palliser Dr.
90 Av.
OAKRIDGE
Oakside Gate
90 Av.

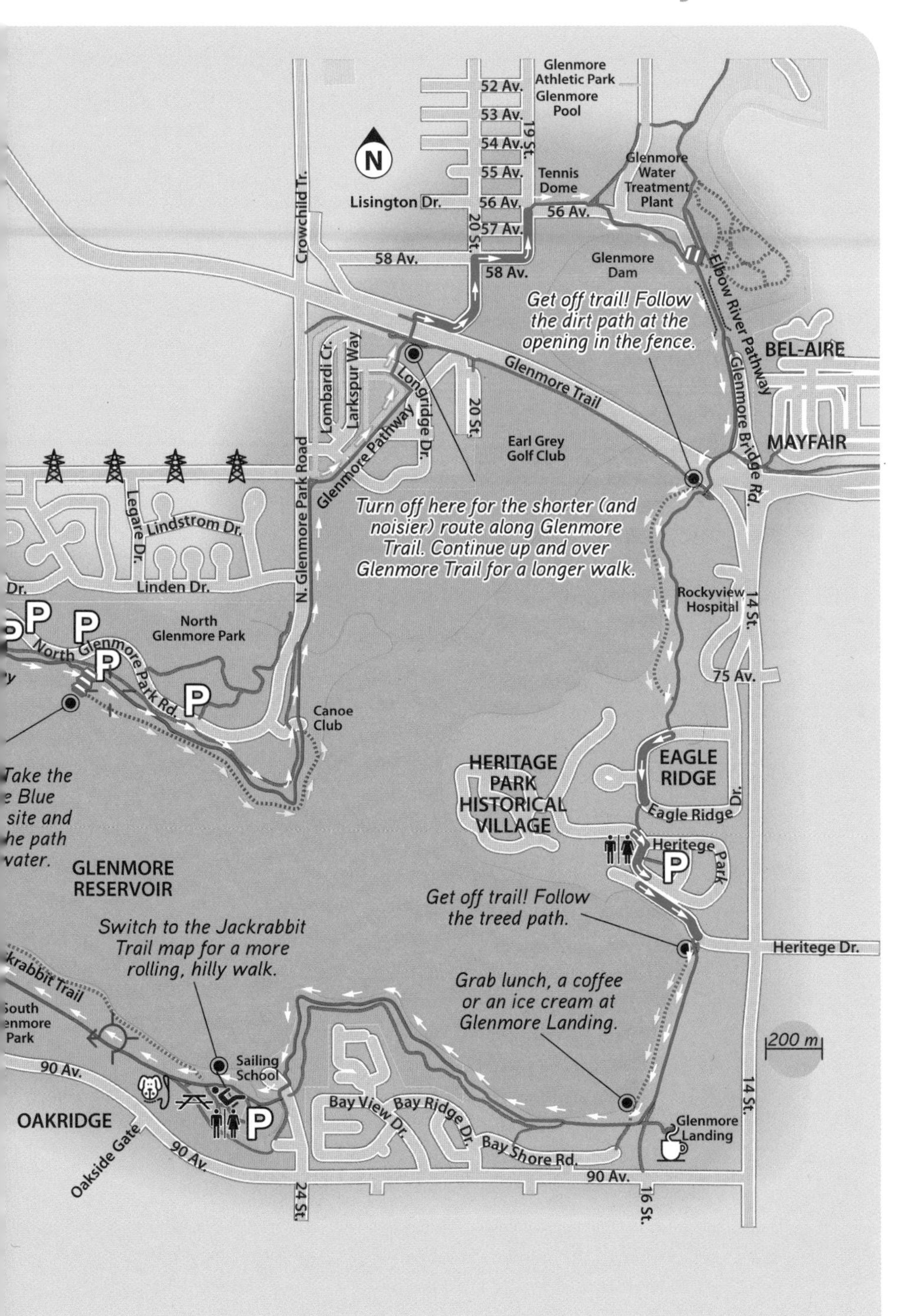
Glenmore Athletic Park
Glenmore Pool
52 Av.
53 Av.
54 Av.
55 Av.
56 Av.
57 Av.
58 Av.
19 St.
20 St.
N
Lisington Dr.
Crowchild Tr.
Tennis Dome
56 Av.
Glenmore Water Treatment Plant
Glenmore Dam
Elbow River Pathway
Get off trail! Follow the dirt path at the opening in the fence.
BEL-AIRE
Glenmore Bridge Rd.
MAYFAIR
Glenmore Trail
Lombardi Cr.
Larkspur Way
Longridge Dr.
Glenmore Pathway
Earl Grey Golf Club
N. Glenmore Park Road
Legare Dr.
Lindstrom Dr.
Linden Dr.
Turn off here for the shorter (and noisier) route along Glenmore Trail. Continue up and over Glenmore Trail for a longer walk.
Rockyview Hospital
14 St.
75 Av.
North Glenmore Park
North Glenmore Park Rd.
Canoe Club
HERITAGE PARK HISTORICAL VILLAGE
EAGLE RIDGE
Eagle Ridge Dr.
Heritege Park
GLENMORE RESERVOIR
Get off trail! Follow the treed path.
Heritege Dr.
Switch to the Jackrabbit Trail map for a more rolling, hilly walk.
Grab lunch, a coffee or an ice cream at Glenmore Landing.
200 m
Sailing School
90 Av.
OAKRIDGE
Oakside Gate
Bay View Dr.
Bay Ridge Dr.
Bay Shore Rd.
Glenmore Landing
24 St.
16 St.

Griffith Woods Park

SW

Walk at a Glance:

Peaceful and pleasant, Griffith Woods Park is the perfect spot to slow the pace and collect your thoughts. The mix of paved and gravel pathways weave through a mature, and at times dense, white spruce forest mixed with stands of balsam poplar.

Route Details

Categories: Dog friendly, Nature, River, Stroller, Trail Running.

Starting-Point Parking: Official parking lot at the end of Discovery Ridge Link SW.

Transit: Bus access to Discovery Woods. Check Calgary Transit at www.calgarytransit.com.

Facilities: Year-round bathrooms at trailhead.

Distance: 4.75 km

Degree of Difficulty: Easy and flat.

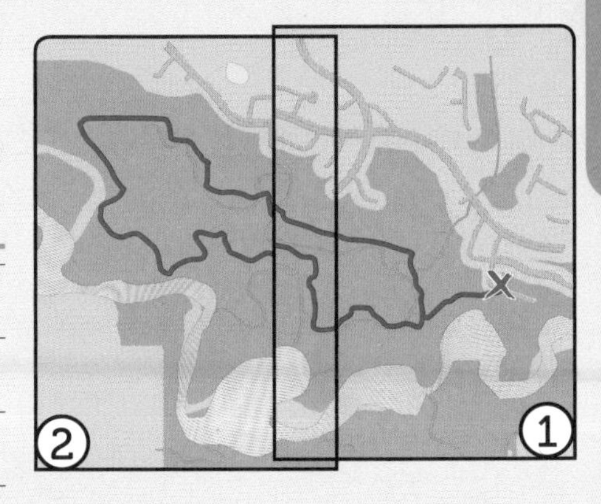

Seasonal Highlights/Cautions

Winter: Post-Chinook, snow-packed trails can be slippery. Traction devices for your footwear will help keep you upright.

Spring and Summer: See spring wildflowers starting in April and continuing through to August.

The coniferous forest is home to mule deer, coyotes, porcupines, and the occasional black bear, so keep an eye out. Oxbow wetlands, created when the river changes course, are home to many birds, such as gray jays and red-breasted nuthatches.

Tucked away in Discovery Ridge, this suburban park was ranch land from the late 1800s until 2000, when the land was donated to the City of Calgary by Wilbur and Betty Griffith to be set aside as a nature preserve.

An oasis of calm, Griffith Woods is a place where you can move slowly and ponder, spend time with family, and enjoy a picnic by the river.

Calgary's Pathways and Rotary/ Mattamy Greenway

When walking along some of Calgary's regional pathways, you might see a tall rectangular signpost with "Calgary Greenway or Rotary/Mattamy Greenway" written along its side. When completed in 2016, the Rotary/Mattamy Calgary Greenway will be a 138-km network of parks and pathways that will encircle the city.

Calgary's first paved pathway was built in in the 1970s in Confederation Park, followed by the Bow and Elbow River pathways. The long-term dream was that Calgarians could walk, run, and cycle the cities' parks and natural areas following a series of interconnected pathways.

The success of the pathway system is evident whenever you head out for a walk or cycle. With 800+ km of pathways, and almost 300 km of on-street bikeways, Calgarians can explore their city without a car. Connecting the Bow and Elbow rivers, Fish Creek Provincial Park, Nose Creek, West Nose Creek, the Western Irrigation District Canal, and the perimeter of Glenmore Reservoir, the pathways allow self-propelled users to circumnavigate the city. The Rotary/ Mattamy Greenway will link the pathways to 55 communities around the city. When complete, it will be the longest urban pathway and park in the world.

Find out more about the greenway by visiting Calgary Parks Foundation at www.parksfdn.com.

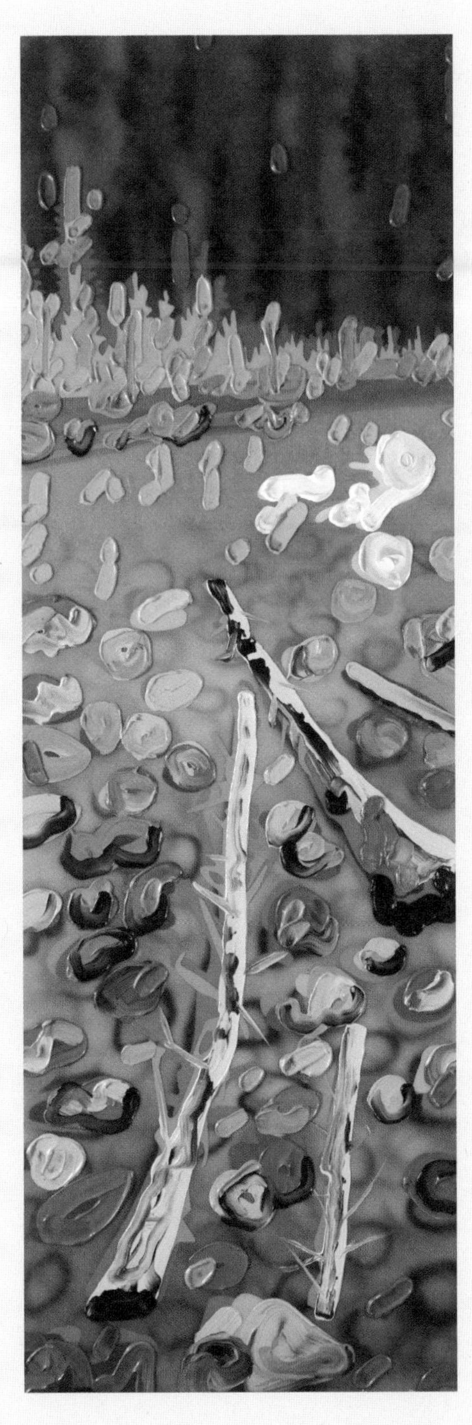

Take My Breath Away
by Sheila Kernan

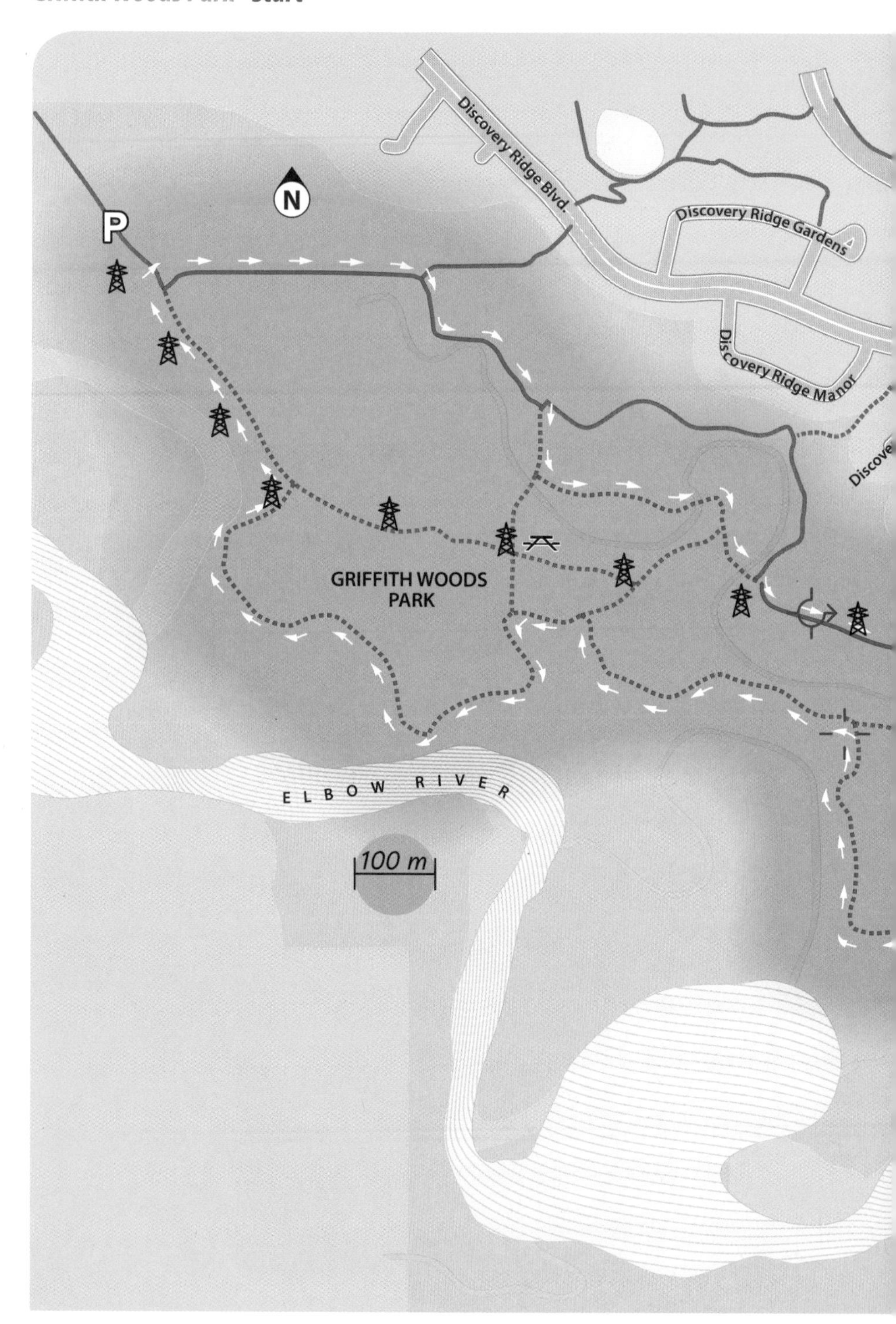
Discovery Ridge Blvd.
Discovery Ridge Gardens
Discovery Ridge Manor
Discove
N
P
GRIFFITH WOODS PARK
ELBOW RIVER
100 m

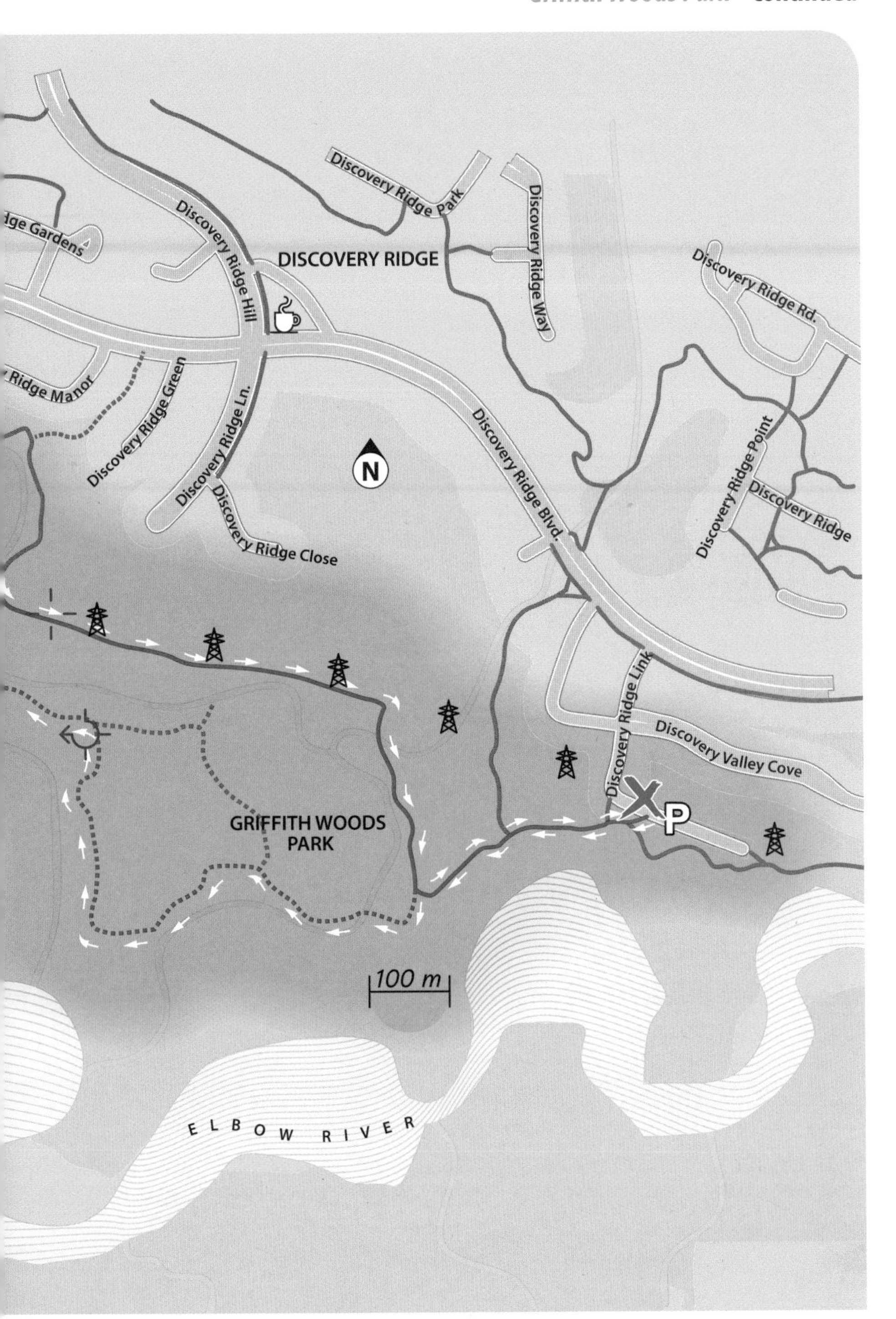

dge Gardens
Discovery Ridge Hill
DISCOVERY RIDGE
Discovery Ridge Park
Discovery Ridge Way
Discovery Ridge Rd.
Ridge Manor
Discovery Ridge Green
Discovery Ridge Ln.
Discovery Ridge Blvd.
Discovery Ridge Point
Discovery Ridge
Discovery Ridge Close
N
Discovery Ridge Link
Discovery Valley Cove
GRIFFITH WOODS
PARK
P
100 m
ELBOW RIVER

Ann and Sandy Cross Conservation Area

SW

Walk at a Glance:

Sandy Cross described his land as a prairie paradise. Consisting of rolling foothills covered in native grasses, aspen forest, and groves of willow, the Cross Conservation Area is Sandy's legacy and taking a walk here is like experiencing a little piece of Alberta heaven.

Unobtrusive trails have been cut into the prairie grasses allowing walkers to navigate the rolling foothills. Aspen forests provide shade and hill climbs get your heart rate up before rewarding you with unobstructed views of the Rocky Mountains. Plunk yourself down, pull out your lunch, and soak up the big-sky views.

Route Details

Categories: Hilly, Nature, Trail Running, Vistas.

Starting-Point Parking: 160 Street W, Calgary. See location map at www.crossconservation.org.

Facilities: Bathrooms at trailhead and along the route.

Distance: 7.4 km

Degree of Difficulty: Moderate, with hills. Numerous interconnecting trails allow users to choose their distance and difficulty level.

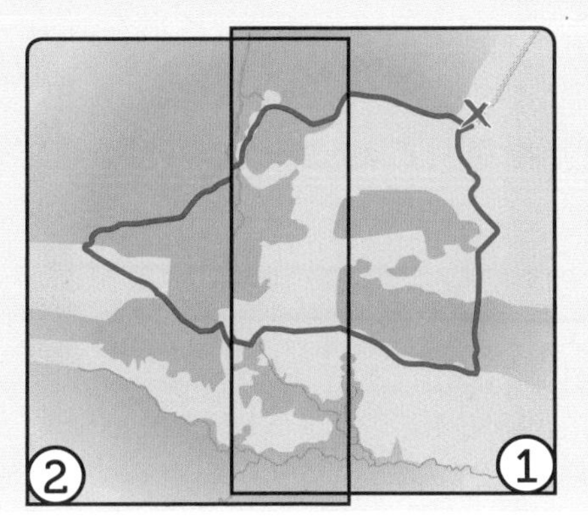

Seasonal Highlights/Cautions

Year-Round: This is a conservation area, a wildlife preserve, not a park. Visitors are asked to book their hike online at www.crossconservation.org and then to register at the kiosk in the parking lot before beginning their hike. A small donation is requested to help with trail maintenance. Be sure to bring your own water and food, and be prepared to pack out all of your garbage. Please note that dogs, bicycles, and strollers are not allowed.

Winter: Practice your animal-tracking skills while snowshoeing.

Spring and Summer: From April through August wildflowers are abundant. Watch for signs that bears have visited the area. Check for paw prints around ponds.

Fall: Listen for the bugling elk in late September. Soak up the colours of the prairie grasses and shrubbery: rich red, burnt yellow, and orange. Mountain views become more spectacular when a dusting of snow covers the distant peaks.

If you hike or snowshoe here after a fresh snowfall your hidden hiking companions will suddenly become evident. Cougar, deer, moose, herds of elk, beaver, porcupine, red fox, snowshoe hare, and coyote are all regulars to the area and their tracks scatter the landscape during the snowy months. Bring your animal tracks book and have some identification fun with the kids.

Ann and Sandy Cross donated 12 km^2 of land to the Province of Alberta to be preserved so that future generations could enjoy this untouched prairie paradise. How lucky we are to have this natural gem so close to the city.

Need a creative boost? Go for a walk.

Creative people walk. The strolling philosopher Friedrich Nietzsche concluded this 125 years ago in *Twilight of the Idols*, in which he claimed, "All truly great thoughts are conceived by walking." This is my experience, too, and the reason this book exists. I needed to walk to research the routes in the book, true enough. But the reason I created this book is because I need to walk, every day.

Recent science has strengthened the link between walking and creativity. A study published early in 2014 in the *Journal of Experimental Psychology* by Stanford University professors Marily Oppezzo and Daniel L. Schwartz found links between physical activity and cognitive abilities, specifically, the effect of walking on creativity. The study, "Give Your Ideas Some Legs: The Positive Effect of Walking on Creative Thinking," concluded that when people walk, on a treadmill or in the great outdoors, creative ideas flow. The walkers had better ideas and more of them compared to the sitting group. And the benefits that came from walking continued after the walk was complete, when participants sat down again.

A walk also offers some downtime from the constant barrage of information that we all experience today. Moving aimlessly through the streets or pathways, picking your pace, letting your thoughts change with the scenery, and getting into a rhythm: that's the power of a walk. When you put yourself in the position of "observer," you allow your mind to wander and to land where it may, which in turn allows you to gain perspective and solve many a problem.

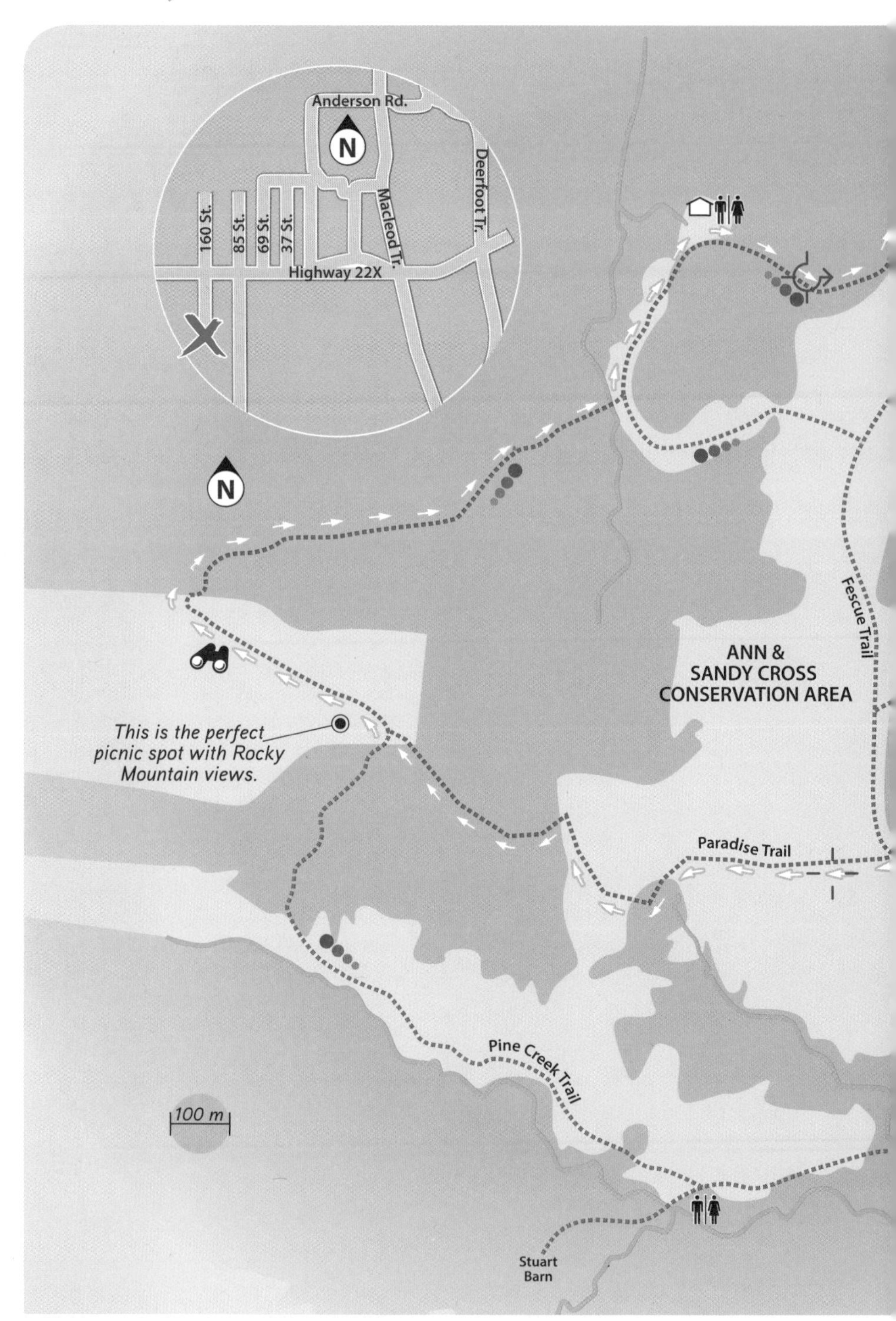
Anderson Rd.
N
Deerfoot Tr.
Macleod Tr.
160 St.
85 St.
69 St.
37 St.
Highway 22X
N
This is the perfect picnic spot with Rocky Mountain views.
Fescue Trail
ANN & SANDY CROSS CONSERVATION AREA
Paradise Trail
Pine Creek Trail
100 m
Stuart Barn

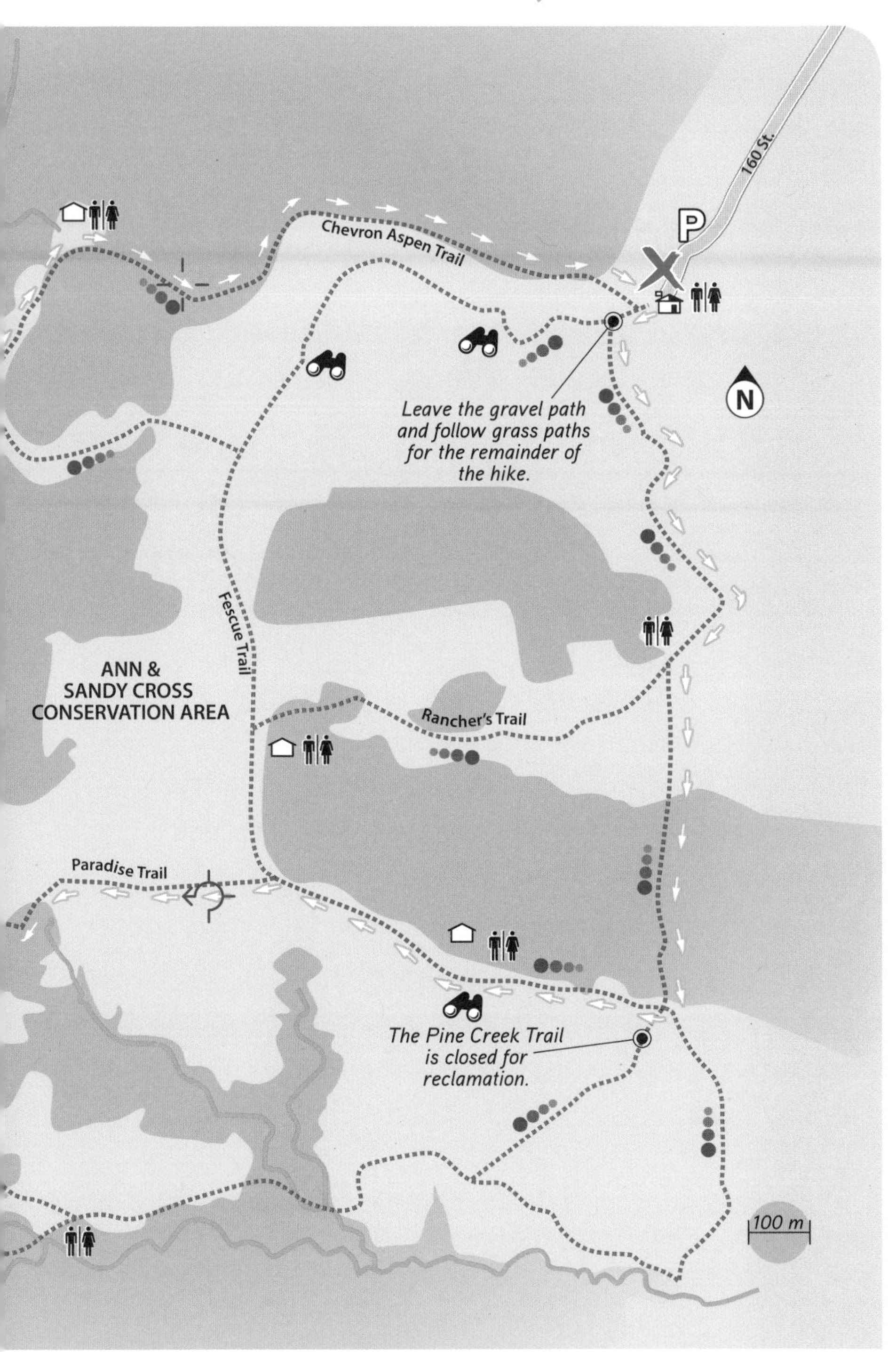
160 St.
P
Chevron Aspen Trail
N
Leave the gravel path and follow grass paths for the remainder of the hike.
Fescue Trail
ANN & SANDY CROSS CONSERVATION AREA
Rancher's Trail
Paradise Trail
The Pine Creek Trail is closed for reclamation.
100 m

Fish Creek Provincial Park

SW-SE

Overview:

Vast and peaceful, Fish Creek Provincial Park offers a complete immersion in nature. Stretching 19 km from east to west and encompassing over 13 km^2, the park is the ultimate, urban-wilderness getaway. Kilometres of pathways, a mix of shale and paved, snake through the park. For those of you inebriated on electronics, the glare of the glass screen consuming all of your waking hours, putting down the device and going for a text- and ping-free walk in Fish Creek will be like hitting the restore button for your mind.

Seasonal Highlights/Cautions

Year-Round: Trail reconstruction is ongoing throughout Fish Creek Park. For more information on this, please check the Fish Creek website (www.albertaparks.ca/fish-creek.aspx). Dogs must be on leash at all times in Fish Creek Provincial Park.

Winter and Spring: The west-end shaded trails can be icy after Chinooks in the winter and throughout April. In a good snow year, cross-country skiing in the park is wonderful. There are no official ski trails, only skier-made tracks.

Summer: Find shaded relief in the west end of the park. The east end has more open-meadow areas, where you can soak up the sun and enjoy a picnic along the Bow River.

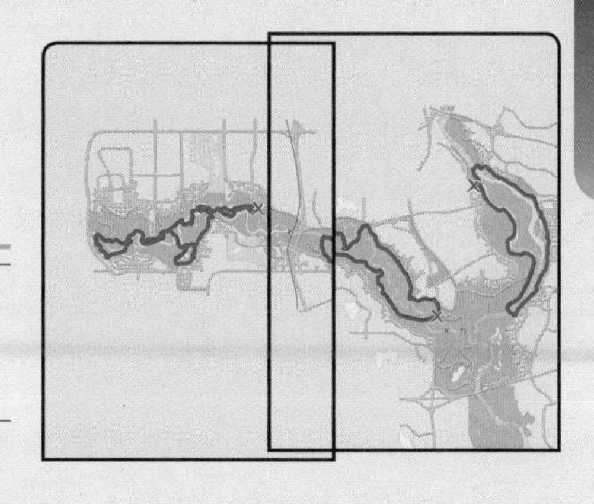

Stay low and follow the creek, or climb the bluffs and skirt the neighbourhoods to the south. The forested west end, nicely shaded by a mix of poplar, aspen, and white spruce, is a joy to walk through on a hot summer's day. When the snow is abundant in January through March, cross-country ski along the creek. Continue east and the terrain changes to grassland with some riparian forest along the creek. Wildflowers are abundant here in the warm months, May through September. Listen for the birdlife in wetlands scattered throughout the park, and spot wildlife as you walk: deer, coyote, snake, frog, and black bear all call the park home or enjoy the occasional visit. Fish Creek Park's vast wilderness is a breath of fresh air for busy urbanites.

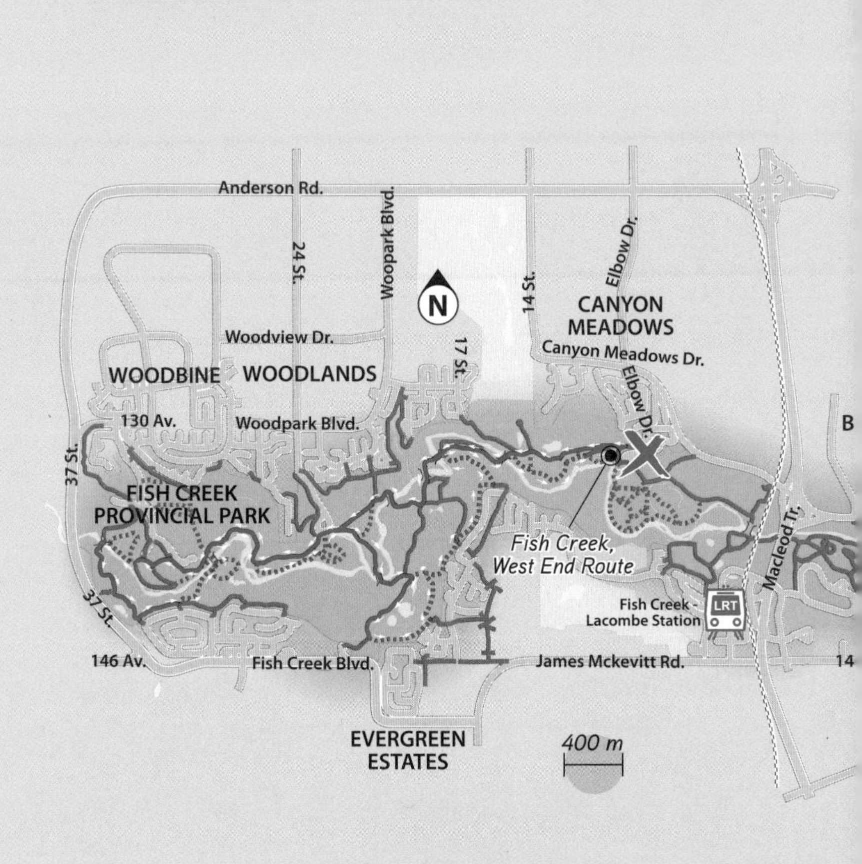
Anderson Rd.
24 St.
Woopark Blvd.
14 St.
Elbow Dr.
CANYON
MEADOWS
Woodview Dr.
17 St.
Canyon Meadows Dr.
WOODBINE
WOODLANDS
Elbow Dr.
130 Av.
Woodpark Blvd.
B
37 St.
FISH CREEK
PROVINCIAL PARK
Fish Creek,
West End Route
Macleod Tr.
37 St.
Fish Creek -
Lacombe Station
LRT
146 Av.
Fish Creek Blvd.
James Mckevitt Rd.
14
EVERGREEN
ESTATES
400 m

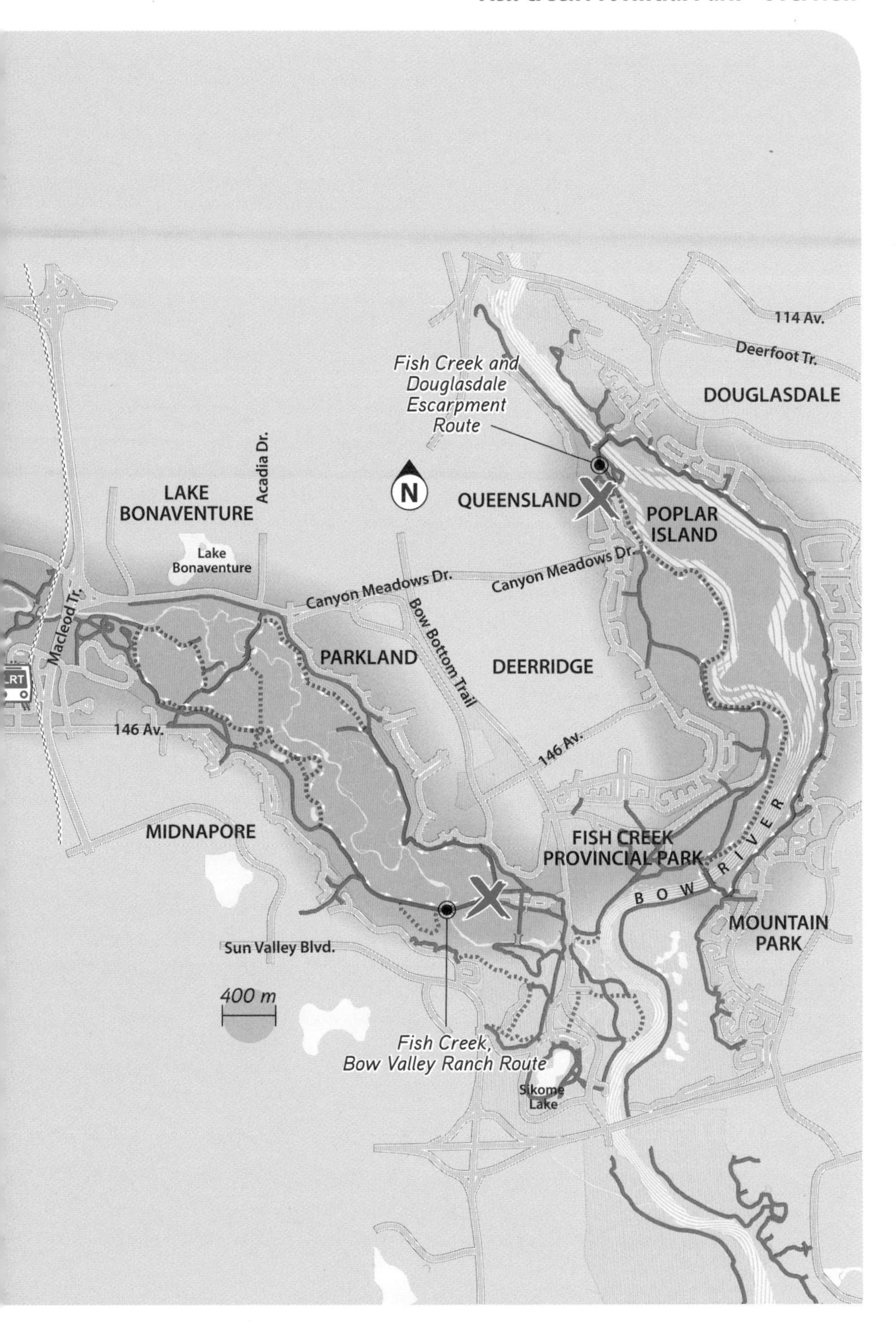
114 Av.
Deerfoot Tr.
DOUGLASDALE
Fish Creek and Douglasdale Escarpment Route
LAKE BONAVENTURE
Acadia Dr.
N
QUEENSLAND
POPLAR ISLAND
Lake Bonaventure
Canyon Meadows Dr.
Canyon Meadows Dr.
Bow Bottom Trail
Macleod Tr.
PARKLAND
DEERRIDGE
146 Av.
146 Av.
MIDNAPORE
FISH CREEK PROVINCIAL PARK
BOW RIVER
MOUNTAIN PARK
Sun Valley Blvd.
400 m
Fish Creek, Bow Valley Ranch Route
Sikome Lake

Fish Creek Park West: Votiers Flats to Shannon Terrace

SW

Walk at a Glance:

Train it to Fish Creek Provincial Park and enjoy a wilderness getaway without having to drive. Walking west along the paved path, you are soon immersed in white spruce and balsam poplar forests. Pass by Bebo Grove parking area and look up and listen. The sandstone cliffs on the north side of the creek are favourite nesting spots for prairie and peregrine falcons and ravens. The ravens' guttural croak can often be heard high overhead.

Route Details

Categories: C-Train, Dog Friendly, Hilly, Nature, River, Stroller, Trail Running, Vistas.

Starting-Point Parking: Votiers Flats parking lot, south end of Elbow Drive SW.

C-Train Start: Fish Creek Station.

Transit: Bus 3 to the trailhead. Check Calgary Transit at www.calgarytransit.com.

Facilities: Bathrooms at trailhead.

Distance: Short route to Bebo Grove return: 6.2 km

Entire route: 12 km

Degree of Difficulty: Moderate, with hill climbs.

Seasonal Highlights/Cautions

Year-Round: Trail reconstruction is ongoing west of Bebo Grove parking area. Strollers may not be able to navigate west of Bebo Grove until the pathway is finished. For more information on this, please check the Fish Creek website (www.albertaparks.ca/fish-creek.aspx). Dogs must be on leash at all times in Fish Creek Provincial Park.

Winter and Spring: The west-end shaded trails can be icy after Chinooks in the winter and throughout April. In a good snow year, cross-country skiing in the park is wonderful. There are no official ski trails, only skier-made tracks.

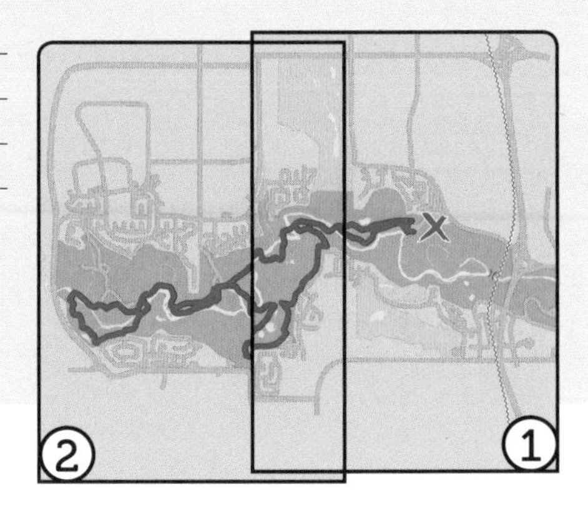

Bunchberry, purple clematis, kinnikinnick (bearberry), buffaloberry, and red-osier dogwood are just some of the native flowers and shrubs that surround you in the far west end of the park. Just past Shannon Terrace, climb to the community of Everglades and continue on paved paths past significant homes that back onto the park. Descend back into the park and follow the creek trails, listening for the call of wetland birdlife. Past the

Raven or Crow?

Ravens are mountain and northern-forest birds, so it is unique for them to nest in the parkland and prairies, as they do at Fish Creek Park. Cliffs are their favourite nesting spots, though, which is where they can be found at Fish Creek. Ravens are usually larger and with heavier bills than crows have, and they soar overhead while crows flap their wings steadily as they fly. Smart scavengers, ravens will eat anything. They talk to each other with "rawks" and "tocks," but it is the guttural "croak" made by the raven that gives it away.

wetlands, a climb leads to mountain views and a good chance of seeing mule deer in the open grassy areas. As you walk the forested trails, keep your eyes high for a chance sighting of a great horned owl atop the poplars.

Enjoy the randomness of nature, the chance sightings of wildlife and disconnect from the city's fast pace. Restore and recharge with a complete wilderness experience in the heart of the city.

Deer Differences

Try your hand at deer identification while walking in Fish Creek Park. Mule deer have large ears rimmed with black and tails that are white with a black tip. They travel in small bands of does, yearlings, and fawns; the bucks travel alone.

White-tailed deer have brown tails. When alarmed they lift their tails to expose the white underside and a white rump patch. They wave this furry flag to warn their friends of possible danger. Being quite solitary and shy, white-tailed does are usually alone or with their offspring from that year.

After the Rain by Mandy Budan

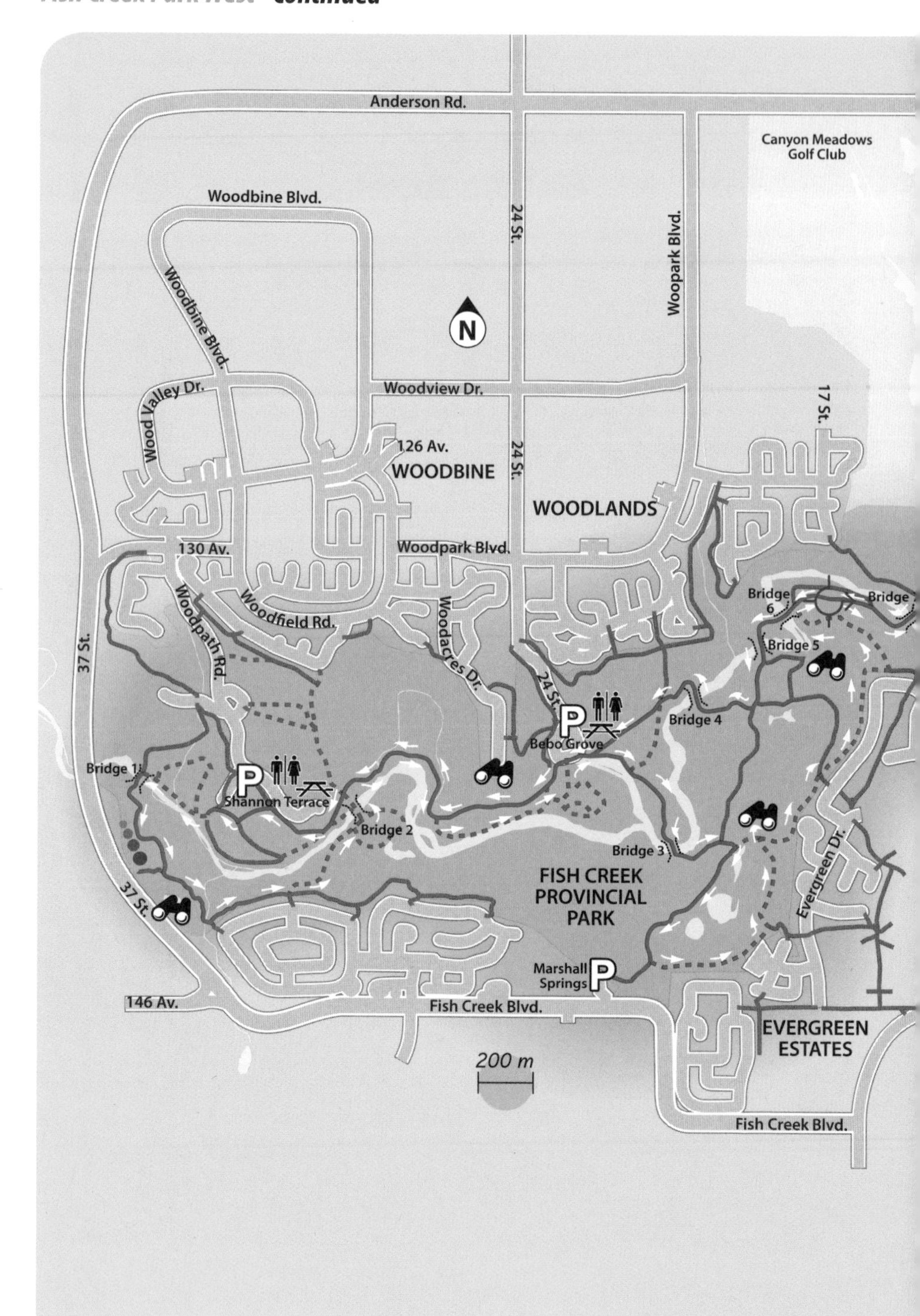
Anderson Rd.
Canyon Meadows Golf Club
Woodbine Blvd.
24 St.
Woopark Blvd.
Woodbine Blvd.
N
Wood Valley Dr.
Woodview Dr.
17 St.
126 Av.
WOODBINE
24 St.
WOODLANDS
130 Av.
Woodpark Blvd.
Woodfield Rd.
Woodpath Rd.
Woodacres Dr.
37 St.
24 St.
Bridge 6
Bridge
Bridge 5
Bebo Grove
Bridge 4
Bridge 1
Shannon Terrace
Bridge 2
Bridge 3
FISH CREEK PROVINCIAL PARK
Evergreen Dr.
37 St.
Marshall Springs
146 Av.
Fish Creek Blvd.
EVERGREEN ESTATES
200 m
Fish Creek Blvd.

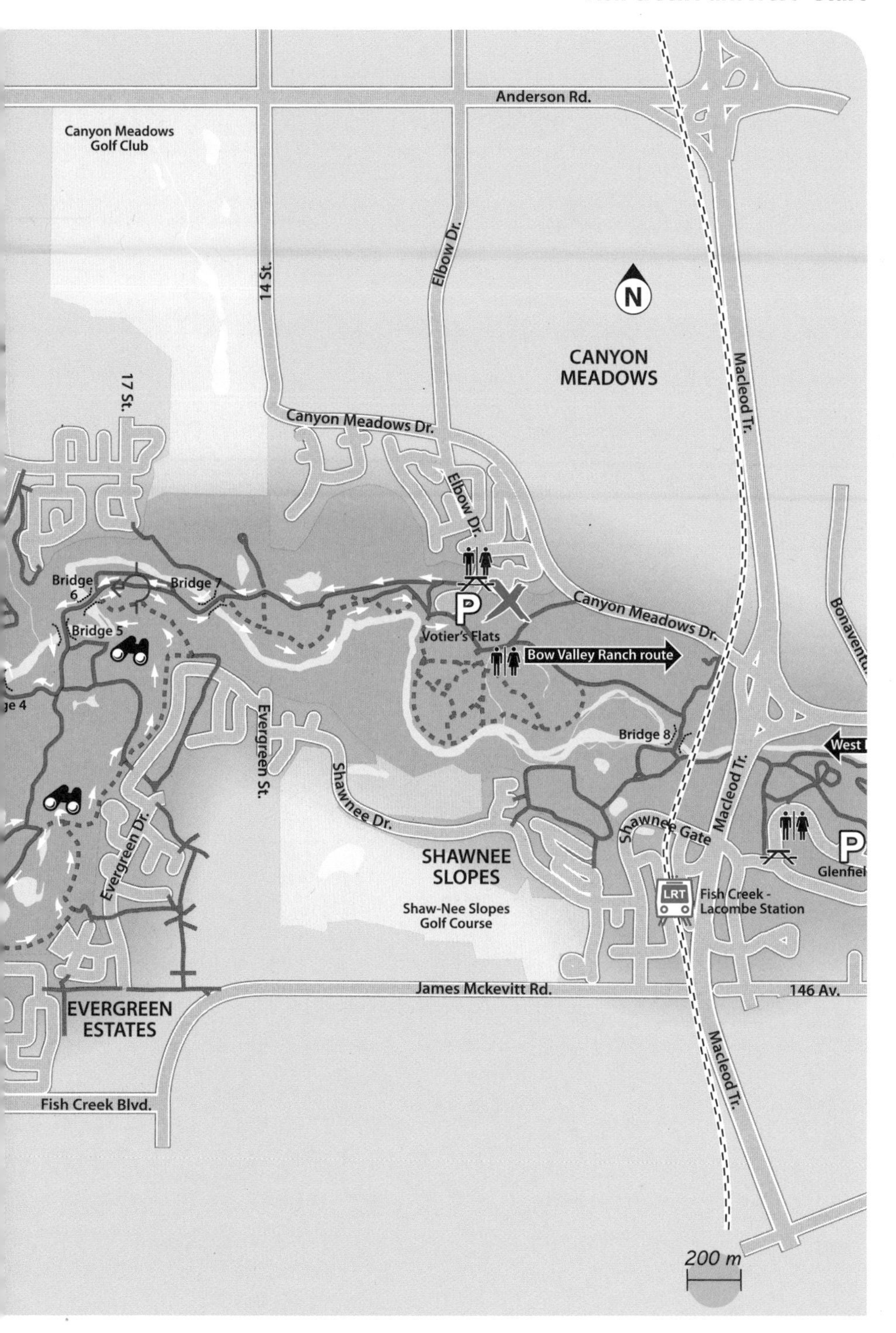

Anderson Rd.
Canyon Meadows Golf Club
14 St.
Elbow Dr.
N
CANYON MEADOWS
17 St.
Macleod Tr.
Canyon Meadows Dr.
Elbow Dr.
Bridge 6
Bridge 7
Bridge 5
Votier's Flats
Canyon Meadows Dr.
Bow Valley Ranch route
Bonaventu
Evergreen St.
Shawnee Dr.
Bridge 8
West
Evergreen Dr.
Shawnee Gate
Macleod Tr.
SHAWNEE SLOPES
Shaw-Nee Slopes Golf Course
LRT
Fish Creek - Lacombe Station
Glenfiel
James Mckevitt Rd.
146 Av.
EVERGREEN ESTATES
Fish Creek Blvd.
Macleod Tr.
200 m

Fish Creek Park–Bow Valley Ranche

SE

Walk at a Glance:

Grassland getaways and vast wilderness tracts tucked into a city of over one million people are unique and wonderful. The Bow Valley Ranche route is an open-prairie, grassland trek that starts with climbs to mountain views. Deer, beaver, and coyote call the park home, and great blue herons visit the creek to fish.

Route Details

Categories: C-Train, Café, Dog Friendly, Hilly, Nature, River, Stroller, Trail Running, Vistas.

Starting-Point Parking: Bow Valley Ranch parking area. Follow Bow Bottom Trail into Fish Creek Park.

C-Train Start: Fish Creek Station.

Transit: Bus access. Check Calgary Transit at www.calgarytransit.com.

Facilities: Year-round bathrooms at trailhead in the visitor centre; café.

Distance: 8 km

Degree of Difficulty: Moderate, with a mix of flats and hills.

Seasonal Highlights/Cautions

Year-Round: At the time of printing, Bridge 9 was still out of service. Fish Creek Park plans on adding a replacement bridge to connect the trails on the east side of the creek with those on the west side in the Spring of 2015. Trails may flood in June, or when beavers have dammed the creek. Check for trail closures at www.albertaparks.ca/fish-creek.aspx, or at the Bow Valley Ranche Visitor Centre. Dogs must be on leash at all times in Fish Creek Provincial Park.

Winter: Peaceful on cold winter mornings when the hoar frost growth on riverside vegetation glitters under blue skies.

Spring to Fall: Enjoy a wilderness walk followed by a picnic lunch, or stop in at Annie's Café.

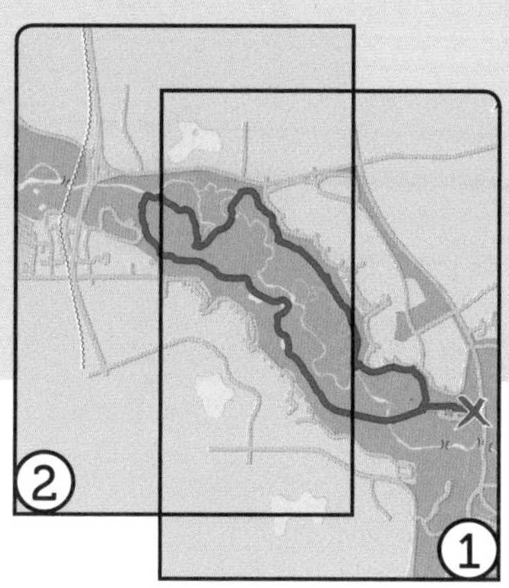

Begin your trek with a stroll past the Artisan Gardens and Annie's café. Climb to the community of Parkland and follow the escarpment trail. Soak up the expansive views of the park below and the Rockies beyond before descending back into the park and continuing along

Artisan Gardens

At Bow Valley Ranche, just north of the visitor centre beside Annie's Café, sits the Artisan Gardens. Here, over sixty established Canadian artists have created 175 pieces or original art that are placed alongside manicured trails. The project is the work of the ranch at Fish Creek Restoration Society. Their vision is to honour the First Nations peoples of the area and the rich history of the Bow Valley Ranche. The benches placed amongst the art provide inspiring places for you to sit down and rest your legs after your walk, and to enjoy some art in a natural setting. You can enjoy the gardens year-round. The artworks are made to withstand all of Canada's seasons.

the valley bottom. Continue on shale paths and narrow treed trails before crossing Fish Creek and travelling into the wide-open grassland. Connect to the popular paved pathway and walk south back to the ranch. Be sure to stop in at the café for a treat. Cafés in provincial parks are, like the blue heron, rare and wonderful.

Workaholic Beavers

Just past the ranch area you'll start to see beaver dams in the streams and many fallen trees along the stream banks. And if the trail you want to walk on is covered by water, you might want to blame a beaver. Beavers use the trees to build dams; they eat the bark, leaves, and twigs. Beavers are bit driven. For instance, they are attracted to the sound of running water. Play the sound of running water on a speaker close to a beaver and watch the building frenzy that erupts as she covers the speaker until the sound is muted. Do beavers ever stop building? They do in the short term, like in the winter, but not in the long term. Their food eventually runs out and they must dismantle the dam, move on, and start from scratch.

Annie's Café

Once part of the Patrick Burns ranching and meat packing empire, Fish Creek was purchased by the provincial government in 1973. In 1997 restoration of the ranch buildings began and Annie's Café was born. Once the foreman's house, this cozy café is named after Annie Bannister, the foreman's wife. The ranch feel is alive at Annie's, where the kitchen uses an antique stove to heat homemade soups, and the rooms are filled with rickety wooden chairs and artefacts from the ranching past. Muffins, scones, and cookies tempt post-hike taste buds. Sit on Annie's deck with a lemonade and watch the world go by.

Location: Fish Creek Bow Valley Ranche, Bow Bottom Trail SE, www.bvrestaurant.com
Phone: 403-476-1308
Hours: Variable, call to confirm

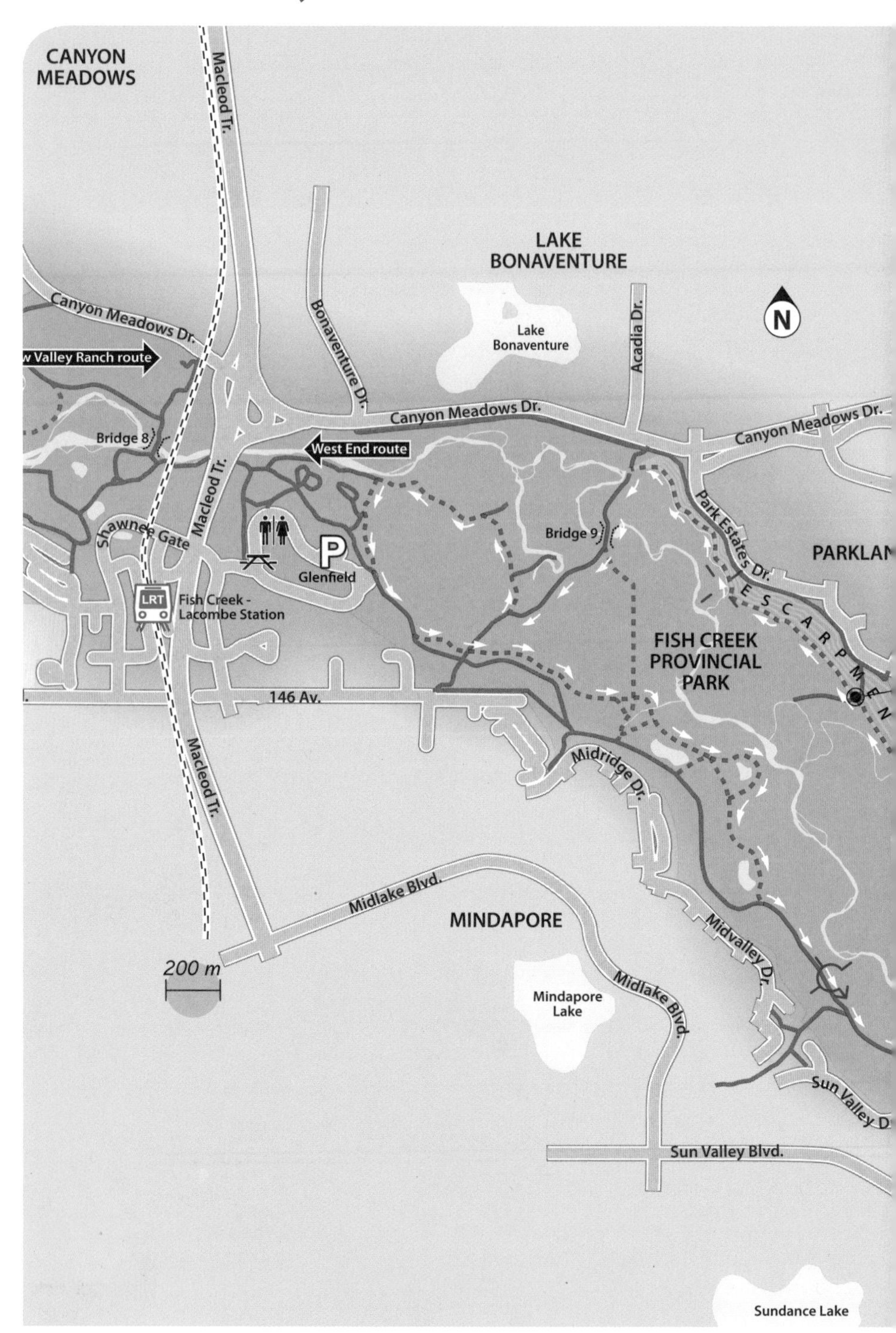
CANYON MEADOWS
Macleod Tr.
LAKE BONAVENTURE
Lake Bonaventure
Acadia Dr.
Bonaventure Dr.
N
Canyon Meadows Dr.
w Valley Ranch route
Canyon Meadows Dr.
Canyon Meadows Dr.
Bridge 8
West End route
Macleod Tr.
Bridge 9
Shawnee Gate
P
Glenfield
Park Estates Dr.
PARKLAN
ESCARPMENT
LRT
Fish Creek - Lacombe Station
FISH CREEK PROVINCIAL PARK
146 Av.
Macleod Tr.
Midridge Dr.
Midlake Blvd.
MINDAPORE
Midvalley Dr.
200 m
Midlake Blvd.
Mindapore Lake
Sun Valley D
Sun Valley Blvd.
Sundance Lake

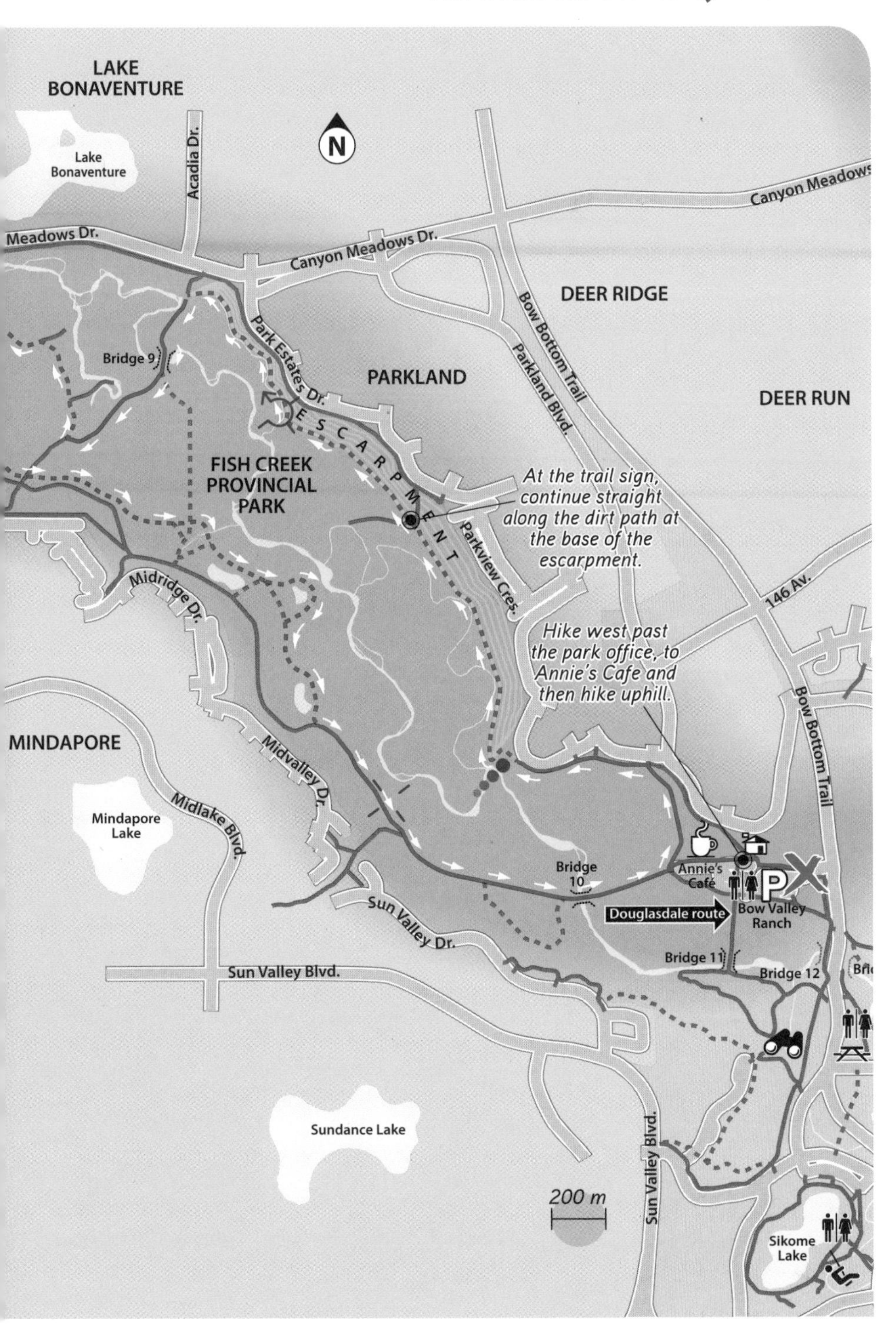
LAKE BONAVENTURE
Lake Bonaventure
Acadia Dr.
N
Meadows Dr.
Canyon Meadows Dr.
Canyon Meadows
DEER RIDGE
Bow Bottom Trail
Parkland Blvd.
DEER RUN
PARKLAND
Park Estates Dr.
Bridge 9
ESCARPMENT
FISH CREEK PROVINCIAL PARK
At the trail sign, continue straight along the dirt path at the base of the escarpment.
Parkview Cres.
146 Av.
Midridge Dr.
Hike west past the park office, to Annie's Cafe and then hike uphill.
Bow Bottom Trail
MINDAPORE
Midvalley Dr.
Mindapore Lake
Midlake Blvd.
Bridge 10
Annie's Café
Douglasdale route
Bow Valley Ranch
Sun Valley Dr.
Bridge 11
Bridge 12
Sun Valley Blvd.
Sundance Lake
Sun Valley Blvd.
200 m
Sikome Lake

Fish Creek Park and Douglasdale Escarpment

SE

Walk at a Glance:

Pelicans visit the Bow River in this area in the spring and summer, so keep your eyes on the river as you climb the escarpment trail to the community of Douglasdale. The views from the community trail above the park are far-reaching. On a blue-sky day in the winter, the Rockies, crisp and white on the horizon, call out to you to grab your skis or snowshoes and come play in the snow.

As you walk, you can ponder the changes to the landscape that have happened here over time. Glaciers covered Fish Creek Provincial Park in 13000 BCE. The glaciers retreated over time, and humans are believed to have first settled in small numbers in the Fish Creek Valley around 6500 BCE. More than eighty archaeological sites have been identified throughout the park. The University of Calgary archaeological team

Route Details

Categories: Café, Dog Friendly, Hilly, Nature, River, Trail Running, Vistas.

Starting-Point Parking: Park at the Mallard Point parking lot at the end of Canyon Meadows Drive SE.

Transit: Bus access to surrounding communities. Check Calgary Transit at www.calgarytransit.com.

Facilities: Washrooms at trailhead, open year-round.

Distance: 9.7 km

Degree of Difficulty: Moderate, with one hill climb.

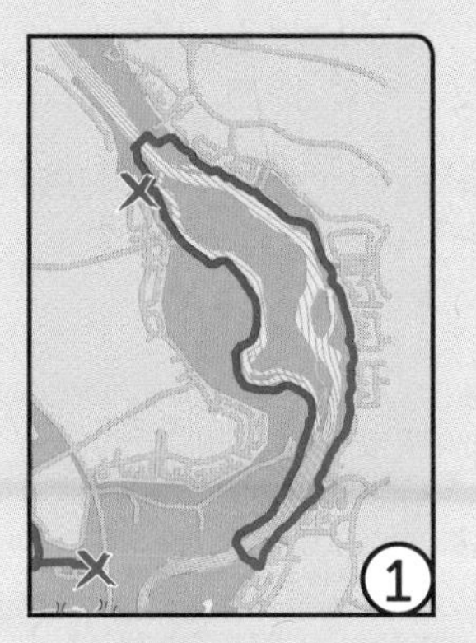

Seasonal Highlights/Cautions

Year-Round: Check for trail closures at www.albertaparks.ca/fish-creek.aspx, or at the Bow Valley Ranche Visitor Centre. Dogs must be on leash at all times in Fish Creek Provincial Park.

Spring and Summer: Watch for pelicans on the Bow River.

has uncovered evidence of early buffalo hunts, Native weaponry, First Nations campsites, cooking utensils, and other ancient artifacts. At least four locations in the park have been identified as buffalo jumps and kill sites used by hunters between 2500 BCE and 1700 CE. The oldest identifiable artifact found in the park to date is a broken atlatl head, dated around 2500 BCE.

In 1873 John and Adelaide Glenn became the first European settlers in the Fish Creek valley. They set up a small trading post and farm in 1874. In 1879 Glenn sold his farm to the Dominion Government, and it became Indian Supply Farm #24 in 1877.

The Blackfoot Confederacy signed Treaty No. 7 in 1877. The First Peoples were paid cash and given reserves totalling close to one million acres. In return, they gave up large tracts of land. The federal government purchased places like that of the Glenns as instructional farms. The idea was to assist the Blackfoot to adjust to their new way of life.

William Roper Hull and John Hull bought Fish Creek Supply Farm in 1892. Experts in the cattle industry, the Hulls had found ranching success through irrigation and hay-stacking efficiencies, using techniques that were copied across Canada. William Roper Hull sold his meat operations and the Bow Valley Ranche to Patrick Burns in 1902. He then moved to Calgary, a two-hour ride away at that time.

Starting with nothing, Patrick Burns came to dominate the western Canadian meat-packing and dairy products industries. To Burns, the Bow Valley Ranche was an integral but small part of his empire. Burns bought out all the nearby ranches and farms. He came to own all the land between the Bow Valley Ranche and his packing plant in the southeast part of Calgary on Blackfoot Trail. The Bow Valley Ranche remained in the Burns family until the provincial government bought it in 1972 and opened it as a park in 1975.

We are lucky to have such a vast park space in the heart of the city. Enjoy the trails as you walk along the Bow River back to your car.

Pelicans on the Bow River

The American white pelican arrives in Alberta in late April. From the Douglasdale escarpment, it is easy to identify these birds, one of the world's largest, because of their distinctive, long, flattened bills and brightly coloured, yellow-orange pouches used for feeding. They fill their pouches with young, warm-water fish such as perch, stickleback, northern pike, and lake whitefish. Pelicans also take salamanders, frogs, and a variety of aquatic invertebrates when they are abundant.

Pelicans are often seen feeding in the same area as double-crested cormorants. When cormorants dive, they flush fish to the surface, making easy pickings for the pelicans. A group of pelicans may mob and rob the cormorants of their fish finds, too. This aggressive behaviour is necessary for the pelicans to reach their daily consumption goal: 2 kg of food.

Young pelicans are fed regurgitated food by their parents. As soon as young chicks can lift their heads, they begin begging by making loud croaking sounds while flapping their wings and weaving their heads back and forth. They bite the base of their parents' bills and pouches to signal that they are hungry. As the chicks get older, they boldly reach into their parents' throats for food, sometimes even farther to extract the gizzard's half-digested contents. The mobbing, persistent harassment by the young, leads the adults to cough up and fly away fast. By late September, the birds head south to the Gulf of Mexico where they winter alongside all the human Canadian snowbirds.

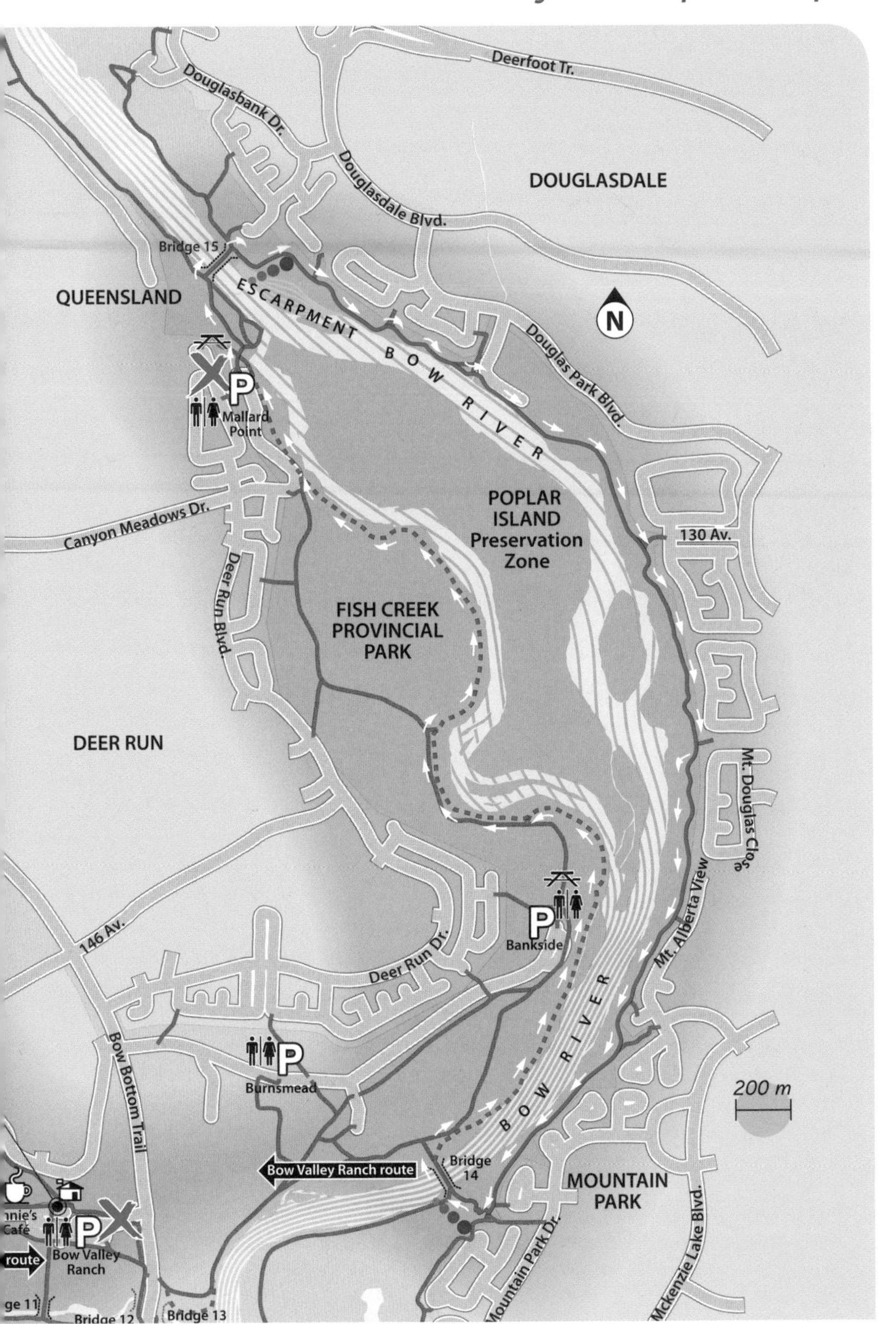
Deerfoot Tr.
Douglasbank Dr.
Douglasdale Blvd.
DOUGLASDALE
Bridge 15
QUEENSLAND
ESCARPMENT
BOW RIVER
N
Douglas Park Blvd.
Mallard Point
POPLAR ISLAND Preservation Zone
130 Av.
Canyon Meadows Dr.
Deer Run Blvd.
FISH CREEK PROVINCIAL PARK
DEER RUN
Mt. Douglas Close
Mt. Alberta View
146 Av.
Bankside
Deer Run Dr.
BOW RIVER
Burnsmead
Bow Bottom Trail
200 m
Bow Valley Ranch route
Bridge 14
MOUNTAIN PARK
Bow Valley Ranch
route
Bridge 12
Bridge 13
Mountain Park Dr.
Mckenzie Lake Blvd.

Carburn Park and Beaverdam Flats

SE

Walk at a Glance:

Families looking for a post-dinner stroll to relax, or to allow the kids to burn off some energy, will enjoy a visit to Carburn Park. This trek is perfect for all ages with its water features, wildlife, and mostly paved pathways. And when the trees are full, this extensive suburban green space becomes a refreshing nature getaway. Balsam poplars offer shade while shrubs like saskatoon, choke cherry, American silverberry, and Canada buffaloberry provide textures and colours along the trail. Pelicans, double-breasted cormorants, and bald eagles all frequent this area, and many deer call the park home.

Route Details

Categories: Dog Friendly, Nature, River, Stroller, Trail Running, Vistas.

Starting-Point Parking: Park at the Carburn Park official parking lot at 67 Riverview Drive SE.

Transit: Bus access to Lynndale and Riverbend. Check Calgary Transit at www.calgarytransit.com.

Facilities: Year-round bathrooms at Carburn Park.

Distance: 8.5 km

Degree of Difficulty: Easy, with one mandatory hill climb.

Seasonal Highlights/Cautions

Year-Round: The 2013 flood destroyed parts of Beaverdam Flats Park and Carburn Park. The City of Calgary continues to work on the trails, building new ones and removing debris. Beaverdam Flats Park is a critical pocket of green in a mostly industrial landscape where parks are scarce. I look forward to when the trails are cleaned up and rebuilt. Check the city of Calgary website, www.calgary.ca , for updates on both Carburn and Beaverdam Flats Parks.

Winter: Enjoy some skating on the Carburn Park pond. When the trees are bare, the traffic on Glenmore Trail makes this a noisy route.

Spring, Summer, and Fall: Bring your fishing rods, canoes, dinghies, and paddle boats and enjoy a float on the two ponds at Carburn Park.

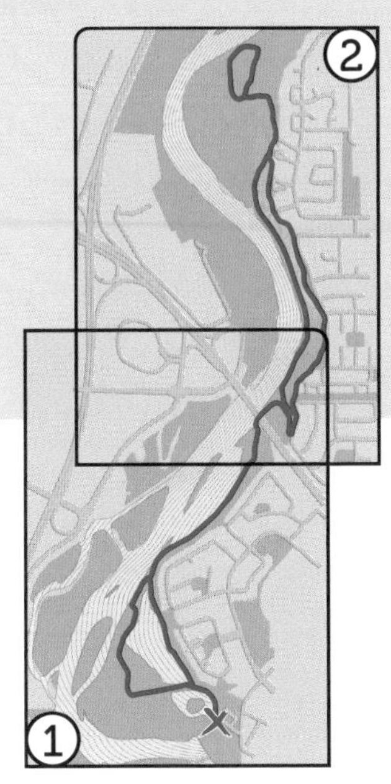

Follow the paved Bow River Pathway through Carburn Park, under Glenmore Trail, and up the escarpment to Lynnwood and views of the Rocky Mountains, the downtown core towers, and industrial Calgary. The southeast of many cities tends to be where industry thrives, and Calgary is no different. In fact, just north of Beaverdam Flats Park along the Bow River Pathway lies Old Refinery Park, a former Imperial Oil Refinery location that has been reclaimed for use as a park.

Continue walking north along the escarpment before descending along a narrow pathway through prairie grasses to the water's edge. Cross the bridge and take a side trip into Beaverdam Flats Park to experience the power of Mother Nature. The park was destroyed by floodwaters in 2013 and has not yet been restored. The City of Calgary removed the bathrooms, playground, and picnic tables and has chosen to let the area recover naturally.

Continue your walk along the river trail, then climb the escarpment toward the big prairie sky. Head south and retrace your steps all the way back to your starting point, or, if you have just got your walking pace, keep on trekking along the Bow River Pathway all the way to Fish Creek Park.

The Industrial East End

In the late 1700s and early 1800s, during the Industrial Revolution, many people flocked to cities for work. As cities in the industrialized northern hemisphere grew, the east end gradually became home to industry: rail yards and factories. As a result, in many cities, the east end is also the most affordable place to live.

But why the east end? Some say the easterly location of industry in northern cities is because the prevailing winds are westerly–blowing from west to east. Homeowners' chimney smoke would have drifted eastward, making air quality much lower in the east end of cities, decreasing peoples' desire to live in that part of town and making it the most obvious choice for industry.

To test this hypothesis, I checked the industrial area for Melbourne Australia, in the southern hemisphere, where the prevailing winds are westerly. Sure enough, the industrial area is situated in the west end of that city.

The east end of Calgary has historically been the affordable place to live. This is changing, however, with the new East Village development. Upscale and vibrant, the East Village connects the central-eastern neighbourhoods of Ramsay, Inglewood, and Victoria Park to the downtown core and the Beltline. The New Central Library, which should be complete in 2018, and the National Music Centre are also in Calgary's east end. In addition, the northeast communities of Bridgeland and Renfrew are hotbeds of real-estate development, desirable for their proximity to downtown.

Thaw by Mandy Budan

Carburn Park and Beaverdam Flats - Continued

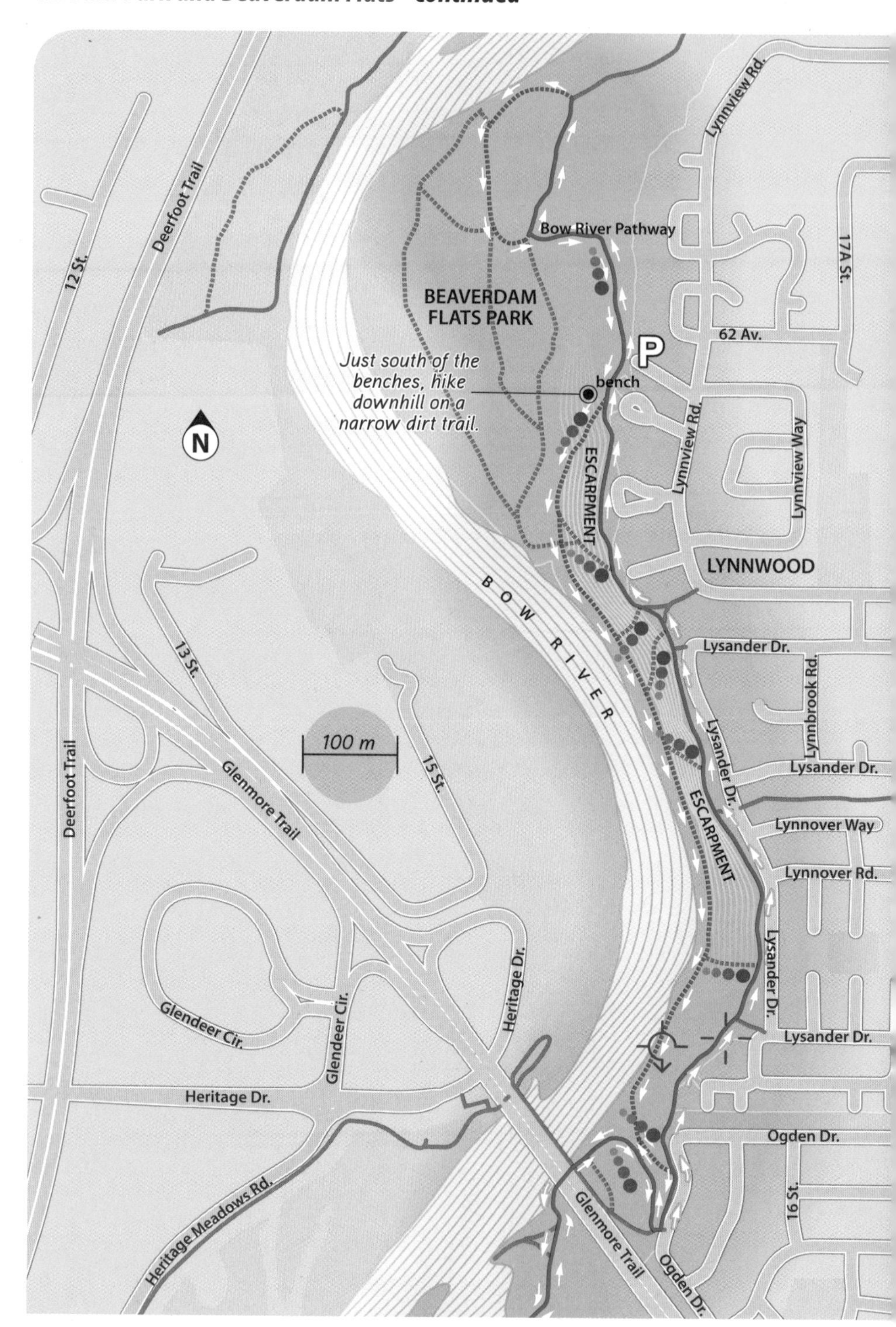

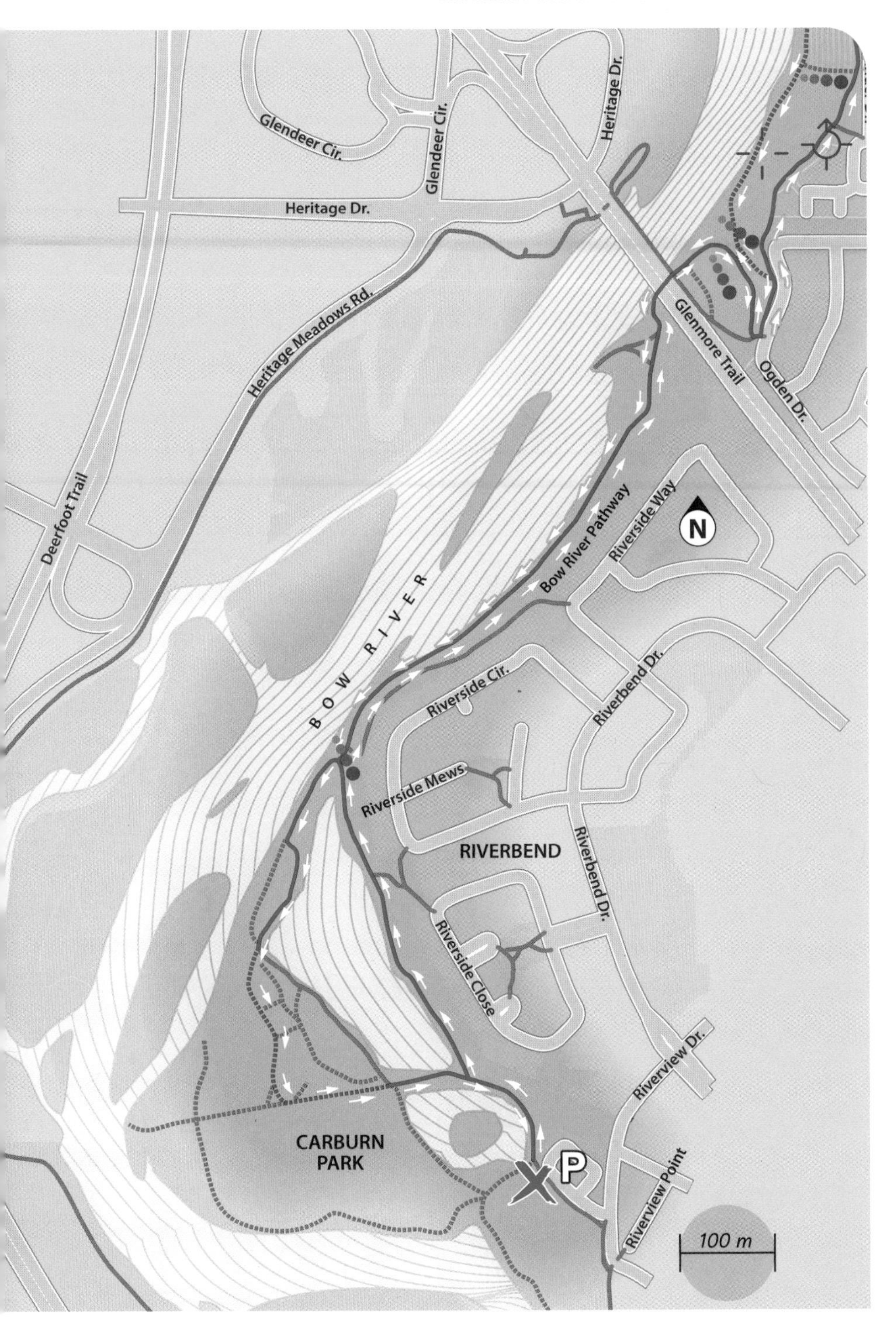
Glendeer Cir.
Glendeer Cir.
Heritage Dr.
Heritage Dr.
Heritage Meadows Rd.
Deerfoot Trail
Glenmore Trail
Ogden Dr.
BOW RIVER
Bow River Pathway
Riverside Way
N
Riverside Cir.
Riverbend Dr.
Riverside Mews
RIVERBEND
Riverbend Dr.
Riverside Close
Riverview Dr.
CARBURN PARK
P
Riverview Point
100 m

Elliston Regional Park

SE

Walk at a Glance:

Small parks offer a taste of nature amidst the urban asphalt. Elliston is a prairie park in the east end of Calgary that is perfect for families with young kids. This route allows visitors to stretch their legs after a nice meal or a shopping spree along International Avenue. Rolling hills surround Elliston's lake, and trees and shrubs have been planted on hillsides. The route circumnavigates the lake, and there are lots of dirt path detours for those who like to explore.

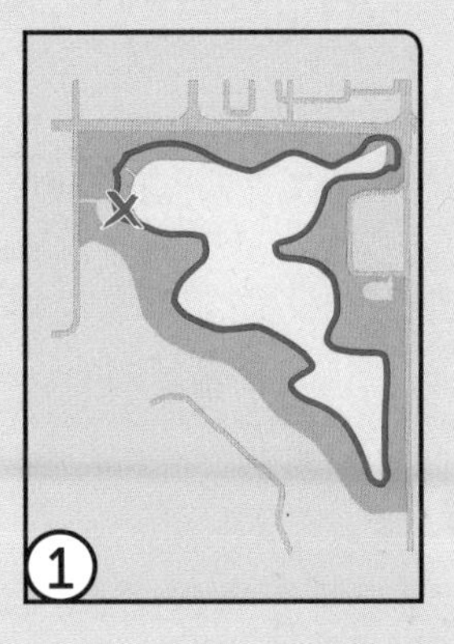

Route Details

Categories: Café, Dog Friendly, Nature, People Watching and Shopping, Stroller.

Starting-Point Parking: Seventeenth Avenue and Sixtieth Street SE.

Transit: Bus access. Check Calgary Transit at www.calgarytransit.com.

Facilities: Seasonal bathrooms at trailhead, open mid-May to mid-October. There are many shops and restaurants along Seventeenth Avenue SE.

Distance: 3.4 km

Degree of Difficulty: Easy.

Seasonal Highlights/Cautions

Year-Round: This park is open to the elements without much shelter. The Around the World in 35 Blocks Food Tour takes you to the shops and eateries along Seventeenth Avenue. This bus tour is offered on various scheduled Saturdays. See www.internationalavenue.com.

Summer: Globalfest, an international fireworks festival, takes over the park during the last half of August. See www.globalfest.ca.

The park is a pleasant and peaceful piece of nature in a part of the city where parks are scarce. Its uses are also practical in that is serves as a storm water drainage lake for the surrounding communities. At times of heavy rainfall, the lake can increase by 35,000 L of water per second. But don't worry: warning bells will ring before the floods descend.

Little Pond by Sheila Kernan

Around the World in 35 Blocks Food Tour

After a walk through Elliston Park, why not take a trip to India, Pakistan, the Mediterranean, Jamaica, Newfoundland, Mexico, Nicaragua, Italy, and Germany. International Avenue, in Forest Lawn, is the most ethnically diverse shopping and eating area in Calgary. A great way to explore the area is to join the bus tour called Around the World in 35 Blocks, offered by the business revitalization zone. The tour provides an introduction to the area and is a fun way to taste foods from around the world or learn how to shop for ingredients for recipes. On various scheduled Saturday afternoons throughout the year, the bus takes salivating "tourists" on a tour of five continents spanning thirty-five blocks.

Walkers should note that unlike Kensington in the northwest and Uptown Seventeenth Avenue in the southwest, International Avenue is more car focused than pedestrian friendly. The community is working on improving the walkability of the area, but with four lanes of traffic, large parking lots at the front of stores, and many turn-offs to shops where cars are always pulling in and out across sidewalks–the area still has a ways to go.

To find out more about the food tour and find a map of the shops, visit www.internationalavenue.com.

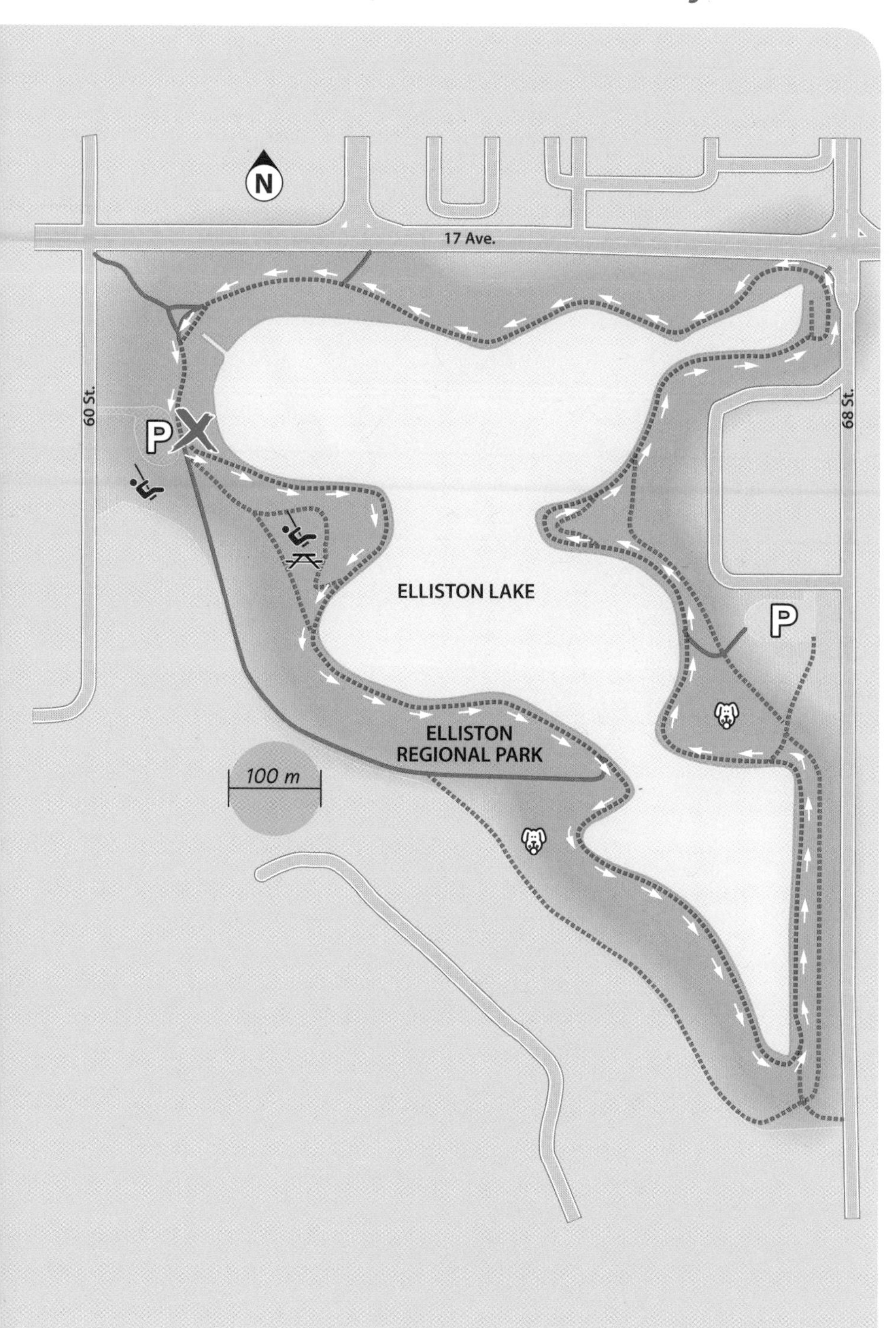
N
17 Ave.
60 St.
68 St.
P
P
ELLISTON LAKE
ELLISTON
REGIONAL PARK
100 m

Inglewood–Pearce Estate Wetland–Inglewood Bird Sanctuary

SE

Walk at a Glance:

This easterly Bow River walk starts with a brief stroll through Inglewood followed by an immersion in nature along the Bow River Pathway. Listen for the howl of the wolves that live across the river at the Calgary Zoo. Continue under the train tracks and soon you are at Harvie Passage, the white-water park that replaces the weir.

Once known as the drowning machine, the weir was a serious hazard for all watercraft, and it is a relief to rescue personnel that paddlers now have a safe route past the churning weir. Completed in 2013, the channel was unfortunately destroyed by the 2013 flood. Mother Nature blasted the fabricated channel and created a new channel. The city will redevelop the area once again to ensure a safe passage.

Route Details

Categories: Café, Nature, Neighbourhoods and Parks, People Watching and Shopping, River, Stroller.

Starting-Point Parking: Park along Fifteenth Street or on New Street SE.

Transit: Bus access at various points along the route. Check Calgary Transit at www.calgarytransit.com.

Facilities: Bathrooms at Inglewood Bird Sanctuary Visitor Centre and Pearce Estate Wetland.
Check www.calgary.ca for visitor centre hours.

Distance: 8.7 km

Degree of Difficulty: Easy and flat.

Seasonal Highlights/Cautions

Winter: Chickadees grace these parks throughout the winter while thousands of ducks and geese spend time on the open-water lagoon and Bow River.

Spring: A variety of waterfowl begin to arrive in March, shorebirds fly in around May, and the songbirds add music to your hike in May and June.

Summer: Watch for pelicans and cormorants throughout July and August. Colourful Baltimore orioles, yellow warblers, fly catchers, and eastern king birds are a common sight in the warm months.

Autumn: August and September are the busy months in this area as a variety of species of warblers pay a visit to the sanctuary at this time.

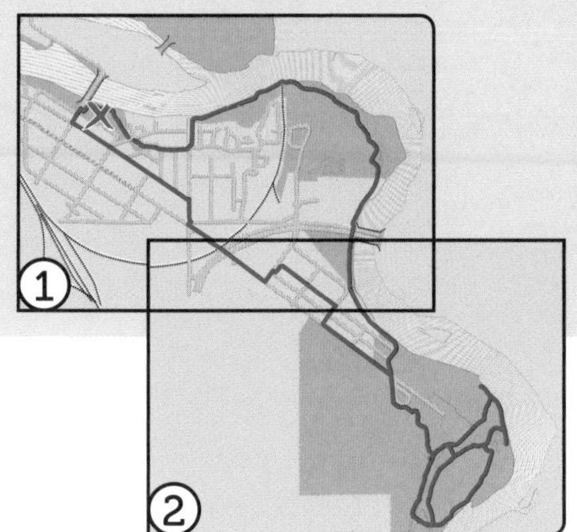

Continue east and soon you have the option of a side-trip walk. Step off the trail and into Pearce Estate Wetland. A meandering interpretive trail system moves through the constructed wetland area. Balsam poplar riverine forest, including willows, water birch, and red-osier dogwood thrive in the area. Keep an eye out for birds such as tree swallows, northern flickers, and common goldeneye–all birds that live in cavities (the holes in old trees) of balsam poplars.

After a short stint on the paved path, the hidden streets of Inglewood emerge. This tucked-away community, consisting of just a few streets, is an interesting diversion from the river pathway walk. In fact, the riverside homes were almost in the river when the flood eroded the banks and consumed the pathway in 2013.

The Inglewood Bird Sanctuary is the next stop. This wildlife reserve was designated a Federal Migratory Bird Sanctuary in 1929. Walk the paved and shale paths that follow the Bow River while keeping a keen eye out for rare birds. Stop by the visitor centre to see which feathered friends are frequently flying and nesting in the area. More than 270 species of birds have been seen here, 53 of which nest on site while the rest are migratory. As well, 21 species of mammals and 347 species of plants have been recorded at the sanctuary. Even if you aren't a birder, the sanctuary is a great place to unwind, have a picnic lunch, learn about birds from the visitor centre staff, and watch binocular-clad birders do their stuff.

If you are feeling the pangs of hunger, help is close by. A brief walk along busy Ninth Avenue leads you past the Blackfoot Truckstop Diner, and anytime, day or night, this Calgary landmark offers you all-day breakfast or a piece of flapper pie with sky-high meringue. The diner is a welcome sight for all walkers and birders who are a little low on sugar. After a slice of pie, continue the walk along the industrial portion of Ninth Avenue and soon emerge at the shopping and walking section of the avenue. Small independent businesses make this a fun street to walk along and window shop. Be sure to walk the length of it before calling it a day.

Blackfoot Truckstop Diner

For over 50 years, the Blackfoot Diner has been serving up all-day breakfasts and down-home food that is filling and reasonably priced. Still a truckstop with an authentic, yet retro, feel, it has a crossover clientele: those who drive semi-tractor trailers and those who just want some good basic food and perhaps a slice of pie with sky-high meringue. My kids love the old-fashioned milkshakes that always come with the extra shake that was leftover. My daughter tells me it's like "drinking cake through a straw." Ah, that's the life!

Location: 1840 Ninth Avenue SE, on the corner of Blackfoot Trail and Ninth Avenue, www.blackfootdiner.ca
Phone: 403-265-5964

Bow Habitat Visitor Centre and Sam Livingston Fish Hatchery

The tagline is: "the experience will leave you hooked!" Bring the whole family and learn all about Alberta's fish, wildlife, water, and aquatic habitats. Spring through fall you can join the Learn to Fish program or rent a fishing rod and give it a go on your own. You can also take a guided tour of the fish hatchery and explore the exhibits and aquariums in the Discovery Centre.

Location: Pearce Estate Wetland, 1440 17A Street SE
Phone: 403 297-6561

Three Mini Islands by Sheila Kernan

Inglewood's Ninth Avenue Shops and Eats

Step away from the mall and take a walk along Ninth Avenue, formally Atlantic Avenue, Calgary's first authentic main street. Packed with an eclectic mix of shops selling clothes, spices, knives, books, home decor, quirky collectibles, as well as restaurants, coffee shops, pubs, live music venues, and art galleries, the avenue is a haven for independent businesses. Many store owners live in Inglewood or neighbouring Ramsay. Top up your spices at Spiceland. Sniff your way around the world and spice up your cooking. So many types of cinnamon! And don't miss ReWorks Upcycle Shop. A clawfoot-bathtub couch, anyone? Be sure to visit the Esker Gallery, a public art gallery at the west end of Ninth Avenue. (For more details on Ninth Avenue, see Walk 35 on page 234.) Plan to visit the area during the Inglewood Night Market, when music, street dancing, and artisans fill the area with energy and people. Check out www.calgary-inglewood.com for more information.

Inglewood–Pearce Estate Wetland–Inglewood Bird Sanctuary - Start

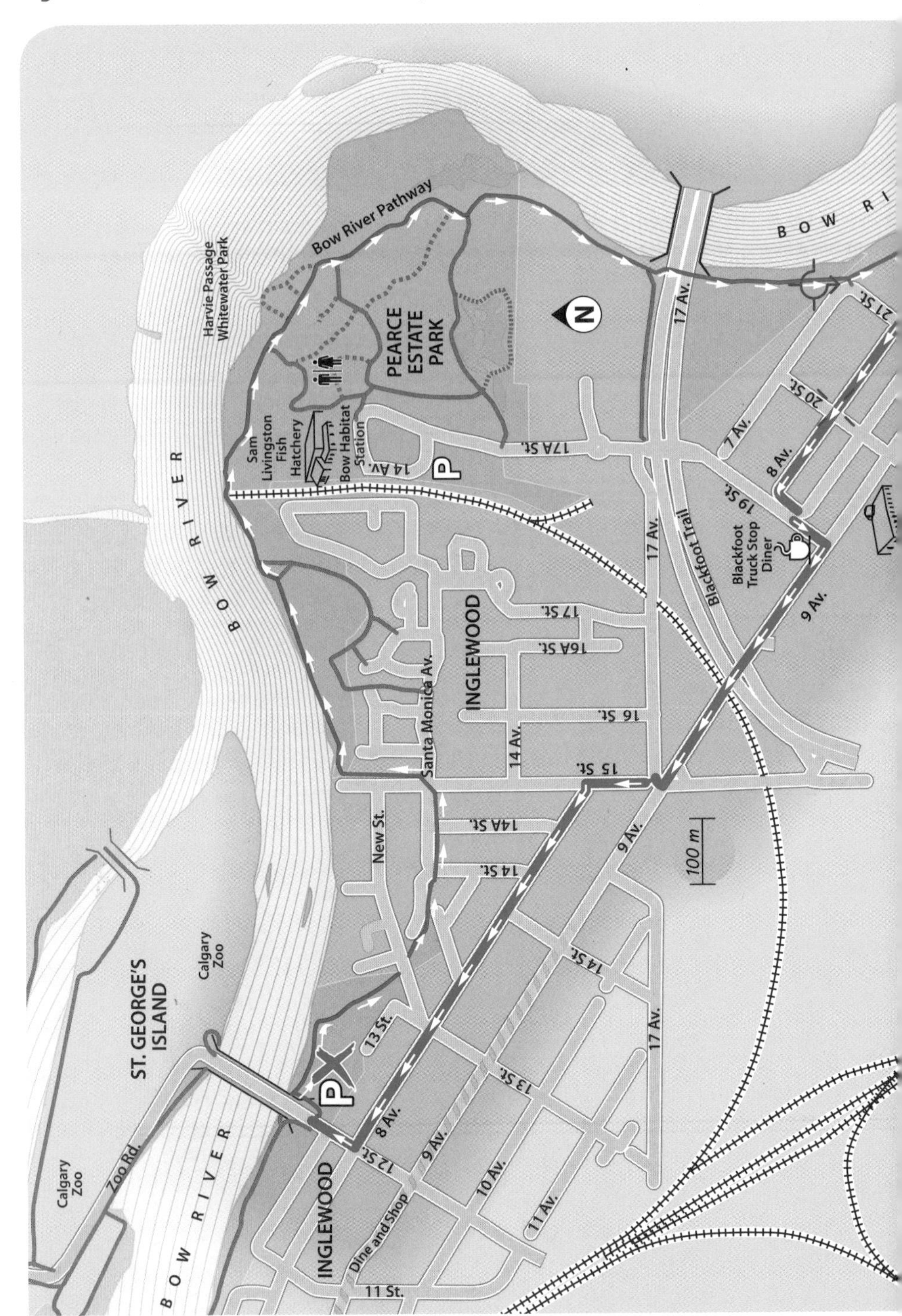

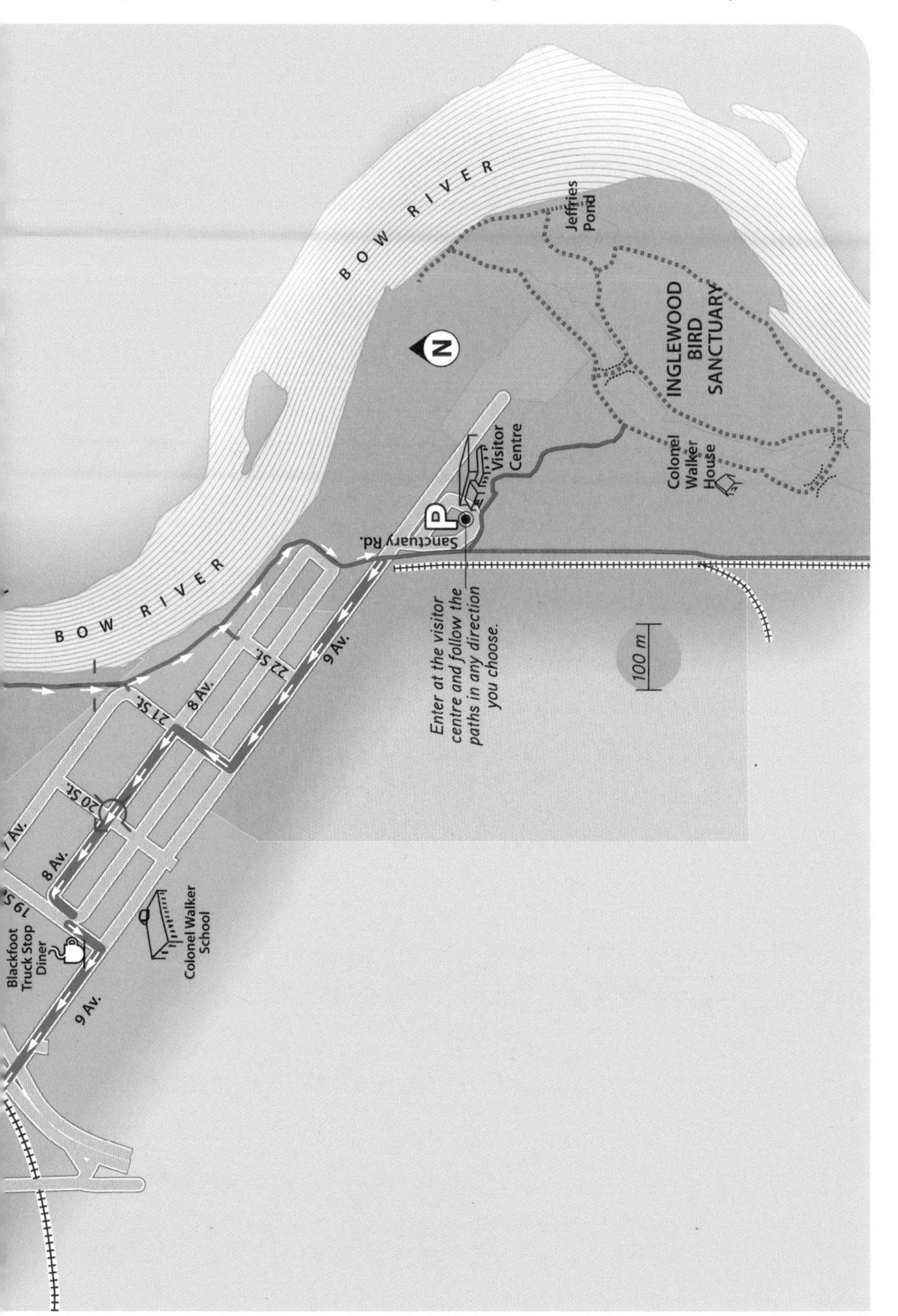

BOW RIVER
BOW RIVER
Jeffries Pond
INGLEWOOD BIRD SANCTUARY
Visitor Centre
Colonel Walker House
Sanctuary Rd.
Enter at the visitor centre and follow the paths in any direction you choose.
100 m
22 St.
21 St.
20 St.
8 Av.
9 Av.
8 Av.
9 Av.
Blackfoot Truck Stop Diner
Colonel Walker School

Inglewood–East Village RiverWalk–Bridgeland

SE

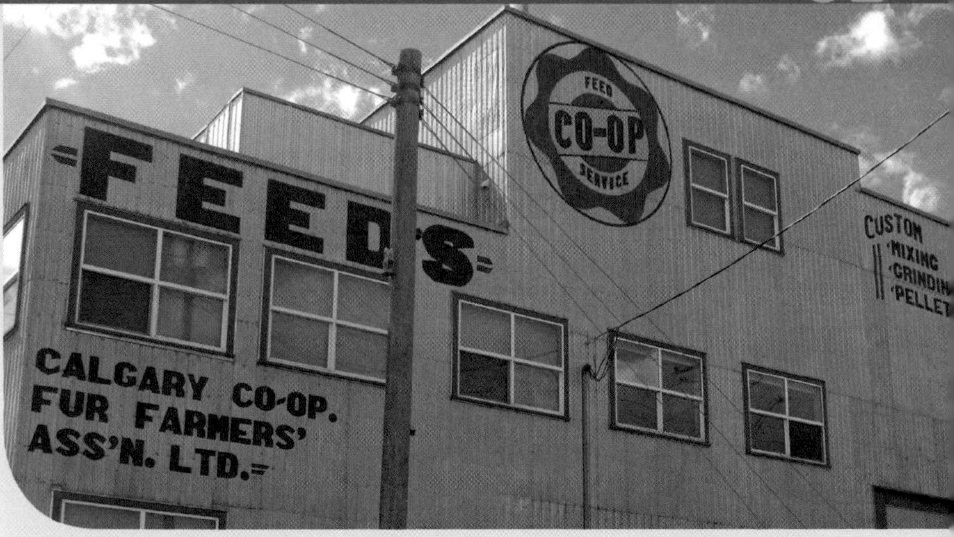

Walk at a Glance:

Eclectic, sometimes gritty, neighbourhoods make for the best urban hikes. Ramsay is home to old-fashioned corner stores, historic homes and buildings from the early 1900s–some renovated and fantastic, some handyman delights. Ramsay is not polished and perfect, and that is what makes walking here so enjoyable, so unpredictable. Red, bright yellow, violet blue, chartreuse, forest green, and turquoise: these are just some of the house colours you will see on this trek. And the gardens here are creative, personalized, and fun. Inglewood and Ramsay's warm microclimate and rich, flood-plain soil makes green thumbs of everyone. The flowers bloom earlier in the season and last longer here than anywhere else in Calgary, and the pear trees hang heavy with fruit in the fall.

Route Details

Categories: C-Train, Dog Friendly, Hilly, Historic, Home and Gardens, Neighbourhoods and Parks, People Watching and Shopping, River, Stroller, Vistas, Café.

Starting-Point Parking: Official parking lot on Twelfth Street, just north of Eighth Avenue SE.

C-Train Start: Bridgeland Station.

Transit: Bus access at various points along the route. Check Calgary Transit at www.calgarytransit.com.

Facilities: Porta Potty at trailhead.

Distance: 7.2 km

Degree of Difficulty: Moderate, with many optional hills.

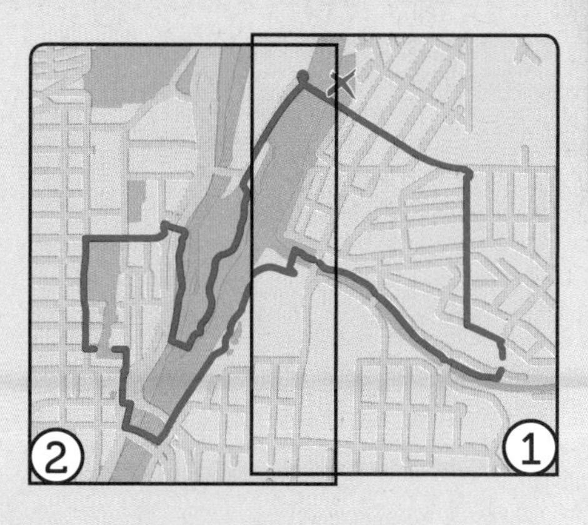

Seasonal Highlights/Cautions

Winter: Observe the impressive ice flows on the Bow River.

Spring and Fall: Gardens start earlier and last longer in Inglewood and Ramsay than in many higher-elevation communities in Calgary.

Summer: The Calgary Stampede takes place in early July and may affect the route.

Scotsman's Hill is the best place to watch the Stampede fireworks. The high point offers a bird's eye view of Stampede Park, where Calgary's annual party takes place each July. The skyscrapers that drive Calgary's economic success backdrop the Saddledome. Look beyond the hardworking core to the Rocky Mountain peaks that offer the physical and mental release that we all crave.

A hidden staircase drops down to RiverWalk, near Stampede Park, which continues north along the Elbow River to the Bow River, past Fort Calgary, and into the East Village. RiverWalk is a beautiful pathway development that connects, or will connect, the East Village, Stampede Park, Lindsay Park, and the community of Mission. With separate pathways for

Esker Foundation Contemporary Art Gallery

Detour along Ninth Avenue and drop by the Esker Art Gallery after your walk. This private non-commercial gallery is impressive, and it is free to all. Tour the latest exhibition–there are three shows each year–or register for and take part in one of the gallery's many educational events. Free contemporary art programming, designed to make art accessible to all ages, is offered to anyone who is interested.
Our family of four enjoyed a mapmaking course at the gallery. An exhibition artist was flown in from Vancouver to facilitate. The gallery owners, Jim and Susan Hill, were also there, ushering and helping visitors enjoy the experience. The gallery is a piece of art in itself. Tour the birds nest boardroom or settle into the comfy couch sitting area, where visitors are encouraged to relax and enjoy the views or to bring their laptops and write a few inspirational words.

Location: Top floor, 1011 Ninth Avenue SE, www.eskerfoundation.com
Phone: 403-930-2490

walkers and cyclists, pull-offs with benches, comfy chairs, art installations, and lush landscaping, this walkway is not to be missed. Continue west along the Bow River past a plaza that sometimes hosts food trucks, and at other times operatic performers. Stop at the historic Simmons Building, the new home of a diverse group of eateries and cafés. Built in 1912, the former mattress factory is a city landmark now filled with tasty treats.

Connect to Bridgeland on the north side of the Bow River. "In transition" is the best way to describe this inner-city community, with young families taking root and building new homes alongside original and renovated character homes. In the early 1900s Bridgeland–then called Riverside–was home to a large, Italian, immigrant community, and you can still find a tasty Italian meal at many restaurants along First Avenue and Edmonton Trail NE.

Picnickers can detour and grab some food along First Avenue before continuing over Memorial Drive and into the manicured St. Patrick's Island, at the confluence of the Bow and Elbow rivers. The park has 1.6 km of pathways, waterparks and picnic spots, wetlands and forests. It is a perfect stop for families.

Creative communities have character. The variety on this walk is due to the uniqueness of the people who choose to live in Inglewood, Ramsay, and Bridgeland–people who enjoy diversity and who embrace unique designs and personal touches. The creativity and ingenuity of the residents give the urban walker a sense of the personalities who live here.

Gravity Espresso and Wine Bar

My favourite café along Ninth Avenue in Inglewood is Gravity. Situated on the ground floor of the Esker Foundation Gallery building, the café is bright with natural light, and full of artwork and a welcoming atmosphere. The coffee is locally roasted and oh, so good. Locally made baked goods are fresh, and the breakfast menu also has healthy, high-energy options like the mason jars filled with Alberta's Vital Green Farms yoghurt, fresh fruit, and granola. For lunch, grab a panini, some soup, or Spolumbo's sausage and beef chili. Plan to drop by in the evening for the nightly special. Gravity hosts live music on many weekends and has fun after-work specials like the "curry and beer" Friday night dinner. I enjoy the eclectic seating arrangements, from the recycled bathtub couch (get your own farther east along Ninth Avenue at the creatively quirky ReWorks Upcycle Shop), to the large rustic tables that are perfect when you and your friends drop by, after a night out at the theatre, for a glass of wine and conversation.

Location: Ground floor, 1011 Ninth Avenue SE, www.cafegravity.com

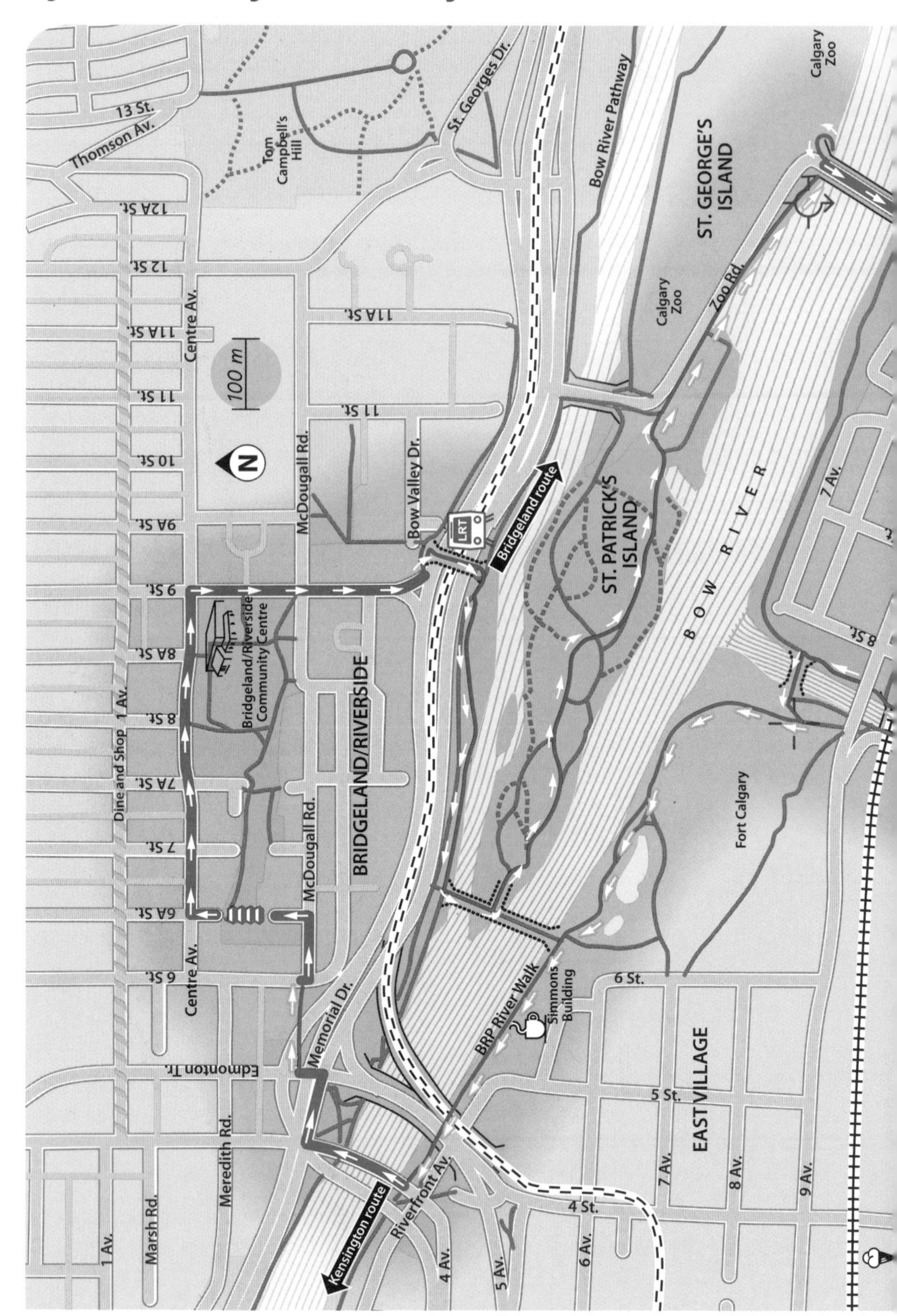

13 St.
Thomson Av.
Tom Campbell's Hill
St. Georges Dr.
Bow River Pathway
ST. GEORGE'S ISLAND
Calgary Zoo
12A St.
12 St.
11A St.
11A St.
11 St.
11 St.
Centre Av.
100 m
Zoo Rd.
10 St.
N
McDougall Rd.
Bow Valley Dr.
LRT
Bridgeland route
ST. PATRICK'S ISLAND
BOW RIVER
7 Av.
9A St.
9 St.
Bridgeland/Riverside Community Centre
BRIDGELAND/RIVERSIDE
8A St.
8 St.
8 St.
Dine and Shop 1 Av.
7A St.
7 St.
McDougall Rd.
Fort Calgary
6A St.
6 St.
Centre Av.
Memorial Dr.
BRP River Walk
Simmons Building
6 St.
Edmonton Tr.
5 St.
EAST VILLAGE
Meredith Rd.
Marsh Rd.
1 Av.
Kensington route
Riverfront Av.
4 St.
4 Av.
5 Av.
6 Av.
7 Av.
8 Av.
9 Av.

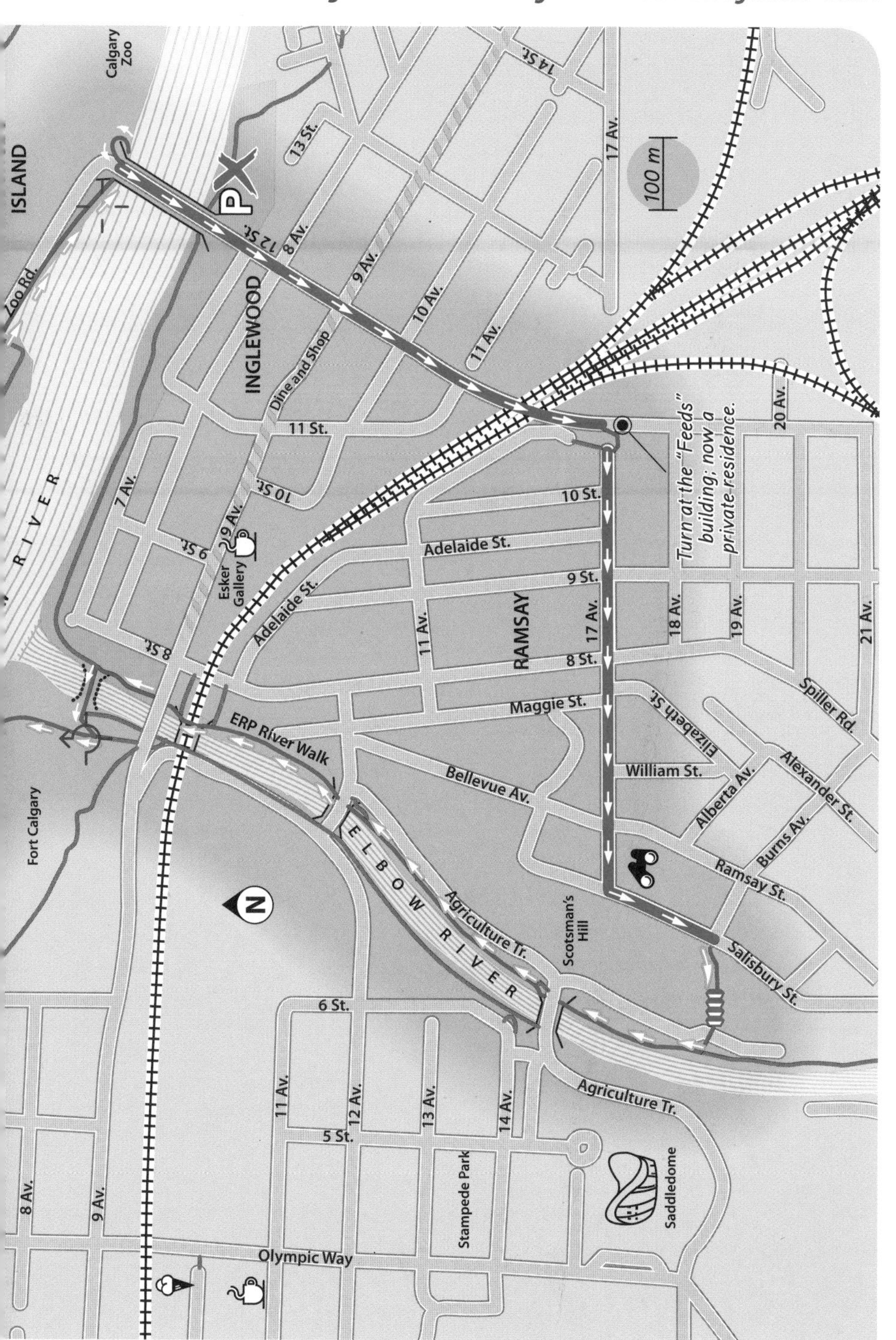
Calgary Zoo
ISLAND
Zoo Rd.
13 St.
14 St.
17 Av.
100 m
12 St.
8 Av.
9 Av.
10 Av.
11 Av.
INGLEWOOD
Dine and Shop
11 St.
10 St.
7 Av.
RIVER
9 St.
9 Av.
Esker Gallery
Turn at the "Feeds" building; now a private residence.
20 Av.
10 St.
Adelaide St.
9 St.
Adelaide St.
11 Av.
RAMSAY
17 Av.
18 Av.
19 Av.
21 Av.
8 St.
8 St.
Maggie St.
Elizabeth St.
Spiller Rd.
ERP River Walk
William St.
Alberta Av.
Alexander St.
Bellevue Av.
Burns Av.
Fort Calgary
ELBOW RIVER
Ramsay St.
N
Agriculture Tr.
Scotsman's Hill
Salisbury St.
6 St.
Agriculture Tr.
11 Av.
12 Av.
13 Av.
14 Av.
5 St.
8 Av.
9 Av.
Stampede Park
Saddledome
Olympic Way

Creative Team

Sergio Gaytan,
Illustrator and Designer

Sergio created the exceptional maps and design of this book. The maps, full colour and to scale, are what makes this book stand out. Sergio has created a guidebook that is beautiful in design and functional on the trails. Thanks to Sergio for taking my guidebook to a whole new level in the guidebook world. You have set the bar very high!

Professional Bio

Sergio takes great pleasure in orchestrating visual communications. The interaction with diverse individuals and organizations presents him with great opportunities to step into different realms and create eloquent, custom-made solutions, each one having original expression. Working together with his clients to understand each case's singularity, complexity, and goals, provides him with the raw material he needs to craft functional, visually appealing, and conceptually convincing communication products punctuated with an exclamation mark!

Sergio's creative work is made possible by his extensive professional experience, which has resulted in a refined, yet robust, skill set. His services incorporate conceptualization, design, illustration, and motion graphics in synergy with meticulous technique.

You can contact Sergio at gaytan07@yahoo.com.

Mandy Budan,
Canadian Abstract Landscape Painter

Throughout my book are many of Mandy's spectacular works. They are simply beautiful. Mandy's use of colour is inspirational. Thanks so much Mandy for teaming up and allowing me to feature your paintings in my book. Original artwork in a guidebook is classy stuff!

Professional bio

Mandy Budan was born in Toronto in 1964. After studying art extensively in high school, and advertising design in college, Mandy worked for many years as a graphic designer in both print and digital media.

Always fascinated by the vibrant colours and shapes that make up the Canadian landscape, Mandy started painting again in 2000. Working with acrylic paint on wood panel, she works to transform the landscape into a series of abstract patterns.

Her work is in private and corporate collections around the world.

Check Mandy's artwork and on-line store at www.budanart.com

Sheila Kernan,
Contemporary Canadian Artist

When I approached Sheila about including some of her paintings in my book, she was interested and enthusiastic (and I was ecstatic!). Her painting, Life's Little Moments, *is featured on the cover. Sheila's paintings bring to life everything that is beautiful about walking in the city from the downtown lights to the solitude of nature. Her use of colour, texture and patterns and the way the light seems to jump off the canvas, is breathtaking. Thanks Sheila, your artwork makes my book beautiful!*

Photo by Amy Cheshire
www.amycheshire.com

Professional bio

Local Calgary artist Sheila Kernan graduated from Alberta College of Art and Design in 2006 and is currently represented across Canada by five elite art galleries.

Sheila finds beauty in large urban centres as well as on remote mountaintops. She is mesmerized by the energy and excitement of translating her experiences onto canvas. Sheila is attracted to unplanned moments, such as stumbling upon a pathway that takes you to the top of a tower overlooking downtown San Francisco during sunset. She loves hiking up a creek and finding herself completely lost in nature. When Sheila paints, she attempts to share her journeys in a unique and vibrant way, utilizing art to express who she is and what she loves. Transposing her vivid imagination into one-of-a-kind works Sheila continues to make her mark in the Canadian art scene, thanks to her extraordinary ability to transform city, prairie, and mountain landscapes onto canvas.

Sheila believes that paintings should be alive, filled with energy and excitement. They should bring a sense of joy. The world is breathtaking and, as Sheila says, "I just have to capture it. The possibilities are endless!"

Check out Sheila's artwork at www.sheilakernan.com